EVEN THE CHILDREN
OF STRANGERS

Even the children of the stranger, that join themselves to the Lord, to serve him and to love the name of the Lord, to be his servants, everyone that keepeth the sabbath from polluting it, and taketh hold of my covenant, even them will I bring to my holy mountain and make them joyful in the house of prayer; their burnt offerings and their sacrifices shall be accepted upon mine altar; for mine house shall be called a house of prayer for all people.

—Isaiah 56: 6–7

Is it not essential to the unity of the Government and the unity of the people that all persons, *whether citizens or strangers, within this land,* shall have equal protection in every State in this Union in the rights of life and liberty and property?

—Congressman John A. Bingham debating in favor of the Fourteenth Amendment in 1866

The questions we have to consider and decide in these cases, therefore, are to be treated as involving the rights of every citizen of the United States *equally with those of the strangers and aliens who now invoke the jurisdiction of the court.*

—Justice Stanley Matthews in Yick Wo v. Hopkins, *1886*

The protection of the Fourteenth Amendment extends to *anyone, citizen or stranger,* who is subject to the laws of a State, and reaches into every corner of a State's territory.

—Justice William Brennan in Plyler v. Doe, *1982*

EVEN THE CHILDREN
OF STRANGERS
Equality under the
U.S. Constitution

DONALD W. JACKSON

UNIVERSITY PRESS OF KANSAS

Published by the University Press of Kansas (Lawrence, Kansas 66049),
which was organized by the Kansas Board of Regents and is operated and
funded by Emporia State University, Fort Hays State University, Kansas
State University, Pittsburg State University, the University of Kansas, and
Wichita State University

Library of Congress Cataloging-in-Publication Data

Jackson, Donald W., 1938–
    Even the children of strangers : equality under the U.S.
Constitution / by Donald W. Jackson.
        p.   cm.
    Includes bibliographical references (p.   ) and index.
    ISBN 0–7006–0547–9 (hard cover) —ISBN
0–7006–0548–7 (paper)
        1. Equality before the law—United States.   2. United
States—Constitutional law—Amendments—14th.   I. Title.
    KF4764.J33   1992
    342.73'085—dc20
    [347.30285]   92–6098

British Library Cataloguing in Publication Data is available.

Printed in the United States of America

10 9 8 7 6 5 4 3 2 1

The paper used in this publication meets the minimum requirements of the
American National Standard for Permanence of Paper for Printed Library
Materials Z39.48–1984.

To Joanne

μείζων δὲ τούτων ἡ ἀγάπη

CONTENTS

PREFACE

The poetry of history lies in the quasi-miraculous fact that once on this earth, on this familiar spot of ground walked other men and women as actual as we are today, thinking their own thoughts, swayed by their own passions but now all gone, vanishing after another, gone as utterly as we ourselves shall be gone like ghosts at cockcrow.

—G. M. Trevelyan

Just as humans often walk and reflect where others have walked and thought much the same thoughts before, books about equality are legion, so much so that my publisher has asked me to explain why this book was written and why it should be read when there are already so many. Both of my reasons are simple, but I trust not simple-minded. I hope the same is true for this book.

My first purpose is to make a case for presumptive human equality and, as a consequence, to urge that the burden of proof ought always to be placed on those who urge that some human beings are better qualified, more intelligent, more deserving, or more fit than others—and thus are entitled to extraordinary rewards or benefits.

My second purpose has been to write an accessible book about a complex subject. The success of this book therefore ought to be measured by the ability both of the interested general reader and of the average American university student to read and understand it without undue effort and without any specialized background or training.

The context for my case for presumptive human equality is found in the Equal Protection Clause of the Fourteenth Amendment and in the decisions of the justices of the Supreme Court of the United States, who since 1868 have interpreted that amendment. The grammar of equality that I employ is that developed by Douglas Rae and his colleagues in *Equalities* (1981).

The case for equality needs a strong voice these days, even with all the books about it. In his recent book on equality, Peter Westen noted that 46 books on the subject had been published in 1988, 65 in 1987, 50 in 1986, and 370 during the decade of 1978–87 (Westen, 1990: 285). It is easy to see why a publisher might be daunted by the prospect of publishing another. Yet many such books are not friends of equality, and those that are friendly have a variety of purposes, most of them different than mine.

Kenneth Cauthen's *The Passion for Equality* (1987), for example, is the work of a "liberal Protestant Christian" and can be viewed, according to its author, as a essay in "Christian natural ethics." It is an accessible book on equality but not at all on the equal protection of the law. Kenneth Karst's *Belonging to America* (1989) is an excellent treatment of equality, with a particular focus on citizenship. Charles Beitz's *Political Equality* (1989) makes a case for political equality as the foundation for modern popular democracy. Peter Westen's *Speaking of Equality* (1990) is a sophisticated study of the rhetorical power of equality in "moral and legal" discourse, written by a scholar who doubts the utility of the concept of equality in rigorous legal analysis.

A Conflict of Rights (1990) by Melvin Urofsky is a first-rate study of a single affirmative action case that culminated with a U.S. Supreme Court ruling in 1987 in *Johnson v. Santa Clara Transportation Department*. Michel Rosenfeld's *Affirmative Action and Justice* and Stephen Carter's *Reflections of an Affirmative Action Baby* (both published in 1991) focus exclusively on a currently "hot" issue. Rosenfeld's book is a complex and sophisticated analysis by a friend of affirmative action but probably is a bit difficult for the novice. Carter's book is a personal account both of the impact of affirmative action on one African-American law professor and on the consequences of affirmative action for young African-American professionals, and indeed for our society in general.

These are all useful books published within the past five years. The book perhaps most similar to my own is a slightly older work, Judith Baer's excellent *Equality Under the Constitution* (1983). With the Supreme Court issuing one hundred or so opinions each year, and with the changing balance of power on the court in the past few years, there will always be room for periodic reexamination of the Court's activities. This is what I have tried to provide in this inclusive history of interpretation of the Equal Protection Clause.

I would like to take the opportunity to acknowledge my debts both to institutions and to friends. My research for this book began with a sabbatical leave at the Bodleian Library at Oxford University made possible by Texas Christian University and by the Brown Foundation, the benefactors of the Herman Brown Chair of Political Science, which

I hold. Much of the material included here was first presented as papers to the Research Committee on Comparative Judicial Studies of the International Political Science Association, chaired by C. Neal Tate of the University of North Texas. For critical reviews, suggestions, and encouragement I am most indebted to Judith Baer of Texas A&M University, to John Brigham of the University of Massachusetts at Amherst, and to Stephen Wasby of the State University of New York at Albany. For friendship and support I owe much to Jim Riddlesperger, Jr., my colleague in the Political Science Department at TCU.

For proofreading and help with the preparation of the manuscript thanks are due to my secretary at TCU, Marilyn Eudaly.

Above all, for patience, inspiration, and loving support I owe an inexhaustible debt to my wife, Joanne Jackson, to whom the book is dedicated.

Fort Worth, Texas
January 1992

1

INTRODUCTION

Now there's always been an undercurrent of resentment out there, espe-
cially among the conservatives, who believe that anybody who really wants
to make it in this country can do so. But when that feeling rose to the
surface, it turned mean. "To hell with the other guy," people said. "I'm
looking out for number one."

Tip O'Neill, *Man of the House,* 1987

Human equality and its conceptual companions, human brotherhood
and sisterhood, often appear to us as strangers these days. The faces of
strangers such as equality and brotherhood are usefully evocative, but
only when we bother to notice them. The quotations that appear on the
frontispiece of this book first caught my notice because of the ways
they include strangers among those who ought to be entitled to the
benefits and protection of society. Perhaps it is because we in the
United States are a nation of strangers who have gathered here from
the corners of the earth that these quotations seem so appealing. However, in this book I will examine not only the claims to equality of
strangers (or, in law, aliens) but also the many distinctions among
people that may be used to justify limiting or excluding some of them
from the economic and social rewards and recognitions that an economy and society may offer.

It is because of frequently claimed preferences for some people over
others (such as the privileges of birth or wealth) that appeals for human
equality and for human brotherhood and sisterhood so often appear to
us as strangers. Competitive individualism, often joined with conspicuous materialistic values, are more familiar companions. "Getting ahead"
and "getting mine" (if necessary, even at great expense to others) are
more likely today to be publicly proclaimed as commendable life goals
than as embarrassing admissions of selfishness and greed.

Equality and its companions are not doing so well these days. Instead, human "pecking orders" are thriving. These pecking orders of-

ten are still associated with race or gender, but they are as likely to be based also on wealth, occupation, education, and the like. Such pecking orders reflect and sustain claims for the extraordinary privileges, status, and rewards that a society can confer upon some of its members.

My purpose in writing this book is to support a premise of pervasive human equality against many (but not necessarily all) claims for privilege, status, or reward. My most challenging task in writing this book is the examination of such pecking orders and their claims for extraordinary rewards (and thus for inequality); I will suggest that many of them may lack a defensible justification. Claims of being extraordinary, and therefore deserving of extraordinary rewards, are usually made by people at the top of the various pecking orders that include us all. African-American or white, male or female, rich or poor, college graduate or not—such pecking orders evoke and sustain inequalities, but often only on the assumption that some people are extraordinary, or better, or more deserving than others. Obviously such assumptions are sometimes wrong, and when they are clearly understood to be wrong, we call them prejudices. A racial pecking order probably represents the most obvious and persistent example of prejudice.

If there is a fairly solid foundation for certain claims of equality in the United States, that is due in no small part to our society's reflections on the meanings and implications of the Equal Protection Clause of the Fourteenth Amendment to the Constitution. At least so it seems to a scholar who spends much of his time reading such constitutional reflections. These reflections are most commonly found in judicial opinions. Of course, our judges have certainly not created, nurtured, or sustained equality single-handedly. Courageous and sometimes incautious litigants have demanded equality as their right, and the lawyers who have represented them have played the crucial role of advocates. Sometimes the stimuli for judicial intervention have been dramatic, even violent, events in the streets of America's cities, with the key heroic parts played by ordinary downtrodden citizens and the villains' roles played by the ostensible forces of law and order. We also must not forget the special gains in equality due to the contributions of such charismatic leaders as Dr. Martin Luther King, Jr. Nonetheless, the interpretations of the Equal Protection Clause contained in judicial opinions offer perhaps the most accessible, continuous, and thoughtful reflections on the possibilities of human equality in our society. In this book I seek to show that since 1865 interpretation of the Equal Protection Clause has evolved toward the achievement of a more inclusive and insightful understanding of human equality (albeit with notable starts, stops, gaps, much delay, and only a few spurts of action). The problem is that many people don't know very much about that evolution and even fewer comprehend its implications.

The 1991 congressional debates over federal civil rights policy and President Bush's continued symbolic opposition to "quotas" illustrate quite well how little even our leaders have understood or acted upon the implications of equality. So equality these days is often like a stranger in our society; we may be familiar with the concept as a lofty abstraction, but not in practical terms, when it affects our own portion in the societal game of "who gets what."

A special irony in this country is that certain versions of equality have often held a high and cherished spot in American popular ideologies, yet even those versions of equality have coexisted (sometimes happily, sometimes not) with glaring and inescapable inequalities for real people in real life. The "American Dilemma" of race (in Gunnar Myrdal's apt characterization) is still the best example of the long-standing coexistence of a norm of equality with the everyday practice of inequality. Sex is another unhappy candidate for such ironic coexistence. And we have only begun to ponder, at least in our recent constitutional reflections, the norm of equality in coexistence with the reality of the distribution of wealth and the victims of poverty or, even worse, of homelessness.

An irony of the twentieth century is that it has witnessed the enduring reality and the abiding prospect of totalitarian oppression (vastly enhanced by the capabilities of modern technology), the insentient horrors of the Nazis and the Holocaust, and, since 1945, the continuing possibility of human extinction through nuclear weapons launched either by design or by accident. Yet at the same time we have been drawn together as human beings (often through much the same technology that has enhanced these evils) who ought to be capable of perceiving and understanding our common humanity—our joys, our hopes, our fears, our terrors, and our sufferings.

Especially as our Western societies have become more secular and as hopes for salvation in some other existence have waned (for those of us who have lost our religious faith), many of us have come more readily to sense the misery and desperation of millions of human lives. We are capable of perceiving that hundreds of millions of humans will experience only that desperation. Our brothers and sisters are often born to suffer, endure, and at the end go out like candles. Yet some of us are born to thrive, prosper, and enjoy life, even if our end is the same.

Others who still have their religious faith may be motivated by theological claims for human brotherhood and sisterhood, though distance has often diffused those claims and proximity has always made them easier to apprehend. The key factor today is that our ability to perceive our human relatedness is now enhanced by modern transportation and communication technology.

Given the size and complexities of the societies in which we live, we can also more readily see that misery and desperation often are not the just desserts of others. Many of the unpleasant realities of our lives are beyond our personal control. When we understand that, it is easier to project ourselves into the misery and hopelessness of others and to understand that we are, all of us, bound together in our efforts to escape the terrors of life—hunger, disease, disaster, discomfort, ignorance, loneliness, old age—and to postpone as long as possible the exquisite and inevitable reality of our own mortality. Certainly in such things all men and women are equal.

Yet we have many mechanisms for escaping from the reality and demands of our common humanity. Whenever we can, we simply try not to think about such depressing and fearsome matters. Even those who seriously seek to follow the moral dictates of a particular religious tradition are often fully capable of avoiding such apparently specific injunctions as: "If you would be perfect, go, sell what you possess and give to the poor, and you will have treasure in heaven; and come, follow me" (Matt. 19:21). Or: "Again I tell you, it is easier for a camel to go through the eye of a needle than for a rich man to enter the kingdom of God" (Matt. 19:24).

Perhaps the easiest escape from such strictures is offered by the justification that others simply get what they deserve. Indeed, that justification thrives in the fertile and well-tilled soil of American individualism, especially when individualism is subsumed under what has been called our "dominant ideology" about economic inequality (Huber and Form, 1973). This ideology begins with the premise that opportunity for economic security and well-being is ample in America, and therefore both are readily achievable through hard work. It follows that individuals are responsible for their own fates. A corollary is that whatever economic inequalities may exist are equitable and fair, for they simply reflect the efforts and abilities of individuals (Kluegel and Smith, 1986: 5).

Our dominant ideology does require equality of opportunity, or, better understood, it requires a particular version of equality of opportunity, one that often doesn't deal adequately with the reality that certain individuals (African-Americans or women, for example) have often been barred or handicapped in the competition for economic success. Our traditional understanding of equality of opportunity rests on the assumption that competition for success is equally open to all and that all are allowed to compete on equal terms under equal rules. Such an understanding of equality of opportunity is the version of equality most compatible with our dominant American ideology. Thus, with equal access and equal rules and through fair competition, people will be allowed to demonstrate their possibly unequal abilities and efforts so that they can be appropriately rewarded for their "successes" or "failures." It is obvious that such an understanding of equality of opportunity, and its primacy within American individualistic ideology, is quite consistent with the ideals of a capitalistic, market-oriented society (Rae, 1981: 64–71). Nonetheless, equality can have other meanings, and some of those meanings are more compatible with the elements of our common humanity (such as our shared fears and aspirations) than is our own traditional American understanding of equality of opportunity.

Yet, it is important to be fair to the American version of equality of opportunity. There is much to be said in favor of incentives and of rewarding individual effort and achievement, and it does appear that insufficient rewards sometimes may stifle individual initiative. Boris Yeltsin's struggle to reform the Soviet economy offers up-to-date evidence of the dysfunctions of centrally directed command economies, as did Deng Xiaoping's earlier modernization program in China. Both have sought to introduce rewards and market principles in the hope of encouraging greater productivity. But it is important to remember that certain normative or structural features of a capitalistic society, like monopolies or racism, may limit the prospects of open and fair competition between individuals. It is important to remember that our society also has dysfunctions, and it is not evident that human beings are motivated solely by material rewards. We may sometimes be capable of altruism as well.

It is true that human nature is often a puzzlement, despite our best efforts to understand who we are. Shortly after President Nixon's surprising visit to China in 1972, American groups began to make three-week tours of China a routine manner, and they often returned reporting that the Chinese regime had apparently "transformed" its young people in some interesting and seemingly important respects. Individualism, the American tourists reported, had been obliterated and replaced by a kind of society-oriented altruism. For example, when uni-

versity students were asked about their life and career goals, they replied that they would go wherever the Party sent them and would willingly serve the people in whatever way the Party might ask.

By 1978 (following the fall of the hard-line Maoists, whose leaders
were by then being vilified as the Gang of Four) when university students were asked the same question, they often gave two-part responses. At first they said that, of course, they were willing to "serve
the people" in any manner that might be asked of them. They then
continued by saying that their own personal preferences would be to
serve as interpreters, translators, etc. (these were English-speaking
university students).

Today, university students asked the same questions would be more
likely to respond readily with their own career preferences and to leave
the Party out of it. Moreover, even given the forcible repression that
followed, the 1989 democracy movement, led chiefly by students, illustrates in still another way the ephemeral nature of the Maoist transformation of human nature. Such a kaleidoscope of attitudes, changing as
they did over roughly a fifteen-year period, should serve to make social
observers suitably skeptical (at least in the short term) about the prospects for fundamental transformations of human nature. The age-old
issues of whether we human beings are inherently selfish and self-
seeking or are capable of genuinely altruistic behavior—and of whether
we are inherently competitive or capable of genuinely cooperative behavior—are certainly beyond the scope of this book. Still, it is intriguing to note that most major world religions have been about the task of
transforming at least the behavior if not the nature of humankind for
many centuries. In this century Marxist leaders set for themselves
much the same task, that is, the stated objective of creating "new socialist men and women." So far Marxists have not had conspicuous success. Instead, the Communist leaders of the Soviet Union and of East-
ern Europe have witnessed the disintegration of their Marxist-Leninist
states, while the people of their countries have largely jettisoned Marxist ideology. Given such failures, it seems extraordinarily unlikely that
even a completely successful effort to establish a proper appreciation
for human equality (an appreciation founded on understanding the elements of our common humanity) would readily produce a broad transformation of people or of society. Ours must be a much more modest
task.

I propose that we examine critically the various pecking orders into
which we sort ourselves, or are sorted by others. Slave or free, African-

American or white, Spanish- or French- or English-speaking, male or female, rich or poor, clever or slow, educated or ignorant, professional or lay, skilled or unskilled—these are the sorts of pecking orders through which certain individuals are sometimes seen as "better" or more deserving than others. Several of these pecking orders have already been examined under the Equal Protection Clause of the Fourteenth Amendment to determine whether they should be sustained— that is, whether they represent compelling or even rational grounds for treating people differently. A few pecking orders have been broadly and firmly rejected through equal protection analysis (race being the best example). Others have been sustained, although in varying degrees and circumstances. No doubt other pecking orders, including ones that we cannot now imagine, will be subjected one day to equal protection scrutiny. The premise for such scrutiny is that the Equal Protection Clause requires public agencies to treat people alike unless there is some rational basis for treating people differently. Given that limited objective, equal protection analysis probably will never eliminate all human pecking orders. Nor should it. It is unlikely that we will reject all criteria for determining differences between people and call for universal equality. But analysis of equal protection requires that we define some objective justifications for any variation in public treatment of people. That is, and will be, no small achievement.

My examination will begin in chapter 2 with an introduction of the key concepts that will help us sort out the various meanings of equality. This chapter frankly is derivative; the source of the concepts I use is Douglas Rae and others, *Equalities* (Rae, 1981).[1] While Rae proposes a number of concepts to encompass the possible meanings of equality, only a few are necessary for understanding how the Equal Protection Clause of the Fourteenth Amendment has been interpreted. I will concentrate mostly on Rae's distinctions between *individual-regarding equality* and *group- or bloc-regarding equality* and on the differences between two versions of equality of opportunity.

History is an important and inevitable part of our effort to understand the possible meanings of the Equal Protection Clause. Chapter 3 will review the antislavery and profreedman antecedents of the Fourteenth Amendment and the debates on that amendment in the first session of the Thirty-ninth Congress, beginning in 1865. We will consider the possible meanings of equality that were attributed to the Equal Protection Clause by proponents and opponents during these debates. Of course, the debates cannot be properly understood apart from the context of ideas and events of the Civil War and Reconstruction, so we will relate the debates in 1865 and 1866 to the social and intellectual history of the period.

In chapter 4 we will review the relatively few early cases that interpreted the meaning of Equal Protection in the contexts of race or sex. We will begin with the ratification of the Fourteenth Amendment in 1868 and conclude with the now notorious decision in *Plessy v. Ferguson* in 1896 and with a few cases that followed *Plessy*, which serve to illustrate how lightly the Supreme Court took its requirement of equal facilities. Probably the most important case from this period was the group of suits joined together as the *Slaughter-House Cases* of 1873. Judicial interpretations of Equal Protection from this time offer to us today a disappointing contrast to the intentions and purposes of the Radical Republicans who made Reconstruction policy. The *Slaughter-House Cases*, however, make some political sense in light of the interests and contending factions that struggled over Reconstruction in the early 1870s and reached their zenith in the contested presidential election of 1876. The political bargain struck to determine the outcome of that election in effect brought the demise of Reconstruction. In turn, the agreement to stifle Reconstruction must have contributed to the reluctance of the Supreme Court justices of that time to give solid substance to the Equal Protection Clause of the Fourteenth Amendment. Instead of equal protection we got the "separate but equal doctrine" in 1896.

We will examine an anomaly in chapter 5. The Equal Protection Clause, as we have seen, written chiefly to protect the status and rights of freedmen, was co-opted and employed by laissez-faire ideologues beginning in the 1880s to protect burgeoning corporate enterprise from the regulatory enactments of the states. The excesses of rapid and heedless industrialization brought human helplessness and misery along with the jobs that were created. Some of the American states responded with legislation designed to protect workers, especially women and children. The use of equal protection to strike down such legislation had much in common with the Court's formulation of "substantive economic due process," also from the Fourteenth Amendment, during the same period. Thus an amendment whose chief purpose was the amelioration of the lot of freedmen produced only the "separate but equal doctrine" for its intended beneficiaries, while yielding a much more rigorous enforcement of equality for business enterprise.

The eventual conversion of the Supreme Court, that is, the voting switch of Justice Roberts in 1937, marked the end of this era. We will analyze the economic equal protection cases from this period in the light of the laissez-faire ideology extant in American society in the last quarter of the nineteenth century and the first quarter of the twentieth. Of course, that ideology lives on in many ways even today, though largely outside the realm of constitutional interpretation.

Chapter 6 reviews the cases that led inevitably to *Brown v. Board of Education of Topeka* in 1954. Much has already been written about these cases, and Richard Kluger's definitive study, appropriately called *Simple Justice*, has given us a detailed account of the yeoman efforts of civil rights activists that began with the work of Charles Houston and the Howard University Law School in constructing the foundation for the legal assault on the separate but equal doctrine. Kluger's account is full and rich, and even if it could be matched here, little purpose would be served by repetition. We can, however, examine in detail the conceptualization of equality that is contained in the decisions that led to *Brown,* in the context of the history of the time.

Chapter 7 is critical in understanding equal protection law since the revolution heralded by *Brown v. Board.* The development of policy that followed *Brown* in 1954–55 and led up to *Swann v. Charlotte-Mecklenburg* in 1971 produced only marginal results. That history of years of resistance, caution, and finally modest efforts to end segregation and to move toward unitary schools is examined.

Chapter 8 begins with *Swann v. Charlotte-Mecklenburg* in 1971 and traces the efforts to integrate and to produce unitary school systems up to its arguable policy limits in *Milliken v. Bradley* in 1974, and through the much-constrained efforts to integrate that followed *Milliken.* Understanding the cases from this period requires close and careful analysis of the various understandings of equal protection of the law contained in judicial opinions, as well as an interpretation of the various meanings of words such as *segregation, desegregation,* and *integration* found in these opinions. As we shall see, the most important development is the Supreme Court's eventual, albeit reluctant, acceptance of a policy that in limited situations involves group-regarding equality. That is simply a way of saying that our courts eventually sought integration through outcomes that involved some measure of group or racial proportionality. In *Milliken* we will see that an intractable obstacle to effective requirement of racial proportionality was confronted when a majority of the U.S. Supreme Court refused to extend the mandate of racial proportionality to encompass the suburban school districts that surrounded Detroit.

Chapter 9 reviews both statutory and constitutional meanings of equality in an effort to understand equality of opportunity in higher education and in employment, both in the context of race. The *Bakke* case, involving the rejection of a white male's application to the medical school of the University of California at Davis when minority applicants with "lesser qualifications"[2] had been admitted, provides one of the best examples of the difficulty of the issues in this area. The apparently irreconcilable conflict between individual-regarding and bloc- or group-regarding equality is examined in depth here. The competing understandings of equality in employment, promotion, and job retention situations make up the balance of this chapter.

Discrimination based on sex is examined in chapter 10. There have been several excellent and extended treatments of sex-based discrimination in recent years.[3] A single chapter, however thorough, cannot do full justice to this subject, but we can examine the ways in which equal protection law has developed with respect to sex in comparison to the previous development of the law on racial discrimination. We will see that a key difference is that while there may be certain legitimate differences between the sexes that the law may take into account (especially regarding pregnancy and childbearing), there are no such differences based strictly on race. Equal protection law must therefore take into account legitimate sexual differences while usually excluding those alleged sexual differences that are based solely on tradition, prejudice, or social attribution.

Chapter 11 is a consideration of other forms of categorical discrimination that have recently been the subject of civil rights cases. These include alienage, elections and voting rights, residency, marriage and the family, poverty, age, and disability. Such distinctions have involved the Supreme Court in determining which rights it ought to recognize as fundamental so as to be accorded equal protection. Since the Equal Protection Clause does not list the possible subjects for categorical discrimination, equal protection analysis must be open ended.

Equality provisions in the basic law of two other countries and under various covenants of public international law are considered in chapter 12. Equality judgments outside the United States are much more friendly to group- or bloc-regarding equality than is U.S. domestic law. It is also interesting to confront the fact that, among advanced industrialized nations, the United States is one of the most reluctant to enter into international covenants that guarantee significant aspects of human equality.

In the conclusion of the book, I stress that the chief conflict in U.S.

cases and policies regarding human equality has to do with the confrontation between individual-regarding and group- or bloc-regarding equality. I argue that while both views represent conceptually acceptable ways of understanding equality, both contain problems. A jurisprudence of equality, based on the individualism of a hypothetical free-market economy, may be unrealistic in a complex world of multinational corporations and huge aggregations of economic power. While most individuals would be frustrated at the prospect of being mere dwarfs relative to such aggregations, in fact they are more like subatomic particles—people as quarks—relative to the mega-aggregations of wealth and power that are now pervasive. Yet group- or bloc-regarding equality unfortunately may perpetuate group distinctions when they are no longer necessarily warranted by the facts—unwarranted, eventually, even by the need to compensate for a history of prior discrimination. We will see that group-based remedies usually are, and must always be, regarded as temporary, remedial, and compensatory expedients. The grounds for accepting such group-based remedies as temporary remedial measures are, I think, clearly demonstrated by the issues and cases reviewed in this book. That is why President Bush's rhetorical rejection of quotas is either cynical or foolish. However, it is likely that in the long run a better solution is possible.

A reconciliation, made possible through a better understanding of the many variables that individual merit may signify, is proposed at the end of the book. The key concept in that reconciliation is what I call the *distance-travelled concept*. The point is that even identical numerical measures of merit, such as grade-point averages in college or standardized test scores, may reflect quite different levels of ability and motivation. One person may have achieved certain scores against usually insuperable social and economic obstacles. Another may have achieved precisely the same scores while having had every conceivable social and economic advantage in his or her favor. If that may be true with respect to identical scores, lower scores by one person may also reflect greater ability and effort than the achievement even of higher scores by another person, depending on a person's socioeconomic starting point and on the obstacles that may have stood in the way.

Another important point is that we often depend on numbers, apart from their socioeconomic context, far too much. For many jobs, for example, higher scores may not be significant to actual performance once a certain level of ability and achievement has been reached. Higher scores may serve only as a means by which society can limit the number of individuals who are eligible for scarce and lucrative positions and render them privileged members of society. The conclusion of the book explores these ideas at greater length.

By now it must be obvious that I take equality seriously, even though I recognize the prospect of being accused of naive idealism or even of fuzzy thinking for writing a book like this. Certainly the critics of equality have had their day. For example, Peter Westen has written in the *Harvard Law Review* that equality is an "empty vessel with no substantive moral content of its own" (Westen, 1982: 547). He argues that equal protection concepts are always susceptible of being translated into more clear and precise claims based on specific rights. His is a long and fairly complex argument, but its best refutation is found by showing the irrelevance of the argument. While his entire argument may succeed according to rules of logic, I contend that it fails within the norms of human experience. Arguments founded on equality are sturdy structures for most of us, full indeed of symbolic moral content. The rhetoric of Martin Luther King, Jr., stripped of its egalitarian appeals, would be more pallid and far less powerful. Revolutions have been launched and sometimes won with such words. Even our best political debates rarely partake of the logic of an article in the *Harvard Law Review.* Yet the most rigorous political debates in our society have contained claims for human equality.

It is interesting that in his book *Speaking of Equality,* published in 1990, Westen acknowledged the rhetorical power of equality, while continuing to insist that equality adds nothing that is necessary to the understanding of rights. Yet conversations about equality involve familiar and well-tempered tools of human communication, and the fact that we may be able to restate equality arguments in other forms simply doesn't advance the prospect of our understanding one another very much. Consider Westen's criticism of this quote from Isaiah Berlin's essay on "Equality as an Ideal":

The assumption is that equality needs no reasons, only inequality does so; that uniformity, regularity, similarity, symmetry . . . need not be specially accounted for, whereas difference, misestimated behavior, change in conduct, need explanation and, as a rule justification. If I have a cake and there are ten persons among whom I wish to divide it, then if I give exactly one tenth to each, this will not . . . call for justification; whereas if I depart from this principle of equal division I am expected to produce a special reason. (Berlin, 1961: 131)

In his 1982 article, Westen's response was that the presumption of equality is essentially meaningless because it offers no basis for distinguishing likes from unalikes and no standards for choosing between "good" and "bad" reasons for treating people differently. While the world might be better if we had such clear and logically absolute rules, we shall have to get on without them. Most of us would regard Berlin's proposed equal division of a cake as the best solution, at least until someone offers a better basis for division. About the best we can do in considering other than equal division—in proposing, for example, that one of the ten potential cake consumers has not eaten all day and warrants a larger piece—is to offer our reasons, discuss them, arrive at a consensus if we can, and do what most of us agree on if we can't. That is generally regarded as preferable to the strongest member grabbing all of the cake (as with the pigs in Orwell's *Animal Farm*: "All animals are equal, but some animals are more equal than others"). Equal division is also clearly seen as preferable to a fight over the cake among the prospective consumers. The presumption of equal division serves the useful purpose of requiring us to propose, discuss, and eventually decide, usually by majority or plurality rule, when to deviate from the principle of equality. Finding no apparently good reasons for deviating from equal division, the presumption of equality prevails. Properly understood, equality is a powerful and valuable human process for considering who gets what.

Our historic difficulty has not been with the principle of equality but with the inferior reasons we have accepted for deviating from that principle. People have too easily been persuaded that reasons such as race, sex, religion, language, or simple right of birth justify differential treatments and rewards.

After more than seventy-five years of desuetude relative to its intended purpose of protecting former slaves, in our time the Equal Protection Clause of the Fourteenth Amendment has at last led us to question critically several of our common reasons for treating some people differently than others. We have finally seen (most of us at least) that some of our traditional perceptions of distinguishing between people are fundamentally flawed.

While distinctions based on race and gender are most prominent in the collective experience of American society, others remain to be examined. This book is for those readers who are willing to become engaged in the process of considering the possible meanings and implications of human equality. No doubt there are many inferior reasons for treating some people differently than others that are yet waiting to be judged critically and then rejected. Many of our human pecking orders may not withstand close scrutiny in the future. Even if we can't always foresee particular outcomes, this book should at least help us to understand the potential claims of equality.

2

UNDERSTANDING KEY CONCEPTS
OF EQUALITY

*Because men are men, social institutions—property rights, and the orga-
nization of industry, and the system of public health and education—
should be planned, as far as possible, to emphasize and strengthen, not the
class differences which divide, but the common humanity which unites
them.*

—R. H. Tawney, *Equality*, 1931

In thinking about equality, it is crucial to begin by considering the
ways in which people are alike rather than the differences that divide
them. If we begin by looking for inequalities, we surely will find them.
The difference between equality and inequality is not just a matter of
semantics or of perceptions; it is not just a matter of seeing a glass as
half-full or half-empty. For example, sociologist Ralf Dahrendorf was
quickly moved when writing about inequality to impose a conceptual
structure on the various ways in which people may be held to be unequal (Dahrendorf, 1969: 18 et seq.).

Dahrendorf, like Rousseau before (in his 1754 *Discourse on the Origin
of Inequality*), first describes inequalities that represent natural capabilities (for example an artistically gifted person) and those that reflect a
social position (an inherited title). He then distinguishes between inequalities that denote some evaluative rank order (differences in intelligence, for example) and those that have no necessary evaluative con-
notation (hair color, state of residence). When these are combined in a
table, inequalities can be represented as shown in Figure 2.1.

Like most sociologists, Dahrendorf was chiefly concerned with cell
d, in which one would find the various indications of social stratification. Since every society that has ever existed has had social differences that reflect the evaluative rank ordering of people, a scholar
studying social stratification will never lack relevant data. Social stratification will vary from one society to another, and comparisons between
societies as to the particular kinds of stratification are fully worthy of

Figure 2.1

	Natural Differences	Social Differences
No evaluative rank order	a	b
Some sort of evaluative order	c	d

study. Nonetheless, without denigrating such studies, it is difficult to see how the description or analysis of social stratification can help very much with the understanding of equality—and especially with our understanding the equal protection of the law under the Fourteenth Amendment.

Questions of equal protection of the law arise when someone has been treated differently than others by some public agency or under some public policy. Our courts have been charged with the duty of deciding whether the reasons offered for such treatment are acceptable. The premise for judicial inquiry is that of equality. Inequalities imposed by public agencies or through public policies require justification. The burden of justification may be heavy or slight, depending to a large degree on the context and on the sorts of inequalities that are imposed.

The premise that people ought to be treated as equals unless differences are demonstrated has been part of Western cultural tradition for a very long time. A related view can be found in Aristotle's *Nicomachean Ethics,* which argues that likes should be treated alike and that unalikes should be treated differently. A corollary, as Rousseau argued in his *Discourse on the Origin of Inequality,* is that social inequality, when enforced by established laws, clashes with "natural rights" whenever it is not proportionate to natural inequality, that is to the demonstrable natural differences between people. Recently Jennifer Hochschild has argued that principles of equality assume that people begin with equal value and can make equal claims on society. Thus differences in treatment must be justified (Hochschild, 1981: 51). Such positions may represent a normative principle, or they may rest on the simple understanding of how people react to everyday situations. The normative principle would be: Treat every person alike, unless there is a good reason to treat her or him differently. The principle may rest on the simple recognition of how we ordinarily behave. Some examples: We are all familiar with the practice of tossing a coin, or of drawing straws, when it is necessary to distribute things that are indivisible and when there is not enough for everyone. We do use such measures. If there is enough for everyone, or if the resource is divisible into equal shares, a norm of share and share alike is more likely to be the initial rule. Deviations from equal chance (tossing a coin or drawing straws) or from equal distribution (share and share alike) do seem to require justification in everyday life. We want to know why a premise of equality is not to be followed. In everyday life someone may occasionally suggest an alternative principle of distribution—based, for example, on differential need or effort. We often accept such alternative principles of distribution, but we do expect that there be intelligible reasons for different treatment—preferably ones on which we can achieve consensus or at least decide through majority rule.

My interest in thinking about such equality principles grew out of a study of two Title VII[1] cases that were decided by the U.S. Supreme Court, *Griggs v. Duke Power Co.* (1971) and *Albemarle Paper Co. v. Moody* (1975). (The eventual implications of these cases in part caused President Bush to raise the specter of quotas.) In first writing about these cases (Jackson, 1976), I focused on the problems entailed in demonstrating significant relationships between tests and actual requisite job skills. At the end of my essay I speculated on the broad implications of being required to justify employment tests.

What if all educational and employment criteria were required to survive empirical validation, even absent showings under prohibited statutory or constitutional categories? What if anyone could challenge educational and employment criteria? The bastions of racism, sexism and credentialism might then fall. Instead of criteria predicated on status—black, white, brown, male, female, high school or college graduate—educational and employment criteria would have to be founded on qualities derived from empirical validation—on the talents, knowledge, experience, and skills (however acquired) that have demonstrable relationships with actual academic or job performance. Under such a policy many criteria that are now only assumed to be valid or that "have always been that way" would be suspect. (Jackson, 1976: 76)

It seems obvious that discriminatory acts have in common the use of a reason for different treatment by someone that others (most often judges or legislators) find to be inappropriate or unconscionable. Yet reasons today held to be unconscionable (race, for example) may once have provided acceptable and commonplace justifications for differential treatment. Even the Radical Republicans, who were the advocates for freedmen during Reconstruction, were markedly racist by contemporary standards (Hyman, 1967: xxvii). As society changes, certain differences between people that were once assumed to be "real" and firmly established may later be entirely rejected.

What produces this transition from commonplace acceptance to complete rejection? What reasons for treating people differently do we use today that may one day be viewed as pinnacles of prejudice? While the first question is intriguing and difficult, the second is impossible because none of us can imagine the unimaginable. All that can be said for certain is that if we require affirmative proof of the validity and utility of the criteria that we use for differential treatment, we will be forced to be aware of them and possibly even to recognize that some of them may be questionable.

Reflect for a moment on the reasons we use in everyday life for treating people differently. In my own field, higher education, we use many criteria that might not withstand close scrutiny. Can the requirement of a specified number of education courses as a prerequisite for teacher certification be demonstrated to bear a significant and strong relationship to competence as a classroom teacher? Is the requirement of a high school diploma or a university degree always clearly sustainable as a precondition for employment? Ought cumulative grade point averages and scores on the Medical College Admissions Test (MCAT) or the Law School Admissions Test (LSAT) be decisive in selecting those young men and women who thereby eventually may earn grand incomes as doctors or lawyers? In education we often help determine life chances—income and various forms of status—through measures that are, at the least, questionable. Conversely, we often limit opportunities by the same measures.

The means by which we attempt to measure the qualities people possess and the relationships between those qualities and expected outcomes are at best highly problematic. It would seem to be a fair requirement of equal protection that we be constrained to do the best job of measurement and validation that the circumstances permit.[2]

To this point we have been considering a premise of equality and the consequent necessary justification of inequalities. To go beyond that, we can best understand the claims of equality by considering the various meanings that equality can have. The most important book on that subject is *Equalities,* a small volume that grew out of a series of seminars involving Douglas Rae and others at Yale University in the 1970s. The book represents an effort to create a "structural grammar of equal-

ity."[3] The work of Rae and his colleagues provides the foundation for the balance of this chapter.

Rae's structural grammar of equality contains many concepts. While many of them represent familiar meanings and content, the words chosen to describe the content may be novel and the carefully worked out distinctions between concepts clearly represent a level of precision and sophistication not ordinarily matched even in serious conversation about equality. A careful reading of the entire book is a rewarding experience; here we can choose only a few concepts that will prove to be especially important in understanding equal protection of the law.

The most important basic concepts and distinctions are between what Rae and his colleagues call *individual-regarding* equality and *bloc-regarding* equalities (Rae, 1981: chapter 2).

Individual-regarding equality involves defining a class of individuals and then demanding that each member of the class be treated equally. The easiest example is to treat all human beings as a class and to demand that each person be treated alike in some respect, for example, that every human being ought to have the right to the minimum necessities to sustain life. A narrower example would be the right of everyone who is prosecuted for a serious crime in an American court to have retained or appointed counsel. The preference for equality represented by the everyday norm of share and share alike is yet another example of simple *individual-regarding* equality.

The question of who is to be treated alike is determined by the definition of the subject class. Classes may be defined narrowly or broadly, implicitly or explicitly. Rae uses the phrase *inclusionary equality* to describe a broadly defined class, such as the class of all human beings. Relative to that broad definition, a class composed of all adult Anglo-Saxon males, each of whom would be entitled to equal treatment, would be an *exclusionary* class. It should already be clear that the point of view expressed in this book essentially is supportive of broad inclusionary equality, coupled with the expectation that all exclusions require justification. Rae suggests, however, that this may involve a paradox. Liberal inclusionary equality, he says, is achievable only through centralized authority, for only centralized authority could have the overall responsibility for broad inclusionary equality. That, of course, is essentially consistent with the long-standing and frequently voiced conservative or laissez-faire criticism of socialism, even of democratic socialism. The argument runs that centralized authority in the long run will prove to be illiberal—in the extreme it might even be the *Road to Serfdom* that Friedrich Hayek wrote about in 1944.

A related point is that while the moral claims of inclusionary equality may be universal, the means to achieve universal equality are usually absent. As Rae notes, if one makes an argument for broad inclusionary equality, what sense does it make to insist on equal treatment for all those within the United States, for example, while dismissing entirely the claims of our neighbors in Mexico? The same moral objection can be raised to the conspicuous consumption of those of us who live in the First World, while many of our brothers and sisters in the Third World suffer famine even unto death.

There are answers to these points, but they admittedly are only partly responsive, that is, they are not logical refutations of the points Rae makes. The first answer is that in the limited domain of equality of opportunity, a presumption of inclusionary equality and a stringent requirement of justification for all exclusions would not necessarily require a monolithic bureaucratic state to enforce individual-regarding equality. It probably *would* require readily accessible judicial or quasi-judicial authorities to strike down those ill-founded exclusions that some of us might prefer to continue to use.

Such a critical revision of equality of opportunity would apply particularly to the sorts of inferior reasons we sometimes offer for excluding individuals from applicant pools for jobs or for higher education. If broad inclusionary equality is well understood and held by most to be legitimate, then we could hope that its recognition would not require frequent resort to coercion, that is, to enforcement by court orders. Ideally, it would be the moral force of our perceived common humanity, of our brotherhood and sisterhood, that would prevail.

A second answer is that there is probably some considerable utility in being mindful of the claims of universal human equality even if the practical means for achieving it do not as yet exist. In recent years, for example, famine in Ethiopia, in sub-Saharan Africa, and in Bangladesh have been portrayed so clearly and so often through television and print media that universal human claims against hunger press upon us, especially those of us in "overstuffed" America, and while the means of food distribution in Africa are not what they might be, there has still been a notable human response to hunger there.

It is easy and tempting to belabor each point as Rae's concepts are introduced, but instead there will be many opportunities in the chapters that follow to apply these concepts in contexts that are often complex. It should be sufficient now to suggest that our review of equal protection cases below will demonstrate long-term trends in the United States that lead toward an ever more inclusive understanding of equality.

Segmental subjects of equality involve the division of people into two or more mutually exclusive subclasses and the requirement of individual-regarding equality within the classes but not between them. Just as the most inclusionary equality would be the absence of subclasses of any sort, exclusionary equality involves the creation of segmental subjects. It is the criteria for exclusion that are significant in segmental equality. Rae points out that military hierarchies of rank are excellent examples of *segmental exclusion,* each rank having its own privileges and its position within the hierarchy. Credentialing processes are segmental as well, though these are often nonhierarchical. If we divide law graduates into those who have successfully passed a bar exam and those who have not, all those who have passed would be accorded the equal right to practice law within a jurisdiction, while all those who have failed would be equally excluded.

There are many measures in our society that involve such divisions into segments, and in some cases their validity is questionable. Others, already recognized as prejudicial, have come to be scorned. For example, the division of some U.S. citizens into African-Americans and whites, with the requirement that each subclass be treated equally, would mean that all whites would be entitled to equal treatment, as would all African-Americans, but the treatment accorded each subclass need not be equal. Thus, race as a criterion for division into subclasses would create a particular form of systematic racial inequality. We would not expect to see this form of racial inequality in a rational world because it is difficult to imagine a sensible reason for such a system, with stringent requirements that all whites and all African-Americans be treated equally within their respective subclasses. Probably the nearest example in our history would be the division along racial lines into slave and freeman, in which legal status would render each subclass equal. The exclusion from the franchise by race prior to the ratification of the Fifteenth Amendment in 1870 would be another example. The best contemporary example would be the sadly paranoid system of apartheid in South Africa, which only now is in the early stage of being dismantled.

Bloc-regarding equality consists of dividing people into two or more subclasses and requiring equality between the blocs but not within each. Rae suggests that the 1896 precedent of *Plessy v. Ferguson,* in requiring separate but equal accommodations for African-Americans and whites in public transportation, was bloc-regarding, since it required overall equal facilities for each subclass but was not concerned at all whether each African-American or white passenger had accommodations equal to other members of their own bloc.

An easy way to illustrate the distinctions between individual-regarding, segmental, and bloc-regarding equality is to apply them to employment and higher education. We can thus examine the uses of education-relevant and job-relevant selection criteria. If we begin with an inclusionary individual-regarding premise, then the relevant class of job or university applicants would consist of all potential applicants with no exclusions, with no subclasses, and without regard to any applicant's membership in a bloc (e.g., race or sex). All applicants would be entitled to equal treatment, except for their differences on some job-relevant or education-relevant criteria. Those relevant differences, when identified, would create segments, that is a division into subclasses of those who possess some relevant criterion (a job-related skill or the ability to read English, for example) and those who do not. Segmental equality would require that those who are equal with respect to some relevant criterion be treated alike. This would be quite different from the pursuit of bloc-regarding equality in which the object would be to create a work force or a student body with some proportional representation by race or sex (presumably still of people with the necessary job-relevant or education-relevant skills). A bloc-regarding policy would suggest that among those with necessary skills the object would be to hire or to admit those who would help achieve the object of racial or sexual proportionality.

A fitting example of these distinctions can be found in the arguments for the respective sides in the *Bakke* case (*Regents of the University of California v. Bakke,* 1978). Bakke was a white male who sought admission to the medical school of the University of California at Davis. He contended that he had been denied admission, while minority applicants with lesser qualifications had been admitted. In one sense his argument was for simple individual-regarding equality, in that he argued that minority or racial status should not be relevant. But he also argued for a form of segmental equality so that applicants would be treated differently (admitted to medical school or not) based solely on their benchmark scores (composed of interviewer's rating, overall grade point average, science GPA, Medical College Admissions Test scores, etc.).

The university's argument was both segmental and bloc-regarding. It was segmental in the sense that the criteria for admitting the 84 students was based primarily on benchmark scores, but it was bloc-regarding in that they had set aside 16 out of 100 entry places for minority applicants to ensure that "disadvantaged" students would be represented in each entering class. The bloc-regarding goal of achieving that proportional representation was obviously antithetical both to simple individual-regarding equality and to segmental equality based solely on benchmark scores.

We will analyze the outcome in *Bakke* in depth in chapter 8; here we only need note that simple individual-regarding, segmental, and bloc-regarding equality each represents a particular kind of equality, each with its own justification. It is important to recognize and to remember that point, for in ordinary conversations involving situations like the *Bakke* case it is commonly claimed that only Bakke's argument is founded on equality. The bloc-regarding claim of affirmative action is usually branded as reverse discrimination rather than as an alternative version of equality. For example, President Bush's rhetorical rejection of quotas simply represents only one of the possible understandings of equality. Understanding the different goals each side intended to achieve with its perspective of equality will not necessarily help us decide which is correct, but it may help us to be more cautious and more thoughtful in the position we take.

Another important concept is what Rae calls the *domain* of equality, that is, what sorts of issues are to be subject to a principle of equality (Rae, 1981: chapter 3). A domain may be narrow or broad, and it is the breadth of the claims for equality that sometimes distinguishes political ideologies. Despite some misleading rhetoric, virtually no one is opposed to the idea of equality—the disputes are usually over its breadth. Conservatives, Rae points out, favor a narrow domain, while people of the left, in their various shadings, favor expanding the domain of equality. Equal employment and equal educational opportunity would represent an important but nonetheless fairly narrow domain.

The next step in Rae's analysis is the difference between *domains of allocation* and *domains of account*. A domain of allocation is the class of things that a given agent or agency controls for the purpose of distribution. A domain of account is the class of things over which a given advocate seeks equal distribution. Thus those who control domains of allocation are those who receive demands for equal distribution, while domains of account are the subjects of those who make demands for equal distribution. Sometimes these may coincide (Rae calls this *straightforward* equality), sometimes not. One instance in which the two do not coincide leads to what Rae calls *compensatory inequality,* which is when a domain of allocation is unequally divided to compensate for inequality in a larger domain of account. In the *Bakke* case, the University of California, for example, was involved in a policy of bloc-regarding equality that can be construed as a policy of compensatory inequality. The university engaged in the unequal distribution of places in its entering class to compensate for the paucity of minority physicians in the larger society.

We come now to two concepts that Rae and his colleagues identified in their analysis of equality of opportunity (Rae, 1981: chapter 4). *Prospect-regarding* equality of opportunity describes situations in which everyone has the same probability of success, as in nonskill games such as a lottery (with a one-ticket limit) or as in the toss of a fairly balanced coin. Nothing about the participants has any effect on the outcome. At first it may not seem obvious why we might distribute opportunity randomly, except in games of chance, but that assumes that we are somehow able to do a better job of selection than does random choice.

Means-regarding equality of opportunity describes situations in which the players have equal rules through which they are enabled to demonstrate their possibly unequal talents, as in a fairly run footrace or in a boxing match. Such situations are quite different than prospect-regarding situations. The ideal of means-regarding settings is that the players will have an equal opportunity to demonstrate their inequality. This is the classic argument for meritocratic forms of competition, but there are a number of difficulties in means-regarding equality. Using the *Bakke* case once again, Bakke's argument would be appropriate and consistent with means-regarding equality, provided that using benchmark scores as the criterion for admitting medical school applicants would result in selecting the best-qualified candidates. The question is whether the benchmark scores do in fact represent legitimate qualifications for admission.

We can all agree that a footrace would be a poor means for selecting say, a reference librarian. It is possible that the benchmark scores, as in the *Bakke* case, are not good enough measures to be used decisively in selected entrants for law school or medical school. Means-regarding equality of opportunity requires that rewards, like places in medical school, be unequally distributed because some applicants have demonstrated more appropriate talents than have others. If we use the wrong measures of talent or if we use egregiously imprecise measures, then we would have made unequal distributions for no good reason. It follows logically that unless the utility and accuracy of a particular measurement of success can be demonstrated, prospect-regarding equality of opportunity may be a better, even if unconventional, outcome. I want to be very clear about the possible use of prospect-regarding equality of opportunity. Once certain minimum qualifications for medical school are established and met by applicants (such as literacy, knowledge of basic science, passing grades in basic science courses, and some minimum MCAT score), we might do just as well by choosing students for admission by lot, for that would at least achieve prospect-regarding equality of opportunity.

The idea of random selection, once minimum requirements are met, may appear startling, yet it is by no means clear that we will do better by choosing for graduate education those students who have the highest test scores or grade averages. Consider, for example, the daily tasks performed by a dentist or by a physician in family practice and ask whether we in fact need to select people of the very highest intellectual talents for such jobs. Perhaps the logic will be clearer if, instead of a recent situation in this country, we consider the traditional nineteenth-century British civil service career track, which involved the study of Latin and Greek classics at Oxford or Cambridge, the achievement of an Honours degree (preferably First Class) at one of those institutions, and the passing of a civil service examination predicated on a rigorous classical education. Through these steps young men (women were then excluded) were selected for the fast track to the upper strata of the British professional civil service. No doubt such a process did select very bright and industrious young men, but it certainly excluded others, some of whom no doubt were equally bright and industrious but had no Latin or Greek. The process had a systematic class bias (as did almost the entire educational system), and it was entirely unsubstantiated that particularly brilliant young men who could master the classics were indeed required for the upper reaches of the British civil service. Also undemonstrated was whether the classical education the process demanded had any particular utility in the work that higher civil servants actually performed. In our time we also may have devised a system through which we award status, prestige, power, and relatively large incomes to those who are able to win a particular kind of race. The qualifications are usually more relevant than the study of Latin and Greek but still may not suit the intended purpose.

The ideal of a meritocracy based on means-regarding equality of opportunity may have some invidious aspects. In any competition in which there are winners there must also be losers, and usually a good many more losers than winners. The rewards of merit are sufficiently great that we need to be sure that the merit we measure is in fact necessary for the achievement of our purposes. But even if we are sure that we have used fair procedures to measure relevant qualities, we still may encounter some intractable problems with means-regarding equality of opportunity. James Fishkin has noted that a strong doctrine of means-regarding equality of opportunity requires both merit that is fairly determined and equal life chances (Fishkin, 1983: 20). Equal life chances would mean that one's chances for success in achieving valued positions in society should not vary systematically with native characteristics such as race or, more broadly, with inherited socioeconomic status. That brings us to the threshold of "Fishkin's trilemma." Fishkin has suggested that the competing claims of means-regarding equality of opportunity, equality of life chances, and a preference in our society for the autonomy of the family create a trilemma. How do we ensure equality of life chances without intruding on other values, such as the autonomy and liberty of the family? The trilemma is raised by the natural tendency of a family to try to enhance the chances for success of its children, by conferring on each child whatever advantages it can in the competition for success in life.

Fishkin's trilemma is based on his assumption of two conditions, the first being moderate scarcity (not plenty for all, but not a life-and-death struggle for survival) and the second being good will (in which society has attempted to be fair and consistent in its implementation of principles such as means-regarding equality of opportunity). If either of those two conditions is absent, Fishkin would concede the primacy of egalitarian values over the value of autonomy and liberty of the family. If some people are in fact dying of starvation, substantial intrusions on the right of private ownership of property, for example, might be warranted. And if there has been no tradition of fairness in implementing means-regarding equality of opportunity, compensatory inequality might be warranted. Leaving those two escape routes aside, Fishkin's assertion is that it is impossible to have perfect (1) means-regarding equality of opportunity, (2) equal life chances, and (3) liberty and autonomy of the family, all at the same time. Whether Fishkin is correct or not, it is easy to see that the successful achievement of means-regarding equality of opportunity in a society is no simple or easy matter.

In the conclusion of this book we will consider the important role that individualism has played in the American understanding of equality. Our traditional understanding of individualism is that each of us has the equal opportunity to succeed or fail based on our own merit and efforts. Yet the liberty of an individual family to favor its own members, whenever possible, means that not all individuals begin life's competition from the same starting line. We will also consider at some length one answer to the particular "trilemma" Fishkin raises. The proposed answer is the use of the *distance-travelled* concept (see chapter 1).

In the next several chapters, as we consider the meanings of equal protection of the law, the distinctions between individual-regarding, segmental, and bloc-regarding equality will be illustrated in several examples. We will find ample evidence that the view of equality in the United States has become much more inclusionary since the Fourteenth Amendment was ratified in 1868. Just as it has become more inclusionary, the domain of equality has expanded. We will see that in our time the legal assault on racial segregation, led by the NAACP through the advocacy of Charles Houston, Thurgood Marshall, and their colleagues, represented an expanding domain of account through which racial equality was demanded. In return, through judicial decisions and eventually in the 1960s through civil rights legislation, the domain of allocation of the federal government expanded nearly to coincide with the NAACP's domain of account to create a condition of straightforward equality. When straightforward equality was not achievable, we will find many examples of compensatory inequality, through which one agency offered recompense within its domain of allocation for inequalities that were largely outside its domain. We will also see that in the United States the particular understanding of equality involves equality of opportunity, which is in fact our version of means-regarding equality of opportunity.

Rae and his colleagues have created this structural grammar of equality. The vocabulary they have proposed will provide a way to describe the evolution of the concept of equal protection of the law in the judicial system of the United States.

3

RECONSTRUCTION AND
EQUAL PROTECTION

I can hardly believe that any person can be found who will not admit that every one of these provisions is just. They are all asserted, in some form or other in our DECLARATION or organic law. But the Constitution limits only the action of Congress, and is not a limitation on the States. This amendment supplies that defect, and allows Congress to correct the unjust legislation of the States, so far that the law which operates upon one man shall operate equally *upon all.*
—Thaddeus Stevens on the Fourteenth Amendment, May 8, 1866

On June 13, 1866, after Radical Republican leader Thaddeus Stevens had delivered in the House of Representatives his judgment of praise for the Fourteenth Amendment—touched, however, with rebuke to the moderates and to the Democrats in the Congress for not having agreed to do more—the Thirty-ninth Congress completed its work on the amendment and submitted it to the states for ratification.

The Fourteenth Amendment has since been a prolific progenitor of constitutional litigation. Its first section, containing the privileges or immunities clause, the due process clause, and provision for the equal protection of the law—each directed at any of the states that might deny them—has been a principal source of constitutional claims.[1] In this book, however, we consider only those claims that are founded on the equal protection of the law. Thaddeus Stevens's words suggest a deceptively simple interpretation of equal protection. He seems to speak of a broad form of inclusionary individual-regarding equality, that is, of a single class of humans, each of whom would be entitled to equal treatment by law. But however broad the single class might be, we know that he was not referring to equality with a particularly large domain. Instead he was then referring to a relatively narrow domain involving the legal status of African-Americans, because he went on to suggest that the amendment should provide that: "Whatever law punishes a white man for a crime shall punish a black man precisely in the same way and to the same degree. Whatever law protects the white man shall afford 'equal' protection to the black man. Whatever means of redress is afforded to one shall be afforded to all" (Hyman, 1967: 323).

Of course, Stevens's domain of equality before the law is not the only possible application of equal protection, and on different occasions his own words suggested others, but it was not generally understood at the time that the proposed amendment ought to encompass full social equality. Eric Foner has noted that the political vocabulary of the day distinguished between natural, civil, political, and social rights. Slavery was seen as a violation of the natural right to life, liberty, and the pursuit of happiness. Civil rights involved equal status before the courts and equal treatment by law. The most important political right, the right to vote, was then more often perceived as a privilege than a right. Social equality, that is, equality in business, social, and personal relationships, was usually seen as a private matter outside the purview of governments (Foner, 1988: 228). Stevens, though for his time a racial egalitarian, did not then imagine the victory of a broad domain for equality. For example, during the war Stevens addressed the House on his bill that would have enlisted former slaves into military service and confirmed their freedom:

> I do not expect to live to see the day when, in this Christian land, merit shall counterbalance the crime of color. True, we propose to give them an equal chance to meet death on the battlefield. But even then their great achievements, if equal to those of Dessalines, would give them no hope of honor. The only place where they can find equality is in the grave. There all God's children are equal. (Korngold, 1955: 209)

In this chapter we will explore the origins of equal protection and its various meanings, especially those suggested in the words of Stevens and his contemporaries while it was being proposed, debated, and ratified. Others have written on the origins of the Fourteenth Amendment in much greater detail than this survey chapter will permit.[2] Our purpose here will be more that of conceptual clarification and comparison than of exhaustive narrative history.

That Stevens was especially focused on a narrow domain consisting of equality before the law was evident in many of his public statements. Citing the Declaration of Independence, he argued that our founding fathers had repudiated the "legal superiority of families or races and proclaimed the equality of men before the law" (*Globe*: December 18, 1866).[3] In the Senate, Radical leader Charles Sumner was a leader

whose career-long theme was the principle of equality before the law
(Foner, 1988: 230). Several historians have written that the year 1865
offered men such as Stevens and Sumner an unusual opportunity to
promote social change. Such occasions—when a major crisis has for a
time torn apart conventional understandings and customary ways of
doing things—are quite rare in American history. When the Thirty-
ninth Congress gathered for its first session in 1865, there was an
emerging consensus within the Republican party that freedmen were
entitled to civil equality, that is, to equality before the law—and possibly
even to more—though for most the outer limit of change would have
been to extend the franchise to freedmen.

The centrality of concerns over the legal status of freedmen suggests
that our understanding of equal protection of the law ought to begin
with the *Dred Scott* case. There, in 1857, Chief Justice Taney held that
"Negroes" could not become citizens because at the time of the writing
of the Constitution they had been considered a "subordinate and inferior class of beings" (*Dred Scott v. Sanford*: 700). Moreover, Chief Justice
Taney compounded his conclusion by this obloquy:

> They had for more than a century before been regarded as be-
> ings of an inferior order; and altogether unfit to associate with the
> white race, either in social or political relations; and so far inferior,
> that they had no rights which the white man was bound to respect;
> and that the Negro might justly and lawfully be reduced to slavery
> for his benefit. He was bought and sold, and treated as an ordinary
> article of merchandise and traffic, wherever a profit could be made
> of it. This opinion was at that time fixed and universal in the civi-
> lized portion of the white race. It was regarded as an axiom in
> morals as well as politics, which no one thought of disputing or
> supposed to be open to dispute. (*Dred Scott v. Sanford*: 701–2)

The contrast between Taney's words in 1857 and Stevens's views in
1865 on legal equality before the law could hardly be more stark. Yet
abolitionist leaders (Sumner, for example) who devoutly embraced the
equal legal status of Negroes nonetheless balked at insisting on social
equality. Sumner conceded that, given the racial views of most whites,
human nature and social degradation could not be overlooked or instantly remedied. Historians have noted that there was then no necessary inconsistency between the goals of abolition and of elimination of
legal discrimination, on the one hand, and the recognition, and even
acceptance, of social inequality, on the other (Donald, 1960: 235). At

best their understanding of equality involved a narrow domain relative to today.

Social prejudice against both free blacks and slaves was commonplace in the North before the Civil War. Even those who agitated for change had varying objectives. Some were concerned chiefly about restricting the spread of slavery. Others were committed abolitionists. Still others went beyond abolition to embrace the objective of free legal status—of equality before the law. On a different dimension, some even favored the colonization of former slaves in Africa (Korngold, 1955: 147 et seq.; Curtis, 1986: chapter 2). For most, social equality remained at best a distant and improbable goal.[4] Even Radical Republican Senator Wade recognized that prejudice against "Negroes" was such that it was "perfectly impossible that these two races can inhabit the same place and be prosperous and happy." His solution: "Let them go into the tropics" (Hyman, 1967: 14).

The distinction between social equality and equality before the law, given the vocabulary of equality of that time, is thus clearly a matter of defining the domain under which equality might apply. Equality before the law is a much more limited domain than social equality, for presumably the protection of social equality would include equality before the law as well. Whatever else the Fourteenth Amendment might eventually do, it is clear that, with the Thirteenth, and in due time the Fifteenth amendments, the equal legal status of freedmen was to be protected and the conclusions of the *Dred Scott* case repudiated.[5] This was still a rather exclusionary version of simple individual-regarding equality (for women were excluded, as we shall see), with a narrow domain of legal rights.

The Thirty-ninth Congress met in its first session on December 4, 1865. On its agenda was the task of reorganizing the government out of the chaos and confusion of the Civil War. On its first day, Thaddeus Stevens offered a resolution to create a joint committee of fifteen members, the committee that would eventually become known as the Joint Committee on Reconstruction (Kendrick, 1914: 37). It was through this committee that the more radical members of the Congress, especially those in the House, eventually challenged President Andrew Johnson's plan for dealing with rebels and rebellious states. On December 5, Stevens introduced a constitutional amendment that provided that "all national and state laws shall be equally applicable to every citizen, and no discrimination shall be made by race or color" (*Globe,* December 5, 1865: 10). The following day Representative Bingham of Ohio offered a resolution to amend the Constitution to "empower Congress to pass all necessary and proper laws to secure to all persons in every state equal protection of their rights, life, liberty and property" (*Globe,* December 6, 1865: 14). Bingham and Stevens became leaders of the Joint Committee on Reconstruction, and their proposed amendments contained the first efforts to formulate federal constitutional equality before the law for freedmen.

It is interesting to note that according to some scholars the first recorded use of the phrase "equality before the law" in English was by Charles Sumner in an oral argument made in 1849 before the Supreme Court of Massachusetts. It is an odd footnote in history that Sumner's first use of the phrase was in an argument contending that the separate public education of whites and "Negroes" was incompatible with the Constitution and laws of the Commonwealth of Massachusetts, one hundred and five years before the decision in *Brown v. Board of Education of Topeka* in 1954 (Frank and Munro, 1950: 136–37).

On December 13, Senator Wilson of Massachusetts offered Senate Bill 9 "for the Protection of Freedmen," which would have nullified any state law or provision that entailed "inequality of civil rights and immunities by reason of color, race, descent or previous condition of servitude" (*Globe,* December 13, 1865: 39). It would be easy to be overwhelmed by the differences in the specific language of the various amendments and bills that were offered late in 1865 or early in 1866 (at one point in January 1866, over seventy constitutional amendments had been introduced) (Foner, 1988: 252). We need not dwell on the vagaries of particular provisions. It is important to recognize and remember that Congress had no dearth either of proponents or of language whose purpose it was to establish some sort of constitutional and legal equality for freedmen. There were good reasons for such great congressional concern about legal equality for freedmen. The leaders of Congress and President Johnson confronted one another regarding Reconstruction late in 1865, and between them there was a growing abyss of suspicion.

In December 1863, Lincoln's Proclamation of Amnesty and Reconstruction had offered pardon and restoration of rights to those rebels who would take an oath of future loyalty and who would pledge to accept the abolition of slavery. When the number of loyal citizens of a state, thus defined, amounted to more than ten percent of the votes cast in 1860, this small minority would be allowed to establish a state government (Foner, 1988: 35).

Lincoln's policy toward the South had not been so different from that first favored by Andrew Johnson, and it was much like that early favored by Congress, at least before the Radical Republicans took the lead. The

Wade-Davis Bill, passed on Independence Day, 1864, provided that seceding states were to be treated as territories over which the president would appoint a provisional governor. The provisional governor would preside over a process for individuals to swear allegiance and to form a state government through a convention called for the purpose of adopting a state constitution. Lincoln accepted the general plan but refused to sign the bill, in part because it would have set aside the state governments that had already been constituted in Arkansas and Louisiana, in part because it would have committed Reconstruction to a single invariable process.

A measure that became known as the Trumbull Resolution marked the intensification of the division between moderates and radicals. Offered in February 1865, it was opposed by the Radicals in Congress. It would have formally recognized the reconstructed government of Louisiana, even though that state denied suffrage to freedmen. Charles Sumner eventually defeated the Trumbull Resolution in the Senate, a victory that Frederick Douglass celebrated with the "friends of freedom all over the country" (Du Bois, 1935: 162).

After Lincoln's assassination in April 1865, the former slave states began to enact "black codes," which denied to freedmen many of the basic rights accorded whites, including the freedom to move, to enter into contracts, to own property, and to bear arms, as well as complicated provisions for the regulation and control of free black labor (Curtis, 1986: 35; Du Bois, 1935: 167 et seq.). One Louisiana community even enacted a pass law, a curfew for African-Americans, and a law barring them from living in town except as servants. By the end of 1865, Mississippi required all African-Americans each January to have written evidence of employment for the year. Any laborer leaving a job before completion of the contract would forfeit wages already earned and would be subject to arrest by any white person (Foner, 1988: 198–99). President Johnson's Reconstruction policy, declared by proclamation in May 1865, was, nonetheless, relatively generous and lenient to the South. He did insist on repeal of secession, ratification of the Thirteenth Amendment, and repudiation of Confederate debt. He urged, but did not require, state protection of civil rights and limited Negro suffrage (Beale, 1930: 44 et seq.).

Johnson's failure to insist on suffrage for freedmen provoked the Radicals to mount a campaign to influence Northern opinion in favor of the black vote. Only five Northern States at that time accorded African-Americans the vote on the same terms as whites. While by the middle of 1865 most Republicans were agreed on equality before the law, the

black vote was not seen as a fundamental issue, except by certain Radicals and by black leaders such as Frederick Douglass. The actions of
southern states in enacting the "black codes" and President Johnson's
own actions added strength to the Radical cause (Foner, 1988: 221, et
seq.).

In February 1866, Johnson's veto of the Freedmen's Bureau Bill,
which continued a protective agency established during the war, drove
the president and Congress even further apart, and that veto was followed by Johnson's Washington's Birthday speech, which accused
Sumner and Stevens of being traitors, who by their extreme actions
were destroying the nation (Beale, 1930: 85). President Johnson's veto
of the Freedmen's Bill was eventually overridden. On March 27, 1866,
he vetoed the Civil Rights Bill of 1866, but within two weeks he was
overridden. The bill conferred national citizenship on African-Americans and accorded them the legal status to make and enforce contracts,
to sue, and to own and dispose of property. The authority to enact such
a bill was said to be drawn from the Thirteenth Amendment, it being
argued that the prohibition of slavery and involuntary servitude implied
that freedmen ought to have the same legal status as whites.

Johnson's veto message rested first on federalism. The national government, he argued, had no authority to enforce civil rights through
legislation, just as it had no authority to confer the rights of state citizenship. But beyond federalism, he expressed doubts that all distinctions between whites and African-Americans as to legal status ought to
be eliminated. Eric Foner has written that Johnson was a racist. He
especially cites Johnson's December 1867 message to Congress in
which the president argued that African-Americans had "less capacity
for government than any other race of people." Foner calls this the
"most blatantly racist pronouncement ever to appear in an official state
paper of an American president (Foner, 1988: 180). Johnson's two vetoes had the unintended effect of uniting his moderate and radical opposition. On April 2, the Senate overrode Johnson's veto by exactly the
two-thirds vote required. A few days later the House also voted to override. Scholars have noted that this was the first legislation ever passed
over a president's veto. Whatever Lincoln might have done in the same
context, Johnson's vetoes destroyed the possibility of cooperation between the president and the Congress (Riddleberger, 1979: chapter 4).
Two months later the Congress proposed the Fourteenth Amendment
for ratification by the states, and among its purposes was the further
provision of equal legal status for African-Americans and whites.

The Thirty-ninth Congress has been studied from a variety of perspectives. Some scholars[6] have examined the debates and other sources to determine whether the Congress intended, through the Fourteenth Amendment, to extend the protection of the original Bill of Rights to the states. Others have examined this period with a particular interest in equal protection, but their interest was chiefly focused on the question of whether the original understanding of equal protection was that it would prohibit racial segregation, especially in public schools.[7] Several recent books are more encompassing, especially that of Judith Baer. She engages in a broad review of the origins of equal protection, but her concerns are often about contemporary issues that were not conceived by the framers of the Fourteenth Amendment (such as the rights of women or gay rights) (Baer, 1983: 9). Like Baer's book, this chapter looks at the origins of equal protection to see whether its original conceptualization could have included categories other than race, that is, how inclusive was the understanding of equality of that time? We must remember, however, that the elimination of unequal racial status before the law was clearly the primary objective of the Fourteenth Amendment.

We will see that the discussion in the Thirty-ninth Congress sometimes went beyond the protection of the legal rights of freedmen. For example, in debating Senator Wilson's bill, which became the Civil Rights Act of 1866 and which sought to eliminate any inequality of civil rights based on race, Senator Cowan of Maryland urged:

> I am in favor and exceedingly desirous that by some means or other the natural rights of all people in the country shall be secured to them, no matter what their color or complexion may be, and may be secured to them in such a way as that States themselves cannot hereafter wrest them away from them. I am in favor of the position that the courts of the country shall be open to everybody, Jews, Gypsies, Chinese, Negroes, all men of every color and condition. (*Globe,* December 13, 1865: 40–41)

Senator Cowan's class of "all people" apparently was as inclusionary as it is possible to be, and the term *natural rights* is possibly a broader domain than that intended by others, even if vague. On the other hand, the suggestion was sometimes equally clear that a more exclusionary class consisting only of Negroes should receive protection, and only for narrow domain of legal rights. Note the following from one of Wilson's adversaries:

There is scarcely a State in the Union that does not make distinctions on account of color. Is it wise for us to legislate in regard to all these various subjects without having full comprehension of what they are? In nearly every State in the Union there is some distinction. In the State of New York a certain portion are excluded from voting—all those who have not property. In the State of Ohio all those nearer black than white are excluded from voting. These are distinctions contained in the laws of what were called the free states—all are free now. Is the purpose of this bill to wipe out all these distinctions? (*Globe,* December 13, 1865: 41–42)

Clearly, the most broad and inclusive interpretation of the intentions of the proponents of equality before the law arose through the apprehensions of the opponents of reform, the Democrats who most feared what "radicals" like Stevens and Sumner stood for. Such Democrats attributed the conflict over the legal rights of freedmen to "one-idea politicians" whose zealotry had "brought on the war" (*Globe,* January 31, 1866: 541). And despite the war and the traumas of Reconstruction, one Democratic Senator was chagrined to find that the Radicals:

falter not in the contest; still they hug to their bosoms the phantom of Negro equality; still they claim for one section the right to control the local affairs of others. They hold that the white and black race are equal. This, they maintain involves and demands social equality; that Negroes should be received on an equality in white families, should be permitted to occupy the same seats in railroad cars and the same pews in churches; that they should be allowed to hold offices, to sit on juries, to vote, to be eligible to seats in the State and national legislatures, and to be judges, or to make and expound laws for the government of white men. Their children are to attend the same schools with white children, and to sit side by side with them. Following close upon this will, of course, be marriages between the races, when according to these philanthropic theorists, the prejudices of caste will at length have been overcome, and the Negro, with privileges of free miscegenation accorded him will be in the enjoyment of his true status. (*Globe,* January 31, 1866: 541)

Of course, Democratic critics such as this were engaging in rhetorical overkill.[8] As we have seen, the Radical Republican leadership was not then committed to the achievement of full social equality. The rhetorical excesses of the Democratic opposition fail to distinguish between equality before the law (a relatively narrow domain) and political equality and full social equality (a much larger domain). It was more than a century after 1866 before the goal of social equality that certain Democrats feared gained fairly wide acceptance, and even today it has been achieved only in part.

The more moderate and mainstream opponents of the Radical Republicans did not embrace the racist apprehensions of some members of the Democratic opposition. The moderates' concerns about enforcement of equality before the law stemmed, they said, from their understanding of federalism. To place in the Congress the affirmative power to legislate against "denials of privileges or immunities" or to secure "equal protection of life, liberty and property" would be to give the Congress affirmative "police power." This was viewed as "in effect a provision under which all State legislation, in its codes of civil and criminal jurisprudence and procedure, affecting the individual citizen, may be overridden, may be repealed or abolished, and the law of Congress established instead." This outcome was seen by these states' rights advocates as an "utter departure from every principle ever dreamed by the men who framed our Constitution" (*Globe,* February 27, 1866: 1063).

There are even some references to sexual distinctions in the debates of 1866. For example, on February 27, 1866, there was an intriguing exchange between Thaddeus Stevens and Congressman Hale of New York, a conservative Republican. In arguing that the proposed Fourteenth Amendment would radically shift power from the states to Congress, Hale suggested this example:

Take the case of the rights of married women; did any one ever assume that Congress was to be invested with the power to legislate on that subject, and to say that married women, in regard to their rights of property, should stand on the same footing with men and unmarried women? There is not a State in the Union where disability of married women in relation to the rights of property does not to a greater or less extent still exist. (*Globe,* February 27, 1866: 1064)

Stevens interrupted to suggest that Hale had misunderstood. When the law treats two people of equal status or condition differently, then it would be unequal and unjust legislation. Thus a law creating a distinction between two married persons or between unmarried women (*feme sole*) would violate the requirement of equality before the law, but where all members of the same class are treated alike, there is no inequality and consequently no violation of the requirement of equality. Instead of Hale having misunderstood, Stevens had misspoken, and Hale delivered the coup de grace:

> The gentleman will pardon me; his argument seems to me more specious than sound. The language of the section under consideration gives to *all persons* equal protection. Now if that means you shall extend to one married woman the same protection you extend to another, and not the same you extend to unmarried women or men, then by parity of reasoning, it will be sufficient if you extend to one Negro the same rights you do to another, but not those you extend to a white man. (emphasis added, *Globe,* February 27, 1866: 1064)

Of course, Hale was right; that certainly was not what the proponents of the Fourteenth Amendment intended. They probably did not mean to reach the question of discrimination between men and women at all, but their inclusionary class (all persons) implied the inclusion of women. In his haste to escape, Stevens was reaching for a rejoinder, and he came up with what amounts to segmental equality, dividing people into two or more subclasses and insisting that there be equality within but not between the subclasses (Rae, 1981: 21 et seq.). Stevens may well have thought that to be an appropriate solution to the distinction between *feme sole* and married women (*feme covert*), but that is not what he had in mind on the racial question. He intended that African-Americans and whites would receive equal treatment before the law, that is, individual-regarding equality. Individual-regarding equality, as we have seen before, involves a single class of individuals (here presumably all male persons) who would be accorded equality before the law.

Hale's question is, nonetheless, intriguing, because it represents an early instance of applying the language of equal protection of the law to distinctions between men and women. Women's suffrage advocates of the day, such as Elizabeth Cady Stanton and Susan B. Anthony, were already active in advocating that principles of equality ought to apply to women as well as to African-Americans. Some of them felt betrayed by the Radicals' lack of concern for women and eventually opposed the Fourteenth Amendment because in its second section the word *male* is used for the first time in the Constitution (Foner, 1988: 255).[9] Had the wording been *all persons* rather than *all males,* the vesting in the Congress of the affirmative power to achieve equal protection of the law would indeed have had the potential for radical social change in 1866. From the perspective of twelve decades later, we can see that Hale was prescient in understanding the possible implications of equal protection applied to the inclusive class of all persons. We can also see that the eventual language of equal protection (no state shall deny its citizens the equal protection of the law) is, on its own, broadly inclusionary, even if its proponents did have a more narrow class and domain in mind.

The eventual equal protection language in Section 1 of the Fourteenth Amendment was passed by the House on May 10, 1866. The affirmative grant of power to Congress to legislate equality before the law in early versions of the amendment was, in the final version, limited to the power to enforce "the provisions of the article" and placed in a separate Section 5, so that the earlier language empowering the Congress to pass "all necessary and proper laws to secure to all person equal protection in the rights, life, liberty and property," was muted. Ten Broek has argued that the shift from the positive form ("Congress shall have the power to pass all necessary and proper laws to secure to all persons equal protection") to the negative form ("Congress shall have the power to enforce this article") provided the basis for a more restrictive interpretation of the enforcement powers of Congress relative to civil rights and hence to the perpetuation of racial discrimination (ten Broek, 1965: 216). Conversely, Foner suggests that Section 1, by affirmatively providing constitutional equal protection of the law, in principle gave federal courts the power of enforcement, while the primary grant of that power to Congress would have subjected equal protection to the vagaries of political competition (Foner, 1988: 258). We can never know what might have been under the positive version, but if the interpretation by the courts of "necessary and proper" had proved to be consistent with Chief Justice Marshall's interpretation of the necessary and proper clause of Article I, Section 8, in *McCulloch v. Maryland,*[10] then the Congress would indeed have been accorded broad implied powers over civil rights enforcement. The political will to act, of course, might have been another matter.

In the Senate on May 23, 1866, Senator Howard of Michigan, a member of the Joint Committee on Reconstruction gave his understanding of the implications of Section 1 of the Fourteenth Amendment:

The last two clauses of the first section of the amendment disable a State from depriving not merely a citizen of the United States, but any person, whoever he may be, of life, liberty or property without due process of law, or from denying to him the equal protection of the laws of the State. This abolishes all class legislation in the States and does away with the injustice of subjecting one caste of persons to a code not applicable to another. It prohibits the hanging of a black man for a crime for which the white man is not to be hanged. It protects the black man in his fundamental rights as a citizen with the same shield which it throws over the white man. Is it not time, Mr. President, that we extend to the black man, I had almost called it the poor privilege of the equal protection of the law? Ought not the time to be now passed when one measure of justice is to be meted out to a member of one caste, both bound to obey the same laws, to sustain the burdens of the same Government, and both equally responsible to justice and to God for the deeds in the body? . . . It establishes equality before the law, and it gives to the humblest, the poorest, the most despised of the race the same rights and the same protection before the law as it gives to the most powerful, the most wealthy or the most haughty. (*Globe*, May 23, 1866: 2766)

Equality before the law—civil equality, but probably not social nor even full political equality[11]—that was probably the intention of the proponents of the Fourteenth Amendment. There is no doubt that the purpose and special focus of the amendment was on the question of race and on the civil rights of freedmen, but it is also evident that the amendment was intended to protect white Union sympathizers in southern states, "whose property, by State legislation, has been wrestled from them under confiscation, and protect them from banishments" (*Globe*, February 27, 1866: 1065). Congressman Bingham of Ohio, one of the principal framers of the Fourteenth Amendment, clearly gave the amendment national scope, "It is to apply to other States also that have in their constitutions and law today provisions in direct violation of every principle of our Constitution" (*Globe*, February 28, 1866).

In their key article on "The Original Understanding of 'Equal Protection of the Laws,' " Frank and Munro identified fifteen insiders who were involved in varying degrees in the drafting and explication of Section 1. They concluded that all fifteen were agreed that equal protection entailed the right to testify, to sue and be sued, and to hold property. Eight of the fifteen, including the leading figures of Bingham, Howard, and Stevens, interpreted the amendment to preclude the use of race as a legal distinction. On the other side, Frank and Munro found that three of the fifteen probably accepted some forms of segregation, most notably relative to miscegenation, as not being barred by the amendment (Frank and Munro, 1950: 142).

Of other scholars who have studied the original understanding, Jacobus ten Broek supports the most expansive interpretation of the amendment. In his 1965 book he argued, "Protection of men in their fundamental or natural rights was the basic idea of the clause." Moreover, he understands the Equal Protection Clause as requiring an affirmative effort to ensure the protection of natural rights. In effect he interprets the clause to mean, "Each State shall supply the protection of laws to men in their natural rights" (ten Broek, 1965: 237).

Ten Broek's most astringent critic is Raoul Berger, who holds that the amendment had only the limited purpose of providing equality before the law, that is, of certain civil rights, rather than political or social equality (Berger, 1977: 169 et seq.). Alexander Bickel, looking at much the same evidence, concluded that congressional moderates (if not the Radical leaders) did not see the amendment as applying to "jury service, suffrage, miscegenation, nor segregation." On the other hand, the right to contract, to sue, to give evidence, to inherit, possess, and dispose of property, and to "equality in the penalties and burdens provided by law" were covered by the Amendment" (Bickel, 1955: 56 et seq.). Finally, Bickel concludes, "Though race was focal at the time, it could not have escaped attention that Fourteenth Amendment language was more general than that" (Bickel, 1955: 60).

Judith Baer poses three questions that can be asked about the intentions of the framers: (1) Why did Congress want to ensure equal protection? (2) What people or groups did equal protection cover or exclude? (3) What rights or interests did the Fourteenth Amendment protect? Her answers rely on Jacobus ten Broek, Howard Jay Graham, and Alfred H. Kelly, as well as on her own reading of the historical record. She concludes that the Reconstruction amendments were intended "to write into the Constitution the principles of equality and natural rights contained in the Declaration" (Baer, 1985: 80). As we have seen, there is certainly language in the debates of the Thirty-ninth Congress to support that conclusion, and the most pertinent language does come from key proponents of the Fourteenth Amendment. Baer's conclusion is sustained also by its breadth, for it rests on all three Reconstruction amendments. The right to vote, eventually protected by the Fifteenth

Amendment but apparently not encompassed by the Fourteenth, otherwise would be an obvious contradiction to her broad conclusion. The
breadth of her conclusion is important because it suggests that the
Fourteenth Amendment was intended to convey equality of rights even
in the face of recognizable inequalities between particular persons—all
human beings, regardless of their stature, physical prowess, intellectual attainments, and the like, would have an equal claim to certain
natural rights. But did the amendment in fact include all human beings,
or were the "natural rights" of whites merely to be opened to include
African-Americans?

Having looked at the same key evidence, that is, the debates recorded in the *Globe,* my conclusion is much the same as Baer's. The
rights protected through the Fourteenth Amendment were clearly to be
extended to everybody, "Jews, Gypsies, Chinese, Negroes, all men of
every color and conditions" (*Globe,* December 13, 1865: 41). The generality of the discussion was such that in theory it would be inclusive of all
male humans, regardless of race or ethnicity. At the time, judging from
the debates, the amendment probably was not intended to include
women, even though the language of the amendment is broad enough
to include them. The omission of women, not by the language of Section 1 itself but by the statements of the proponents during the debates,
does not, however, permanently foreclose questioning sexual distinctions in law, unless we concede that we must be forever bound by
whatever views or prejudices obtained in 1866. The fact that the amendment forbade states from denying any person the equal protection of
the law eventually speaks for itself.

As to the rights that were to be accorded by the amendment, Baer
finds the evidence to be ambiguous, but:

> what emerges from congressional debates is, first, a notion of
> equality based on natural entitlement to rights, derived from the
> Declaration; second, a concern with protecting certain rights, in-
> cluding, but not limited to life, liberty and property; and third, an
> intention to grant people equality under law in order to give them
> protection from those who would oppress and even kill them.
> (Baer, 1983: 104)

On much the same point Eric Foner has written recently:

> The aims of the Fourteenth Amendment can only be understood
> within the political and ideological context of 1866: the break with

the President, the need to find a measure upon which Republicans could unite, and the growing consensus within the party around the need for strong federal action to protect the freedmen's right, short of the suffrage. Despite the many drafts, changes and deletions, the Amendment's central principle remains constant: a national guarantee of equality before the law. (Foner, 1988: 257)

Any careful reading of the debates leaves many questions unanswered. Were such an amendment to be considered in the Congress today, the legislative history would, no doubt, be exponentially larger, and we would be able to infer intention and purpose from a much richer source. The record of 1866 is much more sparse. We can see that the original understanding of equal protection was that its purpose was to create equality before the law for all persons (more properly all male persons), though clearly its raison d'être was the racial question. Equality before the law was then a way of saying that basic civil/legal rights ought not to be distributed according to class, caste, or race. Bingham considered those basic civil rights to be included among the natural rights of men. It was also understood that all should stand equal before the law in the sense of the rules, benefits, and penalties of law that might prove applicable. It seems clear that political rights, especially the right to vote, were not encompassed by the Fourteenth Amendment (though the Fifteenth Amendment was soon to be realized). Radical leaders would have included the vote for freedmen had they been able to do so in 1866. In the event, exclusion of the vote was seen as a necessary compromise.

Most proponents did not see the purpose of the amendment as ending all social distinctions between African-Americans and whites. Stevens and a few others might well have broadened the understanding of equality of the time, had that been possible. That it was not possible at the time is reflected in Stevens's lament of June 13, the date of final passage:

In my youth, in my manhood, in my old age, I had fondly dreamed that when any fortunate change should have broken up for a while the foundation of our institutions, and released us from obligations the most tyrannical that ever man has imposed in the name of freedom, that the intelligent, pure and just men of this Republic, true to their professions and their consciences, would have so remodeled all our institutions as to have freed them from every vestige of human oppression, of inequality of rights, of the recognized degradation of the poor, and the superior caste of the rich. In short, that no distinction would be tolerated in this purified Republic but what arose from merit and conduct. This bright dream has vanished "like the baseless fabric of a vision." I find that we shall be obliged to be content with patching up the worst portions of the ancient edifice, and leaving it, in many of its parts, to be swept through by the tempests, the frosts and the storms of despotism.

Do you inquire why, holding these views and possessing some will of my own, I accept so imperfect a proposition? I answer, because I live among men and not among angels; among men as intelligent, as determined, and as independent as myself, who not agreeing with me, do not choose to yield their opinions to mine. Mutual concession, therefore, is our only resort or mutual hostilities. (*Globe,* June 13, 1866: 3148)

Equality before the law thus probably began as a form of individual-regarding equality with a rather narrow domain of allocation—a fairly short list of explicit legal rights that all persons, that is, all male persons, were to have.[12] It is helpful to remember that of the thirty states that ratified the Fourteenth Amendment, "at least eighteen had laws mandating separate schools or forbidding miscegenation" (Lofgren, 1987: 67). Yet, especially given the words of Congressman Bingham respecting natural rights, equal protection was sufficiently open-ended to include, eventually, unspecified rights—in Dworkin's words, the right to be treated as an equal (Dworkin, 1977: 227).

Two things particularly should be kept in mind after having reviewed the historical record. The first is that the words "any person" from the Fourteenth Amendment have implications in their own right, whatever the intentions of the proponents may have been. The second is that the phrases "equal protection of the law" or "equality before the law" both suggest that any distinctions created or recognized by law are questionable, in the sense that they seem to require some justification.

Social distinctions may or may not be sustained by law. When certain of the proponents of the Fourteenth Amendment said that it was not their purpose to eliminate all social distinctions between African-Americans and whites, that may have been a way of acknowledging the difference between legally sustained differences and those that are strictly a matter of social reality. Whenever a social distinction becomes a matter of law as well, some possible dissonance with the language of the Fourteenth Amendment may exist. The resolution of that dissonance may be easy or difficult, based on our understanding of what sorts of distinctions are tenable. In 1866, legal distinctions based on race were becoming more difficult to justify, while sex-based distinctions were still easy. The evolution of equal protection of the law is an inevitable outgrowth of the tension between the language of the Fourteenth Amendment and each generation's understanding of what sorts of distinctions between people are tenable. Consistent with that point, Eric Foner has argued:

> Even moderates . . . understood Reconstruction as a dynamic process in which phrases like "privileges and immunities" were subject to changing interpretation. They preferred to allow both Congress and the federal courts maximum flexibility in implementing the Amendment's provisions and combating the multitude of injustices that confronted blacks in many parts of the South. (Foner, 1988: 258)

The decisions of the Supreme Court of the United States that are reviewed in the following chapters, will, I think, reveal the correctness of that conclusion.

4

EARLY INTERPRETATIONS OF
EQUAL PROTECTION

We doubt very much whether any action of a state not directed by way of discrimination against Negroes as a class, or on account of their race will ever be held to come within the purview of this provision. It is so clearly a provision for that race and that emergency that a strong case would be necessary for its application to any other.
> —Justice Miller on the Equal Protection Clause
> in the *Slaughter-House Cases* of 1873

Following ratification of the Fourteenth Amendment in 1868, we find in the first thirty years of its existence only about fifteen Supreme Court decisions that interpreted the meaning of the Equal Protection Clause in instances of racial discrimination against African-Americans. Surprisingly, the first interpretation of the amendment in the *Slaughter-House Cases* (1873) did not involve race at all. Nevertheless, it was highly restrictive in its interpretation and dismissive in its perspective.

THE FIRST INTERPRETATION—
THE *SLAUGHTER-HOUSE CASES*

Much has been written about the *Slaughter-House Cases,* but most of the attention has been about Justice Miller's interpretation of the privileges or immunities clause or about his limitation of due process strictly to procedural due process, rather than about the Equal Protection Clause.

The *Slaughter-House Cases* involved an attack on a Louisiana statute that had granted a twenty-five-year monopoly to a corporation to operate stockyards and slaughterhouses within an area of twelve hundred square miles in and around New Orleans. The statute was justified as a "sanitary measure," but the corporation granted the monopoly had to conform only with some minimal health regulations (Crosskey, 1954: 1119). It has been suggested that the measure actually was designed to support the construction of a modern meat-packing facility that would be capable of competing for the Texas cattle trade (Foner, 1988: 529). Whatever the motivation, the effect of the statute was to put all butchers and slaughterhouses out of business—except for the favored monopoly. The losers sought relief under the Fourteenth Amendment but found a five-member majority of the Supreme Court that was intent on giving that amendment the narrowest possible reading.

Justice Miller's interpretation of equal protection does not allow much room for discussion. After acknowledging that others besides "Negroes" might share in the protection offered by the three Reconstruction amendments, since "Both the language and spirit of these articles are to have their fair and just weight in any question of construction" (*Slaughter-House Cases,* 1873: 407), Miller went on to make what has proven to be one of the most mistaken and myopic predictions in our constitutional history. The history of the amendments and their "pervading purpose," he wrote, demonstrated that they were to be applied against discrimination, injustice, and hardship to emancipated Negroes as a class, but he doubted very much that equal protection would ever be applied to anyone other than Negroes. The *Slaughter-House Cases* had nothing to do with race, hence the Equal Protection Clause was not apposite.

The majority's reading of the Equal Protection Clause, while no doubt accurate as to the amendment's primary motivation having been the protection of freedmen, was unnecessarily restrictive in its estimation of the words "equal protection of the law." Justice Miller's opinion represented a highly exclusionary interpretation of the class of persons who would be entitled to make equal protection claims. As we have seen, the debates in the Thirty-ninth Congress did, on occasion, recognize the potential for those words to reach beyond issues of race, and therefore were more inclusionary.

In dissent, Justice Field was emphatic in urging that equal protection included the right to "pursue lawful employment . . . without other restraint than such as equally affects all persons." He held this equality of right to be the "distinguishing privilege of citizens of the United States" (*Slaughter-House Cases,* 1873: 419). We will see in the next chapter that Field's view eventually prevailed in the 1880s. To bring corporations within the ambit of equal protection involved treating them as persons who could claim the protection of individual-regarding equality and also expanded the domain of equality far beyond the imaginations of the proponents of the Fourteenth Amendment. This form of corporate equal protection was eventually abolished by the Supreme Court, mostly after 1937 and emphatically in 1955 in the case of *Williamson v. Lee Optical Co.*

It is ironic that while Field's dissent was claiming broad equality rights for businessmen in the *Slaughter-House Cases,* he found no difficulty concurring in the outright rejection of Myra Bradwell's claim as a woman to an equal right to be admitted to the practice of law in *Bradwell v. Illinois* (1873), a position announced on the day following his dissent in the *Slaughter-House Cases.* It is notable also that, although Justice Miller interpreted equal protection as applying only to race, that the majority of the court was not especially solicitous of cases involving racial discrimination.

To understand the Supreme Court's early reticence in such cases, it is helpful to recall that the disputed presidential election of 1876 contributed to the demise of Reconstruction in the South; perhaps as a consequence, but certainly concurrently, concerns about racial equality moved from the focal point of public policy to the penumbra.

The congressional election of 1874 had brought a Democratic landslide in the South. When Congress convened in December 1874, the Radical Republican leadership, whose control over Congress was about to expire, sought to protect some of the gains that had been made during Reconstruction. Their proposals included what eventually became the Civil Rights Act of 1875. Early on, the bill included a provision that would have required integrated public schools, but that was dropped to make the bill more widely acceptable. As passed, the act included a prohibition against discrimination in public accommodations. Even so, it was passed over intense Democratic opposition, and the will of the Republican party was weakened and close to division. Still, the 1875 act represented a strong assertion of national authority over the recalcitrant Southern states. But as Eric Foner has noted: "The law was more a broad assertion of principle than a blueprint for further coercive action by the federal government. It left the initiative for enforcement primarily with black litigants suing for their rights in the already overburdened federal courts. Only a handful of blacks came forward to challenge acts of discrimination by hotels, theaters, and railroads" (Foner, 1988: 556).

The presidential race of 1876 between Republican Rutherford B. Hayes and Democrat Samuel J. Tilden was conducted on the Republican side by a party and leader who had lost the will to press on with Reconstruction, and on the Democratic side by a party that was ascendent, especially in the South. Even so, the outcome was closely contested. While Tilden apparently had a popular majority, Republicans claimed that his majority was produced, in part, by fraud and intimidation. The disputed results brought the contest into Congress for resolution. In turn, Congress created a special electoral commission to judge the issues. A confusing array of meetings and negotiations took place after that. Accounts of events vary, but all are agreed that the conclusion of the controversy in February 1877 led to Hayes becoming president and to the end of Reconstruction. This outcome boded ill, especially for freedmen. Historical accounts of the period between 1857 and 1877 are especially interesting for the way they reflect the zealotry of the abolitionist Republicans at the beginning and the exhaustion of idealism even amongst the most staunch Republicans at the end.[1]

In the 1880s few of the cases that came before the court on equal protection grounds involved race, and in only a few were the rights of African-Americans vindicated. Yet there were hints that equal protection might not always be limited to the protection of Negroes. In *Strauder v. West Virginia* (1880) a state law excluding "colored men" from service on state grand or petit juries was held to violate the Equal Protection Clause. The case fell quite clearly within the provision for equality before the law that had united most Republicans in the Congress in 1866. The Supreme Court said that the Equal Protection Clause represented a declaration "that the law in the States shall be the same for the black as for the white." The law was to assure "the colored race the enjoyment of all the civil rights that under the law are enjoyed by white persons" (*Strauder v. West Virginia*, 665). But the court added, "Nor if a law should be passed excluding all naturalized Celtic Irishmen, would there be any doubt of its inconsistency with the spirit of the Amendment" (*Strauder v. West Virginia*, 666). Thus it was made clear that while the domain of equal protection might be limited to recognized civil rights, the prohibition against discrimination by race was not to be limited to the "colored race" alone. The class of those who could claim individual-regarding equality before the law was probably inclusionary enough for all men, but not yet for women.

Also in 1880, in another case involving jury service, this one a prosecution in federal court of a state judge who, under Virginia law had excluded "citizens of African race and black color" from jury service, the Supreme Court held that Congress under Section 5 of the Fourteenth Amendment had the authority to provide for federal prosecution of such acts. Once again the court commented on the potential application of the amendment:

The history of the Amendments is fresh in the recollection of all of us. They grew out of the late civil war and the events which followed it. They were primarily designed to give freedom to persons of the African race, prevent their future enslavement, make them citizens, and prevent discriminating state legislation against their lot. The generality of the language used necessarily extends some of their provisions to persons of every race and color; but in constructing the Amendments and giving effect to them, the occasions of their adoption and the purposes they were designed to obtain should always be borne in mind. (*Ex parte Virginia*: 684)

Despite such words, in another 1880 case the Court held that the absence of Negroes on a jury panel was not necessarily evidence of discrimination and that the burden of proof rested on the one alleging discrimination when the laws of the state did not explicitly exclude Negroes. Moreover, a criminal defendant who claimed discrimination in jury selection was required to pursue his claim through the state courts before seeking a federal remedy (*Virginia v. Rives,* 1880). So it seems that while the Supreme Court was probably then willing to apply an inclusionary interpretation of the equal protection clause to instances of racial or ethnic discrimination (not just to African-Americans), it left some serious stumbling blocks in the paths of litigants.

The implications of *Virginia v. Rives* divided the court only a year later in the case of *Neal v. Delaware* (1881). William Neal, a citizen of the "African race," had filed a verified trial petition alleging that African-Americans had been excluded from both the grand and petit juries in his case. While it was true that no African-Americans served on either jury, Neal's petition contained no proof of a general policy of exclusion. The interesting point in the case is that the Delaware attorney general did not contradict Neal's petition but was content to proceed with a hearing on Neal's allegations. The fact that African-Americans had been excluded was conceded in argument, but the chief justice of Delaware remarked that the exclusion was "in nowise remarkable in view of the fact—too notorious to be ignored—that the great body of black men residing in this state are utterly unqualified by want of intelligence, experience or moral integrity, to sit on juries" (*Neal v. Delaware*: 573). The Delaware chief justice acknowledged only "rare exceptions" to his generalization. This was too much for Justice Harlan, who noted that there were more than 20,000 "blacks" in Delaware in 1870 and more than 26,000 in 1880, out of a total population of only 150,000. He found the assumption that all African-Americans were unqualified for jury service to be a "violent presumption" and a denial of Neal's rights (*Neal v. Delaware*: 574). Two justices dissented. One would have rejected Neal's claim based simply on the holding in *Virginia v. Rives* that the absence of African-Americans on a jury is not itself proof of discrimination. The other, also relying on Rives, would have accepted the generalization of the Delaware chief justice (*Neal*: 574–75).

A more significant obstacle to protecting the rights of African-Americans was affirmed in 1883 when in *United States v. Harris* the Supreme Court held unconstitutional a section of the Ku Klux Klan Act of 1871 because it was made applicable to the acts of private persons. The same obstacle was raised that year in a much better known set of cases, the *Civil Rights Cases* of 1883.

It was in the *Civil Rights Cases* that the Civil Rights Act of 1875, the last edifice of Reconstruction, was declared unconstitutional. The court's majority said straight out that, "Individual invasion of individual rights is not the subject matter of this amendment." Only state action or actions under the authority of the state were covered by the Fourteenth Amendment. That point had already been made, albeit somewhat less clearly and forcefully, in *United States v. Cruikshank* in 1876. There it was said that the only obligation placed on the United States by the Fourteenth Amendment was to see that the states do not deny due process or equal protection. This was followed, as we have seen, by *United States v. Harris* in 1883, which held that the efforts of Congress to provide for federal prosecution of those "who conspire or go in disguise upon the highway for the purpose of denying any person the equal protection of the law" to be unconstitutional as applied to the actions of private persons (*United States v. Harris*).

To put the "state action" issue in perspective, it is helpful to remember the language that Congressman Bingham first proposed to the House on December 5, 1865. He would have amended the Constitution to "empower Congress to pass all necessary and proper laws to secure to all persons in every state equal protection in their rights, life, liberty and property" (*Globe*: 14). That is the wording that ten Broek called the "positive form"; he argues that shifting from that form to "No State shall deny its citizens the equal protection of the law" opened the door to an interpretation like that of the *Civil Rights Cases* (ten Broek, 1965: 216 et seq.). Still, ten Broek concluded that the change of language did not represent a serious substantive change of purpose. The difficulties experienced in passing the Fourteenth Amendment came in debates over

Sections 2 and 3 of the amendment, that is, on the issues of representation and disablement of those formerly in rebellion, and not with respect to the equal protection language of Section 1.

Nonetheless, Justice Bradley in the *Civil Rights Cases* took the words
"No State shall" literally to mean that only official acts of the state were
barred by the Fourteenth Amendment. He expressly repudiated the
"positive power" interpretation later proposed by ten Broek:

> It does not authorize congress to create a code of municipal law
> for the regulation of private rights. . . . Positive rights and privi-
> leges are undoubtedly secured by the fourteenth amendment; but
> they are secured by way of prohibition against state laws and state
> proceedings affecting those rights and privileges, any by power
> given to congress to legislate for the purpose of carrying such
> prohibition into effect; and such legislation must necessarily be
> predicated upon such supposed state laws. (*Civil Rights Cases*: 21)

Since the *Civil Rights Cases* involved accommodations in inns, hotels,
or theaters, there was already available to the court the possibility of a
narrowly drawn opinion based on the common-law understanding of
what were "common callings," that is, facilities traditionally open to any
member of the public—mills, public conveyances, inns, restaurants,
theaters. That was the option chosen by the U.S. Supreme Court in 1877
in *Munn v. Illinois* to sustain "police power" regulation of grain eleva-
tors.[2] Businesses that were common callings were not purely private,
but, being open to all, were subject to regulation in the public interest.
Under that reasoning, it would have been possible for the court to
distinguish between three categories: (1) purely private action; (2) state
action; and (3) common callings—which could have been deemed to be
closer to state than to private action. Justice Harlan's dissent developed
that "quasi-public" position, and that solution was suggested also under
Justice Bradley's reasoning, for even he acknowledged, "Innkeepers
and public carriers, by the laws of all the state, so far as we are aware,
are bound to the extent of their facilities, to furnish proper accommodation to all unobjectionable persons who in good faith apply for them"
(*Civil Rights Cases*: 31).

In his solo dissent, Justice Harlan found Bradley's state action concept to be "too narrow and artificial." He believed that the "substance
and spirit of the recent amendments of the constitution have been sac-
rificed by a subtle and ingenious verbal criticism" (*Civil Rights Cases*:
33). From our vantage more than one hundred years later, we can't

determine conclusively which side, Bradley's or Harlan's, was more faithful to the intentions of the proponents of the Fourteenth Amendment. If we look to the intentions of leaders such as Bingham and Stevens, then Bradley's interpretation is almost certainly wrong, but theirs was not the only view in the Thirty-ninth Congress. The important point is that Bradley's view prevailed and became an obstacle that the Supreme Court and the Congress have struggled with since. The domain of equal civil or legal rights did not include protection against purely private discrimination.

Two other equal protection cases came before the Supreme Court in 1883. The first, *Bush v. Kentucky,* was yet another case involving racial discrimination in grand and petit jury qualification. This time the Supreme Court set aside a state court refusal to void a grand jury indictment. Since the Commonwealth of Kentucky had twice since the ratification of the Fourteenth Amendment reenacted statutes that excluded "citizens of the African race" from jury service, the presumption that the state would in good faith comply with the amendment was "overthrown." In the period between the *Civil Rights Cases* of 1883 and the "separate but equal" decision in *Plessy v. Ferguson* in 1896, the Supreme Court wrote opinions in five jury-selection cases, and only one was in favor of the African-American defendant (Lofgren, 1987: 78).

The second case from 1883, *Pace v. Alabama,* poses a more serious problem for equal protection, for there the Supreme Court sustained a state anti-miscegenation law on the ground that the statute prohibited both "whites and blacks" alike from intermarrying and provided the same punishment for each.[3] Surely that was a conceptual precursor to the "separate but equal" doctrine of *Plessy v. Ferguson,* for whites as well as African-Americans were denied the right to integrated transportation under *Plessy.* A disingenuous argument at best, the Supreme Court in *Pace v. Alabama* sustained an explicit distinction based upon race alone. That it did so in the instance of marriage—a social relationship licensed by the state—is probably significant. Marriage commonly leads to procreation, and according to the understanding of race then prevalent, preventing the "mixing of racial blood" and protecting the "purity of blood" were thought by some to be objectively sustainable goals under state police powers.[4]

The understanding that equality is achieved when African-Americans as a group are treated the same as whites as a group is, of course an example of bloc- or group-regarding equality, but one in this instance in which the achievement of equality is illusory. Equality, in this instance, depends on the fact that the law's purpose is to prevent whites from

marrying African-Americans, as well as African-Americans from marrying whites, and that those African-Americans and whites who violate
the law would receive the same punishment. This outcome benefits no
one (unless of course the dubious rationale of preserving "racial purity"
were held to have some merit). In other instances this sort of bloc-
regarding equality may be more appropriate. For example, it makes
certain sense to ask whether African-Americans as a group are doing as
well as whites in instances of admission to graduate schools or of employment in a particular vocation. Such questions may properly be
asked when African-Americans (or some other minority) have traditionally been excluded from a benefit—as in education or a job. In such
instances, past racial discrimination makes the objective of remediation
a relevant question. It makes no sense, however, to seek the objective of
keeping African-Americans from marrying whites as well as whites
from marrying African-Americans, even if they are always punished
equally. Instead, it is the use of the racial category itself that is objectionable.

Two cases from the post-Reconstruction period involved San Francisco laundries. In *Barbier v. Connally* (1884) the Supreme Court upheld
a local ordinance that regulated public laundries for a variety of supposed health and safety reasons. "Class legislation, discriminating
against some and favoring others, is prohibited; but legislation which in
carrying out a public purpose, is limited in its application, if within the
sphere of its operation it affects alike all persons similarly situated, is
not within the amendment" (*Barbier v. Connally*: 360).

And so the stage was set for *Yick Wo v. Hopkins* only two years later.
As in *Barbier,* the city of San Francisco sought to regulate laundries,
this time providing that permission to operate public laundries might
be denied except for laundries conducted in buildings of brick or stone.
The right to deny permission to laundries operated in wooden buildings
was placed in the board of supervisors, and they were given complete
discretion in their approval or denial. The case therefore involved two
points. The first was that most laundries constructed of wood were
operated by Chinese, so that the ordinance, while apparently objective
on its face, was discriminatory in practice. The second point was that
the power to give or withhold permission, without policy guidance, left
open the possibility of arbitrary or capricious decisions. The Court held
that the Fourteenth Amendment protected even Chinese aliens resident in the United States, "These provisions are universal in their application, to all persons within the territorial jurisdiction, without regard
to any differences of race, of color, or of nationality; and the equal

protection of the laws is a pledge of the protection of equal laws" (*Yick Wo*: 1070).

It is remarkable that the first interpretation of the Equal Protection Clause in the *Slaughter-House Cases* expressed the doubt that the clause would ever be used for any purpose other than the protection of "Negroes as a class, or on account of their race," but only thirteen years later the court applied the clause for the protection even of Chinese aliens and used words that inclusively defined the class of males who could claim individual-regarding equal protection.

Yet in 1893, only seven years after *Yick Wo,* the court, in *Fong Yue Ting v. United States,* was less solicitous of the legal status of the Chinese in America. One key difference was that the party accused of discrimination in the *Fong Yue Ting* case was the U.S. government, so the Fourteenth Amendment did not apply (one dissenting justice in the case did suggest that due process of the Fifth Amendment and equal protection might be interchangeable).

Fong Yue Ting's case arose from Congress's passage in 1892 of a provision that required Chinese laborers to obtain and carry with them a certificate of residence. The certificate was much like an internal passport. Any Chinese alien found without such a certificate was subject to deportation, although the alien could attempt to meet an affirmative burden of proving a good reason for not having obtained the certificate and also of proving that he or she had been a lawful resident at the time of enactment of the 1892 provision. The proof of lawful residence in 1892 required "at least one credible *white* witness" (*Fong Yue Ting*: 1028). Moreover, the procedures provided by the act were considerably less than those that would have been required to meet even the minimal procedural due process standard required at that time.

A majority of the court held that requiring at least one white witness was comparable to the requirement in naturalization proceedings of proof, by the oath of a citizen of the United States, of five years' residence. But of course, such naturalization proceedings did not require the oath of a white citizen. Nonetheless, the court held that Chinese had "loose notions" about obligations of an oath, so that the limitation of testimonial rights to white witnesses was judged to have a rational base. Their refusal to protect Chinese aliens was supported by the holding that the power to exclude or expel aliens, with less than normal due process requirements, was within the power of the "political departments" of government. The power of the national government over alienage was seen as being quite different from the police powers of the states to deny Chinese aliens the equal protection of the law. Chinese aliens were at least protected against arbitrary discrimination by the states.

Female U.S. citizens received even less constitutional protection than Chinese aliens in those days. We have already noted that coincident with *The Slaughter-House Cases* in 1873, Myra Bradwell was denied admission to the bar of Illinois. The Equal Protection Clause was not even mentioned by the Supreme Court in her case. However, in his concurring opinion Justice Bradley wrote that "divine ordinance" had accorded men and women different spheres—women were given the "domestic sphere," while men were to be their "protectors and defenders" (*Bradwell v. Illinois*: 446). Two years later, the Supreme Court had no difficulty sustaining the denial of votes to women, and once again the Equal Protection Clause was not mentioned (*Minor v. Happersett,* 1875).

The first few years of interpretation of the Equal Protection Clause thus gave us the "state action" limitation and witnessed an increasingly inclusionary understanding of equality through the occasional application of equal protection to males other than Negroes. Still the domain of equal protection was narrow. The clause was to apply to official state actions that resulted in discrimination based on race, color, caste, or previous condition of servitude. Even then, discrimination was recognized only when it was with regard to clearly established civil rights, such as jury service or the right to equal legal status with respect to the ownership and uses of property or of a business. The court was prepared to look away when issues involving social equality emerged, the best example being the issue of miscegenation in *Pace v. Alabama*. Equal protection of the law had a very narrow domain, and women were not within its purview at all.

THE ADVENT OF THE SEPARATE
BUT EQUAL DOCTRINE

In 1896 in *Plessy v. Ferguson* the U.S. Supreme Court upheld a Louisiana statute that required "equal but separate accommodations for the white and colored races" on passenger trains within the state. Charles Lofgren's book on the *Plessy* case notes that, from our post-*Brown v. Board of Education* vantage, our perception of *Plessy* as a seminal case is anachronistic. As late as 1948, *Plessy* was little noted by constitutional historians. The significance of that omission was explained by Lofgren as a quiet but vivid representation of the reality that racial segregation was, before *Brown,* viewed by many if not most whites (including constitutional scholars) as commonplace and was conventionally understood as unexceptionable (Lofgren, 1987: 5).

Scholars have counted 150 U.S. Supreme Court cases that were decided under the Fourteenth Amendment between the *Slaughter-House Cases* and *Plessy*, but only fifteen of these involved racial discrimination (Lofgren, 1987: 70). Eighty-two state and lower federal court decisions on racial discrimination were considered between 1834 and 1903, and about three-quarters of them were decided between ratification of the Fourteenth Amendment and the decision in *Plessy* (Kousser, 1980; Lofgren, 1987: 79). One review of state cases in which the Fourteenth Amendment was invoked reveals that it was most often ignored (Lurie, 1984; Lofgren, 1987: 78). So the *Plessy* case cannot be counted as the point in our history when the Supreme Court abjured the Fourteenth Amendment's mandate against racial discrimination. Further, the phrase "separate but equal" did not originate in *Plessy*. Lofgren has shown that a Pennsylvania Supreme Court justice, writing in 1867, affirmed a policy of racial separation in a railroad car (*West Chester and Philadelphia Railroad Company v. Miles*). The most interesting aspect of that decision was that the opinion explicitly approved of separation because of "feelings of aversion" between the races, which the policy of separation would wisely recognize (Lofgren, 1987: 119). Other precedents can be cited to the contrary. In 1873, for example, in *Washington, Alexandria & Georgetown Railroad Company v. Brown*, the U.S. Supreme Court enforced a congressional requirement that no person should be excluded from the railroad cars of the company in question, despite the company's response that it had not excluded, it had only segregated. The court found this to be "an ingenious attempt to evade compliance with the obvious meaning of the legislation" (*Washington, Alexandria & Georgetown Railroad Co. v. Brown*: 678). And in 1914, well after *Plessy*, the U.S. Supreme Court held in *McCabe v. Atchison, Topeka & Santa Fe Railway Co.* that a railroad offering luxuries such as dining, sleeping, and chair cars must offer them to "blacks and whites" alike. While that seems consistent with the separate but equal doctrine, the position was sustained by the court against the railroad's argument that there was an insufficient demand from persons "of African descent" to warrant offering such "luxuries" (*McCabe v. Atchison, Topeka & Santa Fe Railway Co.*: 71). The court's words in *McCabe* sound as though it took the "equal" of separate but equal seriously:

It is the individual who is entitled to equal protection of the laws, and if he is denied by a common carrier, acting in the matter under

the authority of state law, a facility or convenience in the course of
his journey which, under substantially the same circumstances, is
furnished to another traveler, he may properly complain that his
constitutional privilege has been invaded. (*McCabe v. Atchison, Topeka & Santa Fe Railway Co.*: 71)

Those words should help us examine the implications of the separate
but equal doctrine in *Plessy*. If it is true that it is the individual who is
entitled to equal protection, then *Plessy* seems to deny that principle in
upholding segregation and in requiring only that African-Americans
and whites as a whole must receive separate but equal treatment. As we
have seen before, that is an example of bloc-regarding equality, and
bloc-regarding equality is race conscious in that it requires only that
whites as group and African-Americans as a group be treated equally
(Rae, 1981: 32). Individual-regarding equality would involve a single
class of individuals and require that they all be treated alike. Clearly,
the majority in *Plessy* did not intend that. To condone separate but equal
facilities seems inevitably to involve a group criterion, for any case
considered under that doctrine would necessitate comparing the facilities generally available to African-Americans with those available to
whites. A showing only of different treatment of two individuals would
be meaningless, unless it could be shown that the difference was attrib-
utable solely to race and was consistently applied, which would thus
make it a general policy rather than an individual outcome. Correctly
understood, therefore, the *McCabe* case stands not for the principle that
African-Americans as individuals must receive equal treatment but
rather that they as a group must be accorded equal facilities, even if
only one member of the group claims service. African-Americans were
thus not treated as equal human beings, and a bloc-regarding policy of
separate but equal was not then intended to be remedial in nature.

As we have noted before, contemporary race-conscious affirmative
action programs are usually seen as remedial in nature, being designed
to compensate for previous racial discrimination. The separate but
equal doctrine, however, was intended as a permanent policy, and the
requirement of separation was based on the assumption of racial aversion.

Of course the consideration of whether the equality protected by the
Fourteenth Amendment ought to be individual or group-regarding is
not the worst of *Plessy*. Instead, the key problem in *Plessy* was pointed
out by Justice Harlan's dissent, when he argued, "Everyone knows that
the statute in question had its origin in the purpose, not so much to

exclude white persons from railroad cars occupied by blacks, as to exclude colored people from coaches occupied by or assigned to white persons" (*Plessy v. Ferguson*: 1145). Harlan was no doubt correct, and thus racial aversion ran only one way. It was aversion by whites against African-Americans, and that being so, aversion inevitably rested on the notion that whites were superior and African-Americans inferior. Lofgren has noted that by 1890, the 1867 Pennsylvania decision in *West Chester and Philadelphia Railroad v. Miles* had been repeatedly cited for its "theorizing" about racial aversion (Lofgren, 1987: 121).

The majority opinion in *Plessy* today seems disingenuous, whether or not we take into account the eventual failure of the Court's resolve to ensure that separate facilities would in fact be equal. Like the decision in *Pace v. Alabama* denying to both "whites and blacks" the right to intermarry, the badge of racial inferiority was not simply in the eye of either the individual white or African-American beholder but in the white society at large. Justice Harlan, a man whose understanding and candor were well ahead of his time, would have denied Jim Crow and would have made differences of class, caste, or race unconstitutional, at least if officially established or condoned. The Constitution, as he said, was "color-blind." The Court's majority, to the contrary, allowed a legal requirement, mandated separation, to confirm extant social distinctions—even to the point of arguing that social inequality based on race could not be eradicated by equal laws. African-Americans were thus to have a narrow domain of protected "civil and political rights," but social equality was clearly outside the domain. The Radical Republican leaders who fought for the Fourteenth Amendment in the Thirty-ninth Congress would probably have been aghast at the facile constriction of the domain of equality that was defined in *Plessy*.

Of course, our reading of *Plessy* today should not lead us to the error of concluding that the Supreme Court in 1896 caused the states to turn to racial segregation. Just as the Compromise of 1877 and the end of Reconstruction did not instantly transform relations between "blacks and whites," *Plessy* did not by itself transform either the Fourteenth Amendment or the status of African-Americans. As C. Vann Woodward has noted in *The Strange Career of Jim Crow,* certain segregation practices arose even during Reconstruction. These included the segregation of Protestant churches and of public schools in the South (Woodward, 1955: 15). Nonetheless, Woodward argues that racism in the South was a phenomenon that rose to dominance in the 1880s and 1890s. In 1881 Tennessee became the first state to enact a separate but equal law for public transportation. Nine states, all southern, had enacted such laws prior to *Plessy.* Five more states enacted such laws following *Plessy* (Lofgren, 1987: 21 et seq.). *Plessy* was thus more an affirmation of "Negrophobia" than a cause (Woodward, 1955: 49 et seq.).

It should be noted in passing that in the North, while the rights of African-Americans were by no means uniformly protected, there were a number of successes. For example, New York's public accommodation legislation dates from 1874, while Michigan first outlawed racial segregation in education in 1867 (Foner, 1988: 471).

Two years after *Plessy,* in *Williams v. Mississippi* (1898), Justice McKenna reviewed a state law that provided for a poll tax that excluded certain convicted felons from voting and that required a literacy test (reading any section of the Mississippi Constitution, or understanding it when read aloud, and giving a reasonably good interpretation of it) and concluded that it did not on its face discriminate between the "white and Negro races." His conclusion avoided the fact that the Mississippi legislature had devised the plan for the disenfranchisement of "black voters" (Woodward, 1955: 54). Apparently Justice McKenna did not want to "open the box to inspect the real contents" (Kluger, 1975: 68).

In 1899 the U.S. Supreme Court in *Cumming v. County Board of Education* held that the separate but equal doctrine did not prohibit a local school board from maintaining a high school for whites, while having none for "black" children in Richmond County, Georgia. To be more precise, the county school board had appropriated money to assist separate high schools for white boys and girls, had provided assistance for a church-related high school for white boys and girls, but provided nothing at all for African-American children of high school age. The local board's rationale was that it had money to support primary education for "300 black students" or secondary education for some "60 black students," but not enough for both. The Supreme Court sustained the local board's discretion in providing only for primary education for African-Americans. The Court expressed its reluctance to interfere with the local management of the schools. The plaintiffs had asked for an injunction that would have stopped all public support for white high schools until equal provision was made for "black students." Even Justice Harlan found that this would merely take educational privileges from whites without providing anything for African-American students. Certainly no support was expressed for integration, but it is surprising that no member of the court could then see this as a violation of the separate but equal doctrine. Thus did the U.S. Supreme Court evidence its degree of commitment to racial equality at the turn of the century.

5

LAISSEZ-FAIRE AND ECONOMIC
EQUAL PROTECTION

The Radicals of 1866 had "entrenched" in the Constitution ... a rule to "curb the many who would do to the few as they would not have the few do to them." In short, corporations were to be protected by Congress against regulation or interference by states.
—H. K. Beale, *The Critical Year*

Given the Supreme Court's quite limited and tentative commitment in the late nineteenth century to enforcement of the Equal Protection Clause even against racial discrimination, its willingness—beginning in the 1880s—to embrace economic equal protection and thus to protect business enterprises may seem astounding. Thus far we have reviewed cases involving discrimination by race in state jury selection, in voting, and in public education, as well as discrimination against persons of Chinese origins. While the Court was often tentative about using the Equal Protection Clause even for these purposes, a short list of protected civil rights nonetheless emerged. Such rights were well within the context of issues that had motivated the proponents of the Fourteenth Amendment in 1865, even if the outcomes were not always what the proponents might have desired.

Some scholars have argued that "economic equal protection" also motivated the proponents of the Fourteenth Amendment. That purpose, if such it was, was well-concealed from the public. The public silence by the proponents of the Fourteenth Amendment on the possibility of economic equal protection led eventually to the accusation that the proponents of the Fourteenth Amendment had conspired to create a national power to protect business enterprise against state interference. This conspiracy theory of the Fourteenth Amendment has been the subject of much controversy. Based on the evidence available today, the more accurate view seems to be that there was no such conspiracy and that economic equal protection was devised by others after the fact and applied for quite different purposes than those intended by the framers of the Fourteenth Amendment.

THE CONSPIRACY THEORY OF THE
FOURTEENTH AMENDMENT

Substantive economic due process—the constitutional alter ego of laissez-faire capitalism[1]—is familiar to most students of the constitution. It is less widely known that in the last decade of the nineteenth century and the first few decades of this century, the Equal Protection Clause was used for much the same purpose, that is, to strike down state regulation of business. Such a usage of the Fourteenth Amendment is a historic fact, but its origins are mired in controversy.

Charles A. Beard, already well known for his economic interpretation of the purposes of the founding fathers in 1787 (Beard, 1965), argued also that the framers of the Fourteenth Amendment intended to undergird corporate power in America. Their use of the word "person" in the Fourteenth Amendment, he asserted, was intended to include artificial persons, that is, corporations. Beard and other scholars who support this view based their position on Roscoe Conkling's oral argument before the Supreme Court in *County of San Mateo v. Southern Pacific Railroad Company* in 1882. Conkling, who had been a member of the Joint Committee of Fifteen on Reconstruction, argued that the *Journal* of the committee affirmed such an intention. According to Conkling, "joint-stock companies" were at the time appealing to Congress for protection against "invidious and discriminating state and local taxes." The Fourteenth Amendment was seen as a means for national protection against ruinous state laws (Beard, 1918: 58). When Conkling's argument was made in 1882, the *Journal* of the committee had not been published. However, in 1914 the *Journal* was edited and published by Benjamin Kendrick (Riddleberger, 1979: chapter 7).

The most prominent refutation of Beard's thesis was published by Howard Jay Graham in 1938, and the prevailing contemporary view is that the *Journal* does not sustain Conkling's argument (Riddleberger, 1979: 165). Beard nonetheless held to his position, and he was by no means alone in his interpretation. In his 1930 book, Howard Beale also argued that "some of the framers and supporters of the Fourteenth Amendment undoubtedly hoped to make it, as it later became, a national bulwark against state regulation," and he also based his position on Conkling's argument (Beale, 1930: 217).

Certainly, Justice Miller's opinion in the 1873 *Slaughter- House Cases* had made no reference to a broader purpose of the framers of the Fourteenth Amendment. Beard had to concede that point, so it was Conkling's argument in 1882 that gave the first public intimation of an economic application of the Fourteenth Amendment. The timing of his argument was apt, for it was at about this time that corporations began to emerge as the dominant form for business enterprise. The corporate process mostly began with the railroads, and in the last years of the nineteenth century and the early years of the twentieth, corporations encompassed banking, insurance, public utilities, textiles, and mining. By 1899, the census reported that two-thirds of all manufactured products were made by corporate enterprises (Berle and Means, 1932: 13 et seq.).

Even if the conspiracy theory ought to be rejected on the best evidence, the fact remains that the Fourteenth Amendment eventually was used by the courts for the purposes that Conkling suggested in his argument. But properly understood, substantive due process and "economic equal protection" had nothing to do with Reconstruction. They are part of a different story.

ECONOMIC EQUAL PROTECTION

Apart from the obvious intention of the framers of the Fourteenth Amendment to protect the civil rights of freedmen, the prohibitions against states denying "life, liberty or property without due process of law" or against any denial of the equal protection of the law are ambiguous. If we accept the proposition that successive generations should not forever be bound by the understanding of due process or of equality that obtained in 1866, when the Fourteenth Amendment was adopted by Congress (lest we also be trapped, for example, by a nineteenth-century perception of sex roles), then the ambiguity of language is coupled with the need to adapt the protection offered by the Constitution to the understandings of due process of law and of equality as they evolve in our society. But therein lies a danger! The meanings that we impute to ambiguous constitutional language are capable of serving a variety of interests and purposes, including ones that may prove antithetical to the values and interests of those who wrote the words.

For example, if one believed passionately in a popularized version of a free market economy taken, more or less, from Adam Smith's, *The Wealth of Nations,* then it would follow that the most efficient allocation of goods and services in a society would flow naturally from the free market interplay of the forces of supply and demand. Happily, these forces would work not only to serve the best interests of suppliers and consumers of specific products but everyone in society would also ben-

efit, at least indirectly, from the achievement of optimal levels of production. It follows that it would be irrational for government to interfere
with the laws of supply and demand through laws that would seek to
serve other identifiable interests. The market, according to this understanding, would always make more rational allocations than would government. There are not many steps from such an understanding of the
economy to a popular form of Social Darwinism, such as that espoused
by Herbert Spencer or by William Graham Sumner. Thus every member of society is seen as engaged in a struggle in which, in the long run,
only the "fittest" will survive. It would be irrational for government to
interfere, for to do so would produce individuals and a society that are
not as fit as they might be if left alone.

It is not difficult to extrapolate a situation in which such an understanding of economics and of society would be prevalent throughout
the intellectual elite of a society and in which a few members of that
elite eventually become justices of the U.S. Supreme Court, where they
are empowered to give meaning to the Constitution. That is roughly
what happened in the 1880s and 1890s and continued, more or less,
through 1936. The United States became the archetypal capitalist, free
corporate enterprise society in the last quarter of the nineteenth century. The interests of all, that is, of "America," were identified in popular
understanding with the interests of business enterprise. Certainly there
were prominent dissenters even then, but they often were identified by
the unenviable nickname "muckrakers." Also known as "reformers"
and "do-gooders," they sometimes tried in progressive state legislatures to improve conditions through remedial legislation.

In *Barbier v. Connally* in 1884 the regulation of laundries in San Francisco was sustained, provided that "it affects alike all persons similarly
situated (*Barbier v. Connally*: 352). Likewise, in *Hayes v. Missouri* (1887)
the Court, in sustaining the provision by Missouri law for fifteen pe-
remptory challenges for juries in capital cases in cities of over
100,000 population (but only eight challenges in cities of 100,000 or
less), said: "The fourteenth amendment to the constitution of the
United States does not prohibit legislation which is limited either in the
object to which it is directed, or by the territory in which it is to operate.
It merely requires that all persons subjected to such legislation be
treated alike" (*Hayes v. Missouri*: 352).

It is easy to see the difficulty lurking in such statements. When are
people (corporations?) similarly situated? In what ways are they to be
treated alike? When is there a reasonable basis for differentiating
people (corporations?) by legislative design? Those may be difficult

questions in themselves, but if those questions are answered from the perspective of laissez-faire ideology, the grounds for judicial intervention are obvious. A requirement that all corporations be treated alike regardless of their economic purpose, for example, would be segmental equality applied with a vengeance to a novel domain to protect corporations and to frustrate remedial legislation. This view of equality would not require that corporations be treated exactly as individual persons, but it would require that all corporations be treated alike. This requirement of segmental equality would hold unless a state legislature had some clear and compelling reason to intervene, sustained by its fairly distinguishing certain businesses from others. The Supreme Court's eventual adherence to laissez-faire economics caused it usually to be poised and inclined to reject a state's asserted reasons.

Predictably, however, the Court early on voiced reservations against too easily overturning state laws, and it was (it said) especially opposed to expecting or requiring precision in legislation when none was possible. For example, in 1898 in *Magoun v. Illinois Trust & Savings Bank,* the Court, in sustaining an inheritance tax law's provision for varying tax rates based on the size of legacies received, affirmed that only "Clear and hostile discriminations against particular persons and classes especially such as are of unusual character, unknown to the practice of our governments, might be obnoxious to the constitutional prohibition" (*Magoun v. Illinois Trust & Savings Bank*: 598). And in 1899 in *Orient Insurance Co. v. Daggs,* the Court, in sustaining a state provision applied to fire insurance companies but not to other insurers, concluded that classifications are not invalid for not "depending on scientific or marked differences in things or their relations. . . . It suffices if it is practical, and is not reviewable unless palpably arbitrary" (*Orient Insurance Co. V. Daggs*: 282).

So the Supreme Court at first seemed to be deferential to the distinctions and classifications drawn by state legislatures. Another example, in 1907, while sustaining a criminal provision that applied only to officers of banks chartered under a particular state law, the Supreme Court announced, "Before we can pronounce its [the legislature's] judgment in conflict with the Federal Constitution it must be made to appear that its decision was one *necessarily* in conflict therewith, and not that *possibly* or even probably it was" (*Bachtel v. Wilson*: 245, *emphasis added*). And in his usually succinct and clear way, Oliver Wendell Holmes, in upholding an Arizona law that exempted female employees in railroad restaurants from certain work hour requirements, wrote in 1919, "The Fourteenth Amendment is not a pedagogical requirement of the impracticable" (*Dominion Hotel v. Arizona*: 274). Again, in 1921 the Court, in upholding a state law that prohibited corporations that operated cotton gins from also being engaged in the manufacture of cotton seed oil or meal, required that "every statement of facts sufficient to sustain such classification which can be reasonably conceived of as having existed when the law was enacted *will be assumed*" (*Crescent Cotton Oil Co. v. Mississippi*: 44, *emphasis added*). In 1900 the Supreme Court even gave us a list of the sorts of discrimination most likely to be held unconstitutional:

> Of course, if such discrimination were purely arbitrary, oppressive, or capricious, and made to depend on differences of color, race, nativity, religious opinions, political affiliations, or other considerations having no possible connection with the duties of citizens as taxpayers, such exemption [here a license tax exemption] would be pure favoritism, and a denial of the equal protection of the law to the less favored classes. (*American Sugar Refining Co. v. Louisiana*: 44–45)

With that body of rhetoric, it would seem that state laws ought to have been virtually invulnerable to equal protection challenge, but the Supreme Court often seemed to protest too much its reluctance to interfere with state authority. Such protestations often serve to obscure the fact that the Court is about to do precisely what it has professed to forswear. The following cases reveal what often actually happened.

Outside the realm of equal protection, the use of the due process clause in the *Minnesota Rate Case* in 1889 to strike down freight rates set by a state railway commission as being an unreasonable deprivation of property rights without due process of law offers an important illustration of the Court's occasional willingness to intervene. That case suggested that federal judges could claim the final right of determining, under the due process clause, the reasonableness of rates set by state agencies. By 1898 such final judicial review had been sustained by the U.S. Supreme Court even when the rates had been set by the state legislature (*Smyth v. Ames*).

The examples of economic equal protection come from the same period. The first two come from Texas, and the first was but a short step from the *Minnesota Rate Case*. In 1894 in *Reagan v. Farmers' Loan and Trust Co.* the U.S. Supreme Court unanimously struck down the rates set by the Texas Railroad Commission as a denial not only of due process (as in the *Minnesota Rate Case*) but also of equal protection, which is the "constitutional right of all owners of property." Equal protection, the Court said, "forbids legislation, in whatever form it may be enacted, by which the property of the individual is, without compensation, wrested from him for the benefit of another, or of the public" (*Reagan v. Farmers' Loan and Trust Co.*: 1055).

In 1897 in *Gulf, Colorado & Santa Fe Railway Co. v. Ellis,* a Texas statute that provided for the recovery against railroads of a $10 attorney's fee on valid claims of less than $50 (which had remained unpaid for more than thirty days after demand) was struck down. Ellis had brought a claim before a justice of the peace to recover $50 for a colt killed by the railroad, but the possibility that the Texas legislature might have taken into account the economic power of railroads relative to those who might bring claims against them did not matter to the Supreme Court's majority. The Court said that it was a denial of equal protection for a state legislature to "arbitrarily select one corporation or one class of corporations, one individual or one class of individuals, and visit a penalty upon them which is not imposed on others of like delinquency" (*Gulf, Colorado & Santa Fe Railway Co. v. Ellis*: 258). Justice Brewer wrote that if this were not judged a denial of equal protection, it would make the guarantee of equality a "rope of sand." It is appropriate to remember that the majority opinion containing the "rope of sand" phrase was written only one year after the separate but equal doctrine had been sustained by the Court in *Plessy!* A state legislature could thus segregate "blacks from whites" in public transportation, but it could not distinguish between small and large claims brought against railroads. All corporations (again an example of segmental equality), but not necessarily all people it seems, were entitled to equal treatment.

Three dissenters in *Gulf, Colorado & Santa Fe* argued that a state legislature must be presumed to have acted for acceptable reasons. They suggested that the Texas legislature might have been satisfied that railroads within the state were "accustomed, beyond other corporations or persons, to unconscionably resist the payment of such petty claims, with the object of exhausting the patience and the means of the claimants by prolonged litigation" (*Gulf, Colorado & Santa Fe Railway Co. v. Ellis*: 261).

In 1901, a Kansas law that regulated the charges of stockyards having a certain business volume was held a denial of equal protection as "a positive and direct discrimination between persons engaged in the same class of business and based simply on the quantity of business which each may do" (*Cotting v. Godard*: 43–44). The business volume proviso in the legislation was included so that the law would apply to the Kansas

City Stock-Yards Company but not to other Kansas stockyards (all of them doing less business volume). The Court stated, "If once the door is opened to the affirmance of the proposition that a state may regulate one who does much business, while not regulating another who does the same but less business, then all significance in the guaranty of the equal protection of the laws is lost" (*Cotting v. Godard*: 43).

In the last chapter we saw the domain of racial equality become smaller by judicial interpretation. We also saw racial equality transformed into an unusual and inappropriate form of group- or bloc-regarding equality in *Plessy.* Now in these remarkable words in *Cotting,* the active domain of equality is moved from race to enterprise, and all enterprises become presumptively entitled to segmental equality. *Cotting* is, for most purposes, an obscure case, yet it should be remembered as one of the vivid examples of the distance in policy and perspective (though not so much distance in time) that separates the Radical Republican proponents of the Fourteenth Amendment from the laissez-faire lawyers and judges of the turn of the century.

An Illinois statute that defined and prohibited trusts and combinations in restraint of trade but exempted from its coverage agricultural products or livestock that was still in the hands of the producer or raiser was declared unconstitutional in 1902 in *Connolly v. Union Sewer Pipe Co.* The Supreme Court held that under the guise of its police powers Illinois had entered the domain of commerce and had discriminated against a particular class by exempting others. The exemption was held to be purely arbitrary.

A Kansas law allowing recovery of reasonable attorneys' fees in suits by shippers who successfully sued railroads for failure to provide railcars, while not providing for fees in suits brought by railroads against shippers, was declared a violation of equal protection in a 1915 case. There a Kansas state court had sustained the law as a valid exercise of police powers, concluding:

> Because of the control of railroad companies over their cars, their capacity to disturb and obstruct trade, and the helplessness of shippers when cars are carelessly or arbitrarily withheld, railroad companies might properly be placed in a class by themselves for the purpose of securing sufficient car service. (*Atchison, Topeka & Santa Fe Railway Co. v. Vosburg*: 675)

The U.S. Supreme Court unanimously reversed the Kansas court. Even though the measure was an exercise of Kansas's police powers, the

Court said that the classifications made in state legislation must be reasonable and not arbitrary. They must rest on "distinctions having a fair and substantial relation to the object sought to be accomplished by the legislation" (*Atchison, Topeka & Santa Fe v. Vosburg*: 676). The Court found the distinction to be arbitrary, even though the State of Kansas clearly had not.

While the subject matter in these cases is no longer of consequence and while they clearly will not make any honor roll of issues involving human liberty, they yet serve to illustrate the willingness of the Supreme Court during this period to make its own judgment of the merits of economic issues. A few more examples will bring us to the end of the period.

In 1921 in *Truax v. Corrigan,* the court overturned an Arizona law that prohibited the issuance of injunctions against striking employees because under that law injunctions could be issued against others who engaged in the same conduct but who were not employees. The striking employees encouraged potential customers (through pickets and handbills) not to patronize their employer's business. Since the encouragement of a boycott could otherwise have been enjoined under state law, the exemption of striking employees from such injunctions by state law was held a denial of equal protection. Chief Justice Taft wrote an opinion for the majority that conceded the inevitability of classification in legislation, but, he said, "it must regard real resemblances and real differences between things and persons and class them in accordance with their pertinence to the purpose in hand" (*Truax v. Corrigan*: 131). Taft, could see no real difference between strikes by employees and other conspiracies in restraint of trade. In dissent, Holmes scorned the majority's search for "delusive exactness." And he added:

There is nothing that I more deprecate than the use of the Fourteenth Amendment beyond the absolute compulsion of its words to prevent the making of social experiments that an important part of the community desires, in the insulate chambers afforded by the several states, even though the experiments may seem futile or even noxious to me and to those whose judgement I most respect. (*Truax v. Corrigan*: 134)

It is evident that these cases protecting businesses under the guise of equal protection have rather little to do with the cases we saw in the last chapter involving race, alienage, or sex. They are, however, precisely like substantive economic due process cases in using judicial power to

determine whether the laws in question are arbitrary or capricious—
under the prevailing laissez-faire economic theory—and such determi-
nations were made despite the clear caveats that the Court itself issued
against such facile decisions.

The simple way to cut through the rhetoric of these cases is to recognize how easy it is to require segmental equality and to dub a state law
arbitrary, capricious, or unreasonable, on the one hand, or to hold it
reasonable and wise, on the other. Such decisions usually result not
from analysis but rather are only an exercise in attribution—in this
instance the attribution is based on laissez-faire ideology. We can better
understand what the Court was about when we examine the situations
in which state laws were held unconstitutional under equal protection
to see what they may have in common. We find one instance of a state
legislature attempting directly to regulate rail freight rates, two instances of state legislatures providing for the recovery of attorneys'
fees in suits against railroads, one instance of a state legislature seeking to regulate the rates charged at the largest stockyard in the state,
one instance of state antitrust legislation exempting farmers and ranch-
ers, and one instance of a state law protecting striking employees from
injunction suits brought by employers. All were held to be arbitrary and
capricious by the Supreme Court. What they have in common is the use
of state police powers to protect persons or interests that state legislatures probably viewed as vulnerable relative to their competing economic adversaries.

In one sense there is little difference between, on the one hand, the
Supreme Court's overturning state laws and enforcing laissez-faire economic values through the equal protection clause by requiring that
corporations be treated alike (beginning in the 1880s and continuing up
through 1936) and, on the other hand, using the Equal Protection
Clause to reject the policy distinctions that legislatures have imposed
based on race, gender, or other personal differences and thereby enforcing egalitarian human values, as it has done during the past several
decades. Both reflect the willingness, and sometimes the eagerness, of
the Supreme Court to reject, under equal protection review, policy distinctions drawn by state legislatures. That is why liberals criticized the
Supreme Court during its laissez-faire activism and conservatives have
criticized the Court's more recent human rights activism.

In another sense, however, there is an important difference. During
the Court's laissez-faire period it rejected legislation because it violated
the Court's presumptions favoring laissez-faire values. Those values
were quite extraneous to the purpose and language of the equal protec-

tion clause, which was written to protect people, not corporations. Contemporary equal protection is, or ought to be, based on a presumption that all people are entitled to the equal protection of the law so that treating some people differently than others requires at least some minimal justification. The rational basis or purpose test conforms with the requirement of minimal justification, and once certain policy distinctions have become suspect (race being the best example) based on the Court's continuing encounter with them, the Court moves on to even more stringent scrutiny.

If we take as a watershed year 1930—the year that followed the crash of 1929, which initiated the Great Depression, but which was before the advent of the New Deal in 1932—A. A. Berle found that as of January 1, 1930, the 200 largest American corporations owned 49.2 percent of all corporate wealth, 38 percent of all business wealth, and 22 percent of the entire national wealth. To put those 200 corporations in perspective, Berle reported that in 1929 there were more than 300,000 nonfinancial corporations in the country, yet only 200 of them controlled nearly half the corporate wealth (Berle and Means, 1932: 33). The states clearly took on some powerful adversaries when they sought to regulate such corporate economic power, and it should not be surprising that allies of corporate power found their way to the benches of federal courts. There they were able to enshrine, for a while, the dictates of laissez-faire capitalism.

What is most obviously missing in the economic equal protection cases is the presence of a disadvantaged categorical group or interest such as race, color, alienage, religion, or sex, which has been the object of state discrimination. Such groups are what Justice Stone eventually called "discrete and insular minorities" (in footnote 4 of *United States v. Carolene Products Co.* in 1938) and which later were held to require the special protection of the court.[2] Instead, in economic equal protection cases the federal courts sought to protect powerful business interests against the sometimes populist policy inclinations of state legislatures.

Lest this conclusion seem to easy or too harsh, let us compare the decision in *Truax v. Corrigan* in 1921, which held as unconstitutional the Arizona law that protected strikers from injunctions, with *Gong Lum v. Rice,* a 1927 decision involving race. In *Gong Lum,* Mississippi classified Chinese students as being "among the colored races" and required them to attend segregated schools with African-Americans. This decision the Supreme Court found to be "within the discretion of the state in regulating its public schools" and not in conflict with the Fourteenth Amendment (*Gong Lum v. Rice*: 94).

Economic equal protection continued through the first three decades of this century. In 1928, for example, Justice Butler, a staunch advocate of laissez-faire capitalism, struck down a Pennsylvania law that imposed a gross receipts tax on corporations operating taxicabs but not on individual taxi owners (*Quaker City Cab Co. v. Pennsylvania*). Holmes and Brandeis predictably dissented.

Almost the last gasp of economic equal protection came in the October 1936 term of the Supreme Court. Justice McReynolds, another strict laissez-faire justice, wrote for the Court's majority in striking down a Georgia law that treated mutual and stock insurance companies differently with respect to their representation by agents (*Hartford Steam Boiler Inspection and Insurance Co. v. Harrison*).

By 1936, Butler, McReynolds, Sutherland, and Van Devanter, the four committed laissez-faire justices, had to rely on the vote of at least one of two centrist justices (Roberts or Chief Justice Hughes) to sustain their economic interpretation of the Fourteenth Amendment. But the four had not just struck down the uses of state police powers, they continued to voice in these years a narrow interpretation of the power of the national government over interstate commerce and a restrictive interpretation of the power to tax and spend for the general welfare. Thus federal power was curtailed as well. The four laissez-faire justices were the last holdouts for such views who actually controlled institutional power at the national level. Roosevelt's re-election in 1936 was followed by his plan to expand the size of the Supreme Court by appointing an additional justice to the court for each sitting justice who was then over the age of seventy. It did not require much political insight to see what Roosevelt was about, and such overt efforts to tamper with the uses of judicial power do not play well in American politics, then or now. Roosevelt was abandoned by some of his key allies, and his "court-packing plan" went nowhere. But in 1937, Justice Owen Roberts, one of the centrists who had sometimes voted with the four laissez-faire justices, began to cast his vote with the other side. Substantive economic due process and economic equal protection, as well as narrow and restrictive interpretations of national power, went down to defeat (Murphy, 1962; Pritchett, 1961). Death and retirement, coupled with Roosevelt's four consecutive elections to the presidency, solidified and extended the judicial victory (Pritchett, 1948).

By 1940 Justice Frankfurter, a Roosevelt appointee, wrote for the majority in *Tigner v. Texas* in upholding a Texas statute that exempted agricultural products from state antitrust legislation. That provision was virtually identical to the Illinois statute struck down by the court in

1902 in *Connolly v. Union Sewer Pipe*. McReynolds wrote a dissent that would have followed *Connolly,* but Frankfurter noted that "time and circumstances had drained [*Connolly*] of its vitality" (*Tigner v. Texas*: 880).

The most explicit epitaph for substantive economic due process came in *Williamson v. Lee Optical Co.* in 1955. The Court upheld an Oklahoma statute that made unlawful the fitting of eyeglasses by anyone not a licensed optometrist or ophthalmologist except by written prescription. The Court said, "The day is gone when this Court uses the Due Process Clause of the Fourteenth Amendment to strike down state laws, regulatory of business and industrial conditions because they may be unwise, improvident, or out of harmony with a particular school of thought" (*Williamson v. Lee Optical Co.*: 464). Economic equal protection had the same fate, but at about the same time—in the late 1930s— that the Supreme Court abandoned substantive economic due process and economic equal protection, it began to evidence a willingness to look anew at racial discrimination in America.

6

THE PATH TO
BROWN V. BOARD OF EDUCATION

*In no event shall a negro be eligible to participate in a Democratic party
primary election held in the State of Texas.*
        —Texas Revised Statutes, Art. 3107, enacted in 1923,
        held unconstitutional in *Nixon v. Herndon,* 1927

Even during the height of economic equal protection, African-Americans experienced some victories, though often illusory ones and ones
that always avoided confronting directly the segregated realm of "separate but equal" in public education and other public facilities. But certain state laws were so blatantly discriminatory and so clearly antithetical to the purposes of the Fourteenth Amendment that sometimes even
the most reluctant justices of the U.S. Supreme Court could see the
contradictions.

In *Buchanan v. Warley* (1917) an ordinance of the city of Louisville
that provided for residential segregation by prohibiting the transfer of
realty from "whites to blacks or from blacks to whites" was challenged.
The ordinance was justified as a police powers measure designed "to
prevent conflict" and to "preserve the public peace." The law provided
that if a residential block had a "white or a black majority," members of
the respective racial minority could not move in. The challenge to the
Louisville ordinance was sponsored by the NAACP, which had been
founded only eight years before (Kluger, 1975: 134).

Conceding a broad zone of deference to local police powers, the Supreme Court nonetheless found that this measure invaded fundamental
rights—indeed, rights that were viewed as of paramount importance at
this time—the rights of property. In sustaining a right to buy, sell, and
hold property, the court distinguished *Buchanan* from *Plessy v. Ferguson.* The Court said that segregation, efforts to prevent "amalgamation
of the races," and efforts to "promote the public peace and prevent race
conflicts," while then constitutionally permissible in general, could not
be accomplished through laws that invaded the rights of property. It is

worth noting that in overturning the ordinance the court relied on due process (the taking of property), rather than on equal protection.[1]

Other victories, however illusory, infrequent, or short-lived, involved the right to vote. In 1915 in *Guinn v. United States,* in which the NAACP filed a brief as a friend of the court, the Supreme Court unanimously struck down an Oklahoma statute containing a patently obvious grandfather clause.[2] In a prosecution brought in federal court against Oklahoma election officials who had excluded "black voters" under the state law, an 1871 federal statute (passed to implement the Fifteenth Amendment) was used for the first time since its adoption to invalidate a discriminatory state law (Kluger, 1976: 104). Oklahoma responded by passing a law that conferred permanent registration on anyone who had voted in 1914 and granting others only a twelve-day period to be registered or to be barred from voting for life, so the victory in *Guinn* was more symbolic than real (Kluger, 1975: 129).

The other apparent voting victories came in the arena of the Texas Democratic primary, challenged in court twice by the long-suffering African-American physician, L. A. Nixon of El Paso, and by the NAACP. The first case, *Nixon v. Herndon* (1927), involved an entirely unambiguous Texas statute that declared Negroes ineligible to participate in the Democratic party primary. It took Justice Holmes little more than a page to reject the statute by invoking the Equal Protection Clause. He noted, "States may do a good deal of classifying that is difficult to believe rational, but there are limits, and it is too clear for extended argument that color cannot be the basis of a statutory classification affecting the right set up in this case" (*Nixon v. Herndon*: 447).

It was also in 1927 that *Gong Lum v. Rice,* introduced in the previous chapter, was decided by the Supreme Court. In *Gong Lum,* Chief Justice Taft's opinion condoned the discretion of local school officials in classifying Chinese-American Martha Lum as a person of color in order to exclude her from attending school with white children in Bolivar County, Mississippi (Kluger, 1975: 149 et seq.). So the "separate but equal" doctrine was alive and well in 1927, even if the requirement of equal facilities was still, at best, a facade.

The fact that Nixon's first victory was illusory is best illustrated by his second case, *Nixon v. Condon* (1932), which was decided by the Supreme Court at the threshold of the New Deal. Texas had repealed the explicit law, which was rejected by the Court in the first *Nixon* case, and replaced it with a law vesting in the Democratic Party State Executive Committee the power to determine qualifications for voting in the primary. The members of the committee then proceeded to adopt a rule excluding African-Americans. This was held in *Nixon v. Condon* to be a delegation of state authority to the Democratic party, and thus still to be state action in violation of the Fourteenth Amendment. Justice Cardozo's opinion in Nixon's favor had, however, only five votes in its favor.

Unfortunately, the Texas Democratic party contrived a "third act." In *Grovey v. Townsend* (1935) the Supreme Court upheld a resolution of the Texas Democratic party gathered in convention, which once again excluded African-Americans but which had no explicit or implicit state authority. The Supreme Court could find no state action sufficient to invoke the Fourteenth Amendment.[3] The Court's commitment to the equal protection of the law was thus still bounded by strict doctrinal constraints, and, given such constraints, it probably was not appropriate to take the requirements of equality very seriously, at least before the late 1930s.

ENFORCING THE "EQUAL" IN "SEPARATE BUT EQUAL"

By 1938[4] in *Missouri ex rel Gaines v. Canada*, the Supreme Court apparently was willing to enforce the separate but equal doctrine more stringently than it had been in *Cumming v. County Board of Education of Richmond County, Georgia*, thirty-nine years earlier.[5] Missouri then operated a segregated state university for whites only at Columbia, where the law school was located. Lincoln University, the segregated state university open to Missouri's African-American students at Jefferson City, had no law school. The state expressed its willingness to open a law school at Lincoln, but in the meantime it provided for legal education for its African-American residents by agreeing to pay their out-of-state tuition (in excess of the tuition that would have been charged by the University of Missouri Law School) in adjacent states. This was held by the U.S. Supreme Court to be a denial of the "equality of legal right to the enjoyment of the privilege which the State has set up" (*Missouri ex rel Gaines v. Canada*: 236). All the court had to do to reach that conclusion was to resort to the language in *Yick Wo v. Hopkins* (1886) that equal protection "is a pledge of the protection of equal laws." However, the provision of a remedy for Gaines did not require repudiation of *Plessy*. He was entitled to attend the law school at the

University of Missouri only until the law school at Lincoln University was a reality.

The key difference between the *Gaines* case of 1938 and the rather more illusory victories that often preceded it is that 1938 was on the New Deal side of the constitutional watershed that had been resolved in favor of the Roosevelt administration in 1937. Only McReynolds and Butler stood against the decision in *Gaines.* Van Devanter had been replaced by Sen. Hugo Black of Alabama, a New Deal Democrat, and Sutherland had been replaced by Roosevelt's solicitor general, Stanley Reed.

Thus began a decade in which the requirement of protection of equal laws for African-Americans was taken more seriously than before. *Grovey v. Townsend,* which had held the Texas all-white primary to be the act of a private association, was repudiated by the Supreme Court in *Smith v. Allright* in 1944. In 1946 in *Morgan v. Virginia,* the Court held a provision of the Virginia code, which required the separation of the races on both intrastate and interstate carriers, to be "an unreasonable burden on interstate commerce," even though Congress had not yet legislated on the subject. The court concluded that "seating arrangements for the different races in interstate motor travel require a single, uniform rule to promote and protect national travel" (*Morgan v. Virginia*: 1058).[6]

Also in 1946, Ada Sipuel applied for admission to the University of Oklahoma Law School but was denied because a new law school for African-Americans would soon be opened. At the trial of her suit brought against the state, Thurgood Marshall sought to prove that a jerry-rigged law school for African-Americans could not satisfy the requirements even of the *Gaines* opinion. He lost the trial and the appeal before the Oklahoma Supreme Court. His brief before the U.S. Supreme Court argued that "the terms 'separate' and 'equal' can not be used conjunctively in a situation of this kind; *there can be no separate equality,*" he argued (Kluger, 1975: 325).

In its unanimous per curiam opinion in 1948, the Supreme Court ordered Oklahoma to provide Sipuel a legal education as soon as it would any other applicant, but Oklahoma's response was only to open the sort of makeshift school that Marshall had scorned in this argument. The U.S. Supreme Court was at that time unwilling to require more of Oklahoma, although it would indirectly through a Texas case only two years later.

In 1950 in *Henderson v. United States,* the court confronted the rules of an interstate railroad that provided preferences for white passengers in railroad dining cars.[7] Justice Burton found that such rules violated the Interstate Commerce Act, which had made it unlawful to subject a person to any "undue or unreasonable prejudice or disadvantage." After the initial challenge to their rules, the railroad had amended them to set aside one table with four chairs unequivocally for "Negro passengers," but a curtain was still to be drawn between that table and others during meals. That revised rule was approved by a divided Interstate Commerce Commission, the majority sustaining the rule because the single table and four chairs were "adequate to service the average number of Negro passengers" and therefore proportionately fair (*Henderson v. United States*: 846).

Justice Burton's opinion in *Henderson* rejected the proportionate allocation of chairs, which, if sustained, would have provided chairs as a form of bloc- or group-regarding equality. Under the ICC rule, as long as adequate provision was made for Negro passengers as a whole, there would be no discrimination even if on a particular day certain "excess" numbers of Negroes might not find seating in the dining car. Instead, the court's opinion in *Henderson* required that each individual black passenger be accorded facilities equal to each white passenger. Burton's opinion recalls the 1914 decision in *McCabe v. Atchison, Topeka & Santa Fe,* which required that dining, sleeping, and chair cars be offered to African-Americans and whites alike. The opinion in *McCabe* suggested that each individual under the separate but equal doctrine was entitled to equal treatment, but in *McCabe,* as now in *Henderson,* that suggestion was misleading as long as the separate but equal doctrine remained.

The requirement of the separate but equal doctrine, for example, might be satisfied by dividing the dining car into two equal parts. "White or black" passengers, finding no seats in their respective halves, would be accorded equal treatment. Another solution under separate but equal would be to adjust the seating proportionately to the patrons who actually present themselves for service, that is, moving the "boundary line" between blacks and whites. Both solutions were employed in attempting to live with the separate but equal doctrine in the segregated South, but neither of them involves true individual-regarding equality. For one thing, priority seating was often accorded white passengers in the South, even if that might be in violation of ICC rules. The main objection, however, is that any form of separate but equal seating involves treating "blacks as blacks and whites as whites," as witnessed in the instance of Rosa Parks, who grew tired of it all on a

Montgomery bus on December 1, 1955, and refused to give up her seat to a white passenger (Garrow, 1988: 11).[8]

Unlike *McCabe,* Justice Burton's opinion in *Henderson* actually came close to repudiating the separate but equal doctrine. In *Henderson,* the U.S. Solicitor General Philip Perlman was supported by Att. Gen. J. Howard McGrath in arguing before the Supreme Court that *Plessy* should be overruled. The Justice Department also filed friend of the court briefs in pending cases from Oklahoma and Texas, which involved segregated graduate and law schools, respectively; it argued in both cases for overruling *Plessy.* The decisions in *Henderson* and in the cases from Oklahoma and Texas were announced by the court on the same day, June 5, 1950. They marked the beginning of the end of the separate but equal doctrine.[9]

The sort of petty nastiness reflected in the railroad's dining car policy in *Henderson* was also reflected in the policies of the University of Oklahoma as revealed in the case of *McLaurin v. Oklahoma State Regents* (1950). Given the rules in the *Gaines* and *Sipuel* cases, it was inevitable that Oklahoma would have to admit African-American students to its principal white universities when Oklahoma's "black universities" had no comparable programs. The state's only other option was to create makeshift programs in response to the varying demands of African-American students. Still, sixty-eight-year-old George McLaurin was rejected by the University of Oklahoma in his effort to gain a doctoral degree in education and was forced to sue (Kluger, 1975: 334). It was only under a federal court order that he was admitted. The Oklahoma legislature, however, sought a way out of that court order by requiring that such education be conducted on a segregated basis, and it vested in the president of the University of Oklahoma the authority to make rules and regulations respecting segregation.[10] The rules in force and applied to McLaurin when his case was argued before the U.S. Supreme Court required him to sit in a row in the classroom designated for colored students, to use an assigned table in the library, and to eat at a specifically assigned table in the cafeteria. Chief Justice Vinson's opinion for a unanimous court was emphatic in rejecting rules whose "result is that appellant is handicapped in his pursuit of effective graduate instruction. Such restrictions impair and inhibit his ability to study, to engage in discussions and exchange views with other students, and, in general to learn his profession" (*McLaurin v. Oklahoma State Regents*: 853). One response from Oklahoma was that even if such rules were repealed, McLaurin might still be "set aside" by the views and conduct of his fellow students. To this Chief Justice Vinson replied, "There is a

vast difference—a Constitutional difference—between restrictions imposed by the state which prohibit the intellectual commingling of students, and the refusal of individuals to commingle where the state presents no such bar" (*McLaurin v. Oklahoma State Regents*: 853–54).

Given such words it is difficult to see how any policy requiring separate but equal facilities could be preserved, yet Vinson's opinion did
not expressly repudiate *Plessy.* Nonetheless, the Court's language in
McLaurin, taken with its decision on the same day in *Sweatt v. Painter*
regarding the University of Texas Law School, made the repudiation of
the separate but equal doctrine all but inevitable.

The law school created by the State of Texas to provide a legal education for African-American postal worker Heman Sweatt had, by the
time his case was argued, "five full-time professors, twenty-three students, [and] a library of 16,000 books" (Kluger, 1975: 354). It had been
created under court order in 1946, and classes had been set to begin in
1947 with three part-time faculty members and a library of 10,000 books
(Kluger, 1975: 328). Sweatt for some reason still preferred the University of Texas Law School, but the Texas courts dutifully found that the
newly established "black law school" offered opportunity for the study
of law that was "substantially equivalent" to that offered at the University of Texas Law School. It would have been easy for the U.S. Supreme
Court to decide the case simply by comparing tangible resources, such
as libraries, student-faculty ratios, physical facilities, and the like. By
almost any honest measure, application of the separate but equal doctrine would have found the newly created "black law school" unequal.
But would the provision of equal tangible resources by the state have
made the new law school equal to that at the University of Texas?

Anyone who might have wished to speak honestly in defense of the
University of Texas Law School faced a dilemma in which pride, or even
the customary inclinations of "Texas Brags," would clash with the implications of Heman Sweatt's lawsuit. Certainly no representative of the
University of Texas Law School was keen to claim that the provision of
equal tangible resources would automatically make the newly created
school the equal of the old. There was in fact considerable support on
the university's campus for Sweatt's lawsuit. An all-white NAACP chapter had by then been formed on the campus. It had 200 members, and
more than 2,000 gathered at a mass meeting to support integration just
before Sweatt's case went to trial (Kluger, 1975: 328).

Chief Justice Vinson's opinion in *Sweatt* is most important for taking
intangible factors into account:

What is more important, the University of Texas Law School possesses to a far greater degree those qualities which are incapable of objective measurement but which make for greatness in a law school. Such qualities, to name but a few, include reputation of the faculty, experience of the administration, position and influence of the alumni, standing in the community, traditions and prestige. It is difficult to believe that one who had a free choice between these two schools would consider the question close. (*Sweatt v. Painter*: 850)

The point was made with equal force regarding the student body at the University of Texas Law School:

The law school to which Texas is willing to admit petitioner excludes from its student body members of the racial groups which number 85% of the population of the State and include most of the lawyers, witnesses, jurors, judges, and other officials with whom petitioner will inevitably be dealing when he becomes a member of the Texas Bar. With such a substantial and significant segment of the society excluded, we cannot conclude that the education offered petitioner is substantially equal to that which he would receive if admitted to the University of Texas Law School. (*Sweatt v. Painter*: 850)

Given the language of the Court, especially in *Sweatt* and *McLaurin,* the filing of a case like *Brown v. Board of Education* became inevitable. It was only a matter of time and place. More important, it was a matter of combining the resources of the NAACP with the talents of Thurgood Marshall and others that would make the inevitable a reality.

On the day following the Court's unanimous decision in *Henderson, McLaurin,* and *Sweatt,* Georgia's Gov. Herman Talmadge vowed in response, "As long as I am governor Negroes will not be admitted to white schools. The line is drawn . . . the threats that have been held over the head of the South for four years are now pointed like a dagger ready to be plunged into the very heart of Southern tradition." Strom Thurmond, governor of South Carolina and 1948 Dixiecrat nominee for president, proclaimed, "These decisions are the fruits of the campaign President Truman and his cohorts have been waging against the South for many months. It is apparent that they are part of the effort to destroy states' rights in this country."

Those states' rights included, in addition to Texas's omissions before *Sweatt* in legal education, the right not to have any Southern public university that would educate African-American medical students and none that would award a Ph.D. to African-Americans. The head of Georgia's public school system said that it would take $100 million to bring that state's "black schools" up to par with white schools. From New York, the NAACP issued a statement which said that the three decisions "emphasize once more that the courts of the land are far in advance of the Congress in recognizing the legal and moral obligations of our government to grant civil rights to all citizens. . . . This is a great step forward" (*Austin Statesman,* June 6, 1950).

The following day, the Austin *Statesman*'s headline announced: "Two Negroes Enter UT." One was a doctoral candidate in government, the other a candidate for a master's degree in architecture. No comparable graduate programs were available in any Texas "Negro state institution." An editorial column in the same paper noted that Homer Rainey, a former president of the University of Texas who had been "ousted for his radical views," had earlier warned that "unless equal educational facilities were provided for Negroes by Texas, the Supreme Court of the United States one day would accord them equality rights." For those views, "Dr. Rainey was proclaimed in every quarter of Texas to be a communist, despite the fact that he was an ordained Baptist minister and a loyal and patriotic American" (*Austin Statesman,* June 7, 1950). Rainey was right; that day had come.

Eighty-five years had passed since the Fourteenth Amendment was proposed by the Congress to the states for ratification in 1866. In 1950, the Supreme Court was much closer to the intentions of the Radical Republican proponents of the Fourteenth Amendment than it had ever been before. The NAACP was also correct in saying that the Court was far ahead of the Congress in its willingness to protect the civil rights of African-Americans.

RACE AS A "SUSPECT CLASSIFICATION"

We should not overlook the emergence, even before *Brown,* of the Court's treatment of race as a suspect classification. In his terse opinion in *Nixon v. Herndon* in 1927, Justice Holmes had already hinted that certain statutory classifications might be so extreme as to be presumptively invalid. That notion was revived and strengthened, at least rhetorically, in two World War II cases involving persons of Japanese ancestry. The problem with those cases is that the Japanese-Americans won only the rhetoric. They lost their liberty and often their property as well.

In *Hirabayashi v. United States* in 1943, the Court's majority sustained wartime curfews for persons of Japanese ancestry, despite its statement that "distinctions between citizens solely because of their ancestry are by their very nature odious to a free people whose institutions are founded upon the doctrine of equality." Hence the idea of a suspect classification—as the court said, "legislative classification or discrimination based on race alone has often been held to be a denial of equal protection" (*Hirabayashi v. United States*: 1385).

In *Korematsu v. United States* (1944), the far more onerous wartime exclusion and internment orders were also sustained, even in the fact of Justice Black's pronouncement:

> It should be noted, to begin with, that all legal restrictions which curtail the civil rights of a single racial group are immediately suspect. That is not to say that all such restrictions are unconstitutional. It is to say that courts must subject them to rigid scrutiny. Pressing public necessity may sometime justify the existence of such restrictions; racial antagonism never can. (*Korematsu v. United States*: 194)

The same day that *Korematsu* was decided, the Supreme Court found that the constitution of the Brotherhood of Locomotive Firemen and Engineers and the conduct of that union in negotiating a contract that was disadvantageous to "black" railway firemen (despite its being the bargaining agent for the entire unit of firemen, "blacks and whites" alike) violated the Railway Labor Act's requirement of fair representation, for "here the discriminations based on race alone are obviously irrelevant and invidious" (*Steele v. Louisville & National Railroad Co.*: 203). The wartime Japanese-American cases aside, race was becoming a suspect classification in the fundamental sense that the Supreme Court was coming to see it as a distinction that was a largely irrelevant and inappropriate basis for treating people differently.

CONCLUSION

While we have come forward much more than halfway in time from our beginning in the debates in the Thirty-ninth Congress in 1865 and

1866, conceptually we have not travelled very far. Before *Brown v. Board* the equal protection of the law denoted a fairly simple and limited domain and understanding of equality. After *Brown* we will see what may fairly be called an explosion of complexity, both as equal protection comes to relate to racial distinctions in new ways (e.g., in attempting to reach de facto[11] segregation and affirmative action through group-regarding equality) and as it expands to encompass new categories such as sexual discrimination.

The chief difficulty in confronting racial discrimination between the ratification of the Fourteenth Amendment in 1868 and the cases that led up to *Brown* was for the Supreme Court to find the *will* to enforce what, under any reasonable interpretation, had been in the Equal Protection Clause all along. The separate but equal doctrine was never a reasonable interpretation of the Equal Protection Clause, and the unwillingness of federal courts to enforce the requirement of equality even in racially separate institutions until the period following World War II belied the honesty of the separate but equal doctrine.

Most of the racial cases we have reviewed involved an expectation of individual-regarding equality. Equality was commonly viewed as an individual right to be claimed by those males, of whatever ethnic origin, who had personally experienced some form of de jure discrimination. This was true with respect to a short list of rights, which included jury service, the right to vote, and the right to possess and transfer property. The occasional exception, when justices of the Supreme Court required only group- or bloc-regarding equality (that is, requiring only that African-Americans as a group be treated equally), unfortunately covered a large domain under the separate but equal doctrine. Group-regarding equality was required in outcomes that in this particular context invariably were negative for African-Americans, as best exemplified in *Plessy.* Before World War II, group-regarding equality was a means for keeping blacks down through segregation, and the requirement of individual-regarding equality would have liberated African-Americans from de jure segregation. That, of course, would have been true only if the Supreme Court had also been willing to expand the domain of individual-regarding equality to include public education and the use of other public facilities. The conflicts between individual-regarding and group-regarding over "affirmative action" that came later in the 1960s, and still continue today, were by and large not foreseen in the days of *Plessy.* It is important to remember, however, that while the cases before *Brown* often spoke of equal protection as providing a remedy for individuals, the discrimination that African-Americans experienced was not directed toward individuals but toward their race. Racial discrimination is a form of group or categorical discrimination that sometimes may require affirmative group-regarding equality for its remedy. The conflicts and issues between individual-regarding and group-regarding equality in the context of race are indeed manifold and complex. No doubt both the Congress and the Supreme Court will have to deal with them even into the 1990s—and beyond?

Before *Brown* the domain of equality, whether individual or group-regarding, was narrow, although offering room for expansion. Economic equal protection (and segmental equality for business enterprises) came and went along with substantive economic due process, but the economic equal protection cases offer a still useful caveat—the sort of warning the Justice Oliver Wendell Holmes was prone to give—that judges in applying the Fourteenth Amendment should not require impracticable precision in legislation. Unless thoughtfully contained, Holmes feared that government by the judiciary might rise again in a different context. For some that might be a "consummation devoutly to be desired." For others that outcome might be a fearsome specter.

7

SEGREGATION AND DESEGREGATION— THE CONSEQUENCES OF *BROWN*

There were no separate waiting rooms at the train and bus stations, and Negroes did not have to ride in the back of the local buses, but in other ways it was segregated by law and, more effectively, by custom. There were eighteen elementary schools for whites and four for blacks. There was one colored hotel, the Dunbar, and all the rest were for whites. Almost no restaurants downtown served colored customers.
—Richard Kluger, *Simple Justice,* describing
Topeka, Kansas, in 1951

Brown v. Board of Education of Topeka is one of the few decisions of the Supreme Court of the United States whose name is instantly recognizable to a great many people. Many of them believe that they know what it says, even though most of them may never have read the full text of the opinion, or indeed even excerpts from it. Most people would simply say that *Brown v. Board* did away with racial segregation in public education—that separate schools for "blacks and whites" were judged in *Brown* to be unequal. While that is broadly correct, the implications of the opinion in *Brown* are more complex, and it may well be that close study and reflection on the opinion in *Brown* is more likely to confuse than to clarify. As one commentator has said, "Its brevity was a mask for ambiguity" (Wilkinson, 1979: 29). Close inspection of the opinion does reveal a greater complexity, yet understanding the implications of *Brown* is crucial in coming to grips with the contemporary meaning of equality within the Equal Protection Clause of the Fourteenth Amendment. *Brown* and its progeny are necessary ingredients for understanding not only cases involving race; it can fairly be argued that the entire body of contemporary equal protection law follows proximately from the implications for equality that *Brown* heralded. And if indeed certain modern equal protection concepts are not strictly required by the logic of *Brown,* it was the Court's commitment to equality in *Brown* that marked heightened concern for the application of the

Equal Protection Clause to instances of discrimination long overlooked or ignored.

PUBLIC SCHOOL DESEGREGATION

The question of whether the Fourteenth Amendment was intended by its proponents to outlaw racial segregation in public education was addressed in *Brown,* but the Court found the historical evidence to be inconclusive, despite the best efforts of counsel on both sides to demonstrate the necessity of a single interpretation, the amicus curiae briefs of various allied interest groups, and the follow-up research by the talented young law clerks who were at the command of the nine justices.

The historical record is sufficiently ambiguous that advocates on both sides could choose quotes from the *Congressional Globe* to sustain their respective positions (see chapter 2). However, the problems encountered in inferring the intent of Congress respecting public school segregation from the historical record are much greater than the simple selective use of sources. The debates on the Fourteenth Amendment in the Thirty-ninth Congress are largely devoid of careful or complete explication of the philosophy, purposes, or possible consequences of the amendment. Thus, the advocates who attempted in *Brown* to inform the Supreme Court about the intentions of the Congress in proposing the Fourteenth Amendment were reduced to arguing from an ambiguous historical record, one easily presented to the Court in the light most favorable to each side. Indeed, the solicitor general, speaking on behalf of the government, concluded that the debates "are too sketchy under the rules laid down by this Court to rely on." The evidence, he said, "does not sustain the plaintiff's position nor the position of the states" (Friedman, 1969: 241). It is thus not surprising that the Supreme Court eventually found the record to be "At best . . . inconclusive." Of course, not all scholars have agreed with the Court's conclusion regarding inconclusiveness. As we have seen, Raoul Berger has argued at length for a narrow interpretation of the intentions of the framers, while Jacobus ten Broek was equally insistent in arguing for a broad interpretation of the framers' intentions.[1]

Supreme Court decisions after *Plessy v. Ferguson* but before *Brown* were not particularly helpful. The previous opinions in school segregation cases were few in number and arguably were oblique to the key questions presented in *Brown*. Chief Justice Warren's opinion in *Brown* noted that there had been only six cases involving the application of the separate but equal doctrine in public education. According to Warren, in none of them was the propriety of applying the doctrine of separate but equal to public education directly questioned. Of course the propriety of that application *was* directly questioned in *Brown,* so the court had to consider the "effect of segregation on public education" (*Brown v. Board of Education I*: 691). The key question, according to the Supreme Court, was, "Does the segregation of children in public schools solely on the basis of race, even though the physical facilities and other tangible factors may be equal, deprive the children of the minority group of equal educational opportunities?" (*Brown I*: 691). The Court's short and simple answer was, "We believe that it does." Separation by race, "generates a feeling of inferiority as to their [the "black school children's"] status in the community that may affect their hearts and minds in a way unlikely ever to be undone" (*Brown I*: 691). Chief Justice Warren then adopted that language of the lower court in the Topeka case, that is, the reasoning that a sense of inferiority affects a child's motivation to learn and thereby retards the "educational and mental development of negro children." And this was seen by the Court especially to be the case when the separation had the force of law. The inevitable conclusion was that "in the field of public education the doctrine of separate but equal facilities has no place. Separate educational facilities are inherently unequal" (*Brown I*: 692).

THE IMPLICATIONS OF *BROWN*

Several prominent court observers have written that it was not at all clear how the Supreme Court reached its conclusions in *Brown*. It is true that the opinion is rife with ambiguity. We know that Chief Justice Warren worked long and hard to achieve a unanimous opinion in *Brown,* so some of the ambiguity may have been the result of negotiated language. More important is the fact that looking back on *Brown* from the perspective of subsequent efforts to enforce it readily reveals difficulties that the Court did not anticipate in its opinion.

One key difficulty lurks in the distinction between de facto and de jure discrimination.[2] If racial segregation generates feelings of inferiority in those who are being kept separate, then those feelings presumably would result even if separation occurs only because of private housing patterns or private customs. If "purely private" racial segregation damages those who are deemed by it to be inferior and thus to be kept apart, then it also would seem to call for remedy. Under this reasoning it is the fact of segregation, as well as its enforcement by law, that does the damage.

Of course state or local governments may (within the boundaries of their state constitutions) use their police powers to eliminate private racial segregation or discrimination. The South, however, had a traditionally segregated social system and (possibly with a few local deviations) no will to change. So the difficulty lay in finding the basis for federal intervention, if segregation was in fact to be ended.

The Fourteenth Amendment is directed only at state action, so federal courts were required to find state action for the Fourteenth Amendment, or for federal legislation based on the Fourteenth Amendment, to be sustained and enforced. That at least was the holding in the *Civil Rights Cases* of 1883, and that holding has never been repudiated. Thus in our time the U.S. Supreme Court was impelled by the reality of the evils done by racial segregation (whether public or private) to search for acts that could plausibly be called state action so as to invoke federal intervention under the Fourteenth Amendment.

Simply requiring the demise of de jure segregation would have accomplished little. Alexander Bickel has noted that during the first argument in *Brown,* Justice Frankfurter asked Thurgood Marshall (then acting as counsel for the petitioners) whether a favorable decision would "entitle every mother to have her child go to a nonsegregated school?" Marshall replied that the only requirement of school boards would be that they draw attendance zones "on a natural basis" and that they not be gerrymandered so as to include or exclude African-American school children (Bickel, 1978: 117–18). It is worth remembering that by the time the NAACP position had prevailed in *Brown I* and enforcement had become the issue in *Brown II* (1955), Marshall had become much more insistent on a prompt and real remedy.[3] Nonetheless, the crux of his complaint continued to be against deliberate de jure segregation (Friedman, 1969: 439).

It is obvious today that there is a large and important difference between simply doing away with officially prescribed racial segregation in public schools and actually achieving racial integration in those schools. That distinction was also evident to some when *Brown* was decided. In a 1955 opinion in *Briggs v. Elliot* (one of the NAACP-sponsored companion cases to *Brown*), John J. Parker, writing for a three-judge federal court sitting in South Carolina, suggested:

If the schools which it [a public school system] maintains are open to children of all races, no violation of the Constitution is involved even though the children of different races voluntarily attend different schools. Nothing in the Constitution or in the decision of the Supreme Court takes away from the people the freedom to choose the schools they attend. The Constitution, in other words, does not require integration. It merely forbids discrimination. It does not forbid such segregation as occurs as the result of voluntary action. It merely forbids the use of governmental power to enforce segregation. (*Briggs v. Elliot*: 777)

If all that *Brown* was to require was the end of formal de jure segregation, then the mere striking from the statute books of discriminatory laws might have sufficed, even if no actual desegregation ever occurred. The elimination of those ostensible "badges of inferiority" might have had some marginal impact on the psychological well-being of black school children, but the fact of segregation would have remained. Surely the Supreme Court meant to require more than that. The purpose of *Brown I* must have been more than the mere elimination of explicit discriminatory laws—at the least, it must have had the purpose of requiring actual desegregation in those instances in which racial segregation had previously been required or permitted by force of law. Only by removal of the *fact* of segregation in those instances of prior de jure segregation might the feelings of inferiority produced by deliberate racial segregation be undone. Only by removing the *fact* of segregation through de facto desegregation might the motivation of African-American school children to learn be enhanced. Only by removing the *fact* of segregation would the mental and educational development of African-American school children be improved—that seems to be the clear implication of the Court's language in *Brown*.

The problem of what to do about segregated public schools when there has been no history of de jure segregation remained. One scholar has argued that the de facto/de jure distinction is one that African-Americans are likely to find irrelevant:

Now it is not easy to maintain the position that the impairment and inequality result only from segregation imposed by official legislative or administrative action, and not from segregation as such, however it may have come about, by official or by private initiative, exercised recently or long ago. If a Negro child perceives

his separation as discriminatory and invidious, he is not, in a society a hundred years removed from slavery, going to make fine
distinctions about the source of a particular separation. (Bickel,
1978: 119)

The point seems irrefutable, but the Supreme Court was still constrained by the state action requirement of the Fourteenth Amendment, as that had been interpreted since the 1880s.

Another difficulty in *Brown* lurks in a possible distinction between
integration and *desegregation*. Whether there is a precise difference between an objective of de facto desegregation and an objective of de facto
integration is not clear. It is possible to argue that a policy of de facto
desegregation might admit some element of tokenism, while a policy of
de facto integration is likely to require more substantial results. A
policy of de facto integration is likely to be measured by targets, goals,
or quotas that depend on some mathematical measure of achievement.

What vision of equality does *Brown I* entail? The simple acknowledgment that race may not be a de jure factor in public school assignment
or attendance, or in the quality of public education offered, is an instance of individual-regarding equality, in which there is only one class
of public school students and all are to be treated alike. A policy of
desegregation also seems to be consistent with individual-regarding
equality, in the sense that all that might be required by a desegregation
policy would be the elimination of explicit discrimination against African-Americans, the elimination of barriers such as attendance zones,
and possibly the closing of certain schools and the opening of others.
Such steps could be designed in such a way as to produce some actual desegregation, while leaving the basic concept of neighborhood
schools substantially intact. Likewise, the assignment of teachers and
staff randomly, or otherwise in a racially neutral way, could be done
consistently with individual-regarding equality. The key to evaluating
policies of desegregation would be to be sure that school district policies, including attendance zones and the location of schools, would be
carried out in a racially neutral way.

The pursuit of an affirmative policy of integration, however, represents a different sort of equality. To the extent that policies of integration are measured in their outcomes by the achievement of targets or
goals that involve percentages or ratios (that reflect racial distributions), then the policies seem to represent a form of group- or bloc-
regarding equality. They are group or bloc regarding if the view of

equality they represent is measured by the group's success, for example, by the ratio of "black and white" students attending various schools within the system.

Individual-regarding policies, on the other hand, would be measured by their racial neutrality, that is, by showing that policies did not have the direct or indirect effect of causing or of maintaining racial segregation. Equally, the integration of faculty and staff would be bloc or group regarding if its success were measured by the ratio of "black to white" teachers and staff in each school, relative to the racial staffing ratios in the system as a whole.

A counterpoint to Judge Parker's 1955 opinion in *Briggs v. Elliot*—on the point that the Fourteenth Amendment did not require anything more than the demise of de jure segregation—can be found in another Fifth Circuit opinion by John Minor Wisdom. His response to *Briggs* reflects the different understandings of policy that can be found in these cases. In 1966 Judge Wisdom wrote:

> The Constitution forbids unconstitutional state action in the form of segregated facilities, including segregated public schools. School authorities, therefore, are under the constitutional compulsion of furnishing a single-integrated school system. . . . The school children in still-segregated grades in Negro schools are there by assignment based upon their race. This assignment was unconstitutional. They have an absolute right, as individuals, to transfer to schools from which they were excluded because of their race. This has been the law since *Brown*. . . . But there should be no misunderstanding now as to the right of any child in a segregated class to transfer to a formerly all "white" class regardless of the slow pace of systematic desegregation by classes. (*Singleton v. Jackson Municipal Separate School District*: 869–70)

Still, Judge Wisdom's opinion in *Singleton* does not go far enough, even if it does require more than Judge Parker would have required in *Briggs*. Wisdom's words possibly would have led to some African-American students actually attending predominantly white schools, but at their own instance. He seemed at this time to place no burden on the school district itself to achieve de facto desegregation. Are there good reasons for requiring affirmative efforts to integrate on the part of school districts in which there previously had been de jure discrimination?

There are suggestions in *Brown I* that segregated education probably is inferior for everyone concerned. That can be inferred from the Supreme Court's reference in *Brown I* to language in the *McLaurin* and *Sweatt* opinions to the effect that excellent graduate or professional education was not as likely to occur when members of the community were isolated from one another. If that is so, then it follows that public schools have an "equalizing, socializing—assimilationist and secular mission" (Bickel, 1978: 120–21). On the other hand, even if segregated education is viewed as inferior only for African-American school children (because it is they, presumably, who suffer feelings of inferiority), it is nonetheless the fact of segregation that must be ended, rather than simply eliminating racially discriminatory policies. In either instance, the most appropriate inference from *Brown I* is that some sort of affirmative policy of integration is required—at least where there previously has been *de jure* segregation. Otherwise, the evils that *Brown I* described would, in large part, continue untouched by the court's decision.

Brown II sheds little light on the distinctions we have been considering. If anything, it is even more terse and enigmatic than *Brown I.* Nevertheless, at several points the court's opinion in *Brown II* suggests that something more than the simple demise of discriminatory policies is required where there previously has been de jure segregation. At a minimum, lower federal courts were charged to "achieve a system of determining admission to the public schools on a nonracial basis" and to assess the adequacy of a school district's plan "to effectuate a transition to a racially non-discriminatory school system" (*Brown II*: 300–301).

The key phrase in *Brown II,* the enforcement decision announced on May 31, 1955, was that the federal courts below were directed to "make a prompt and reasonable start with compliance" and then to proceed with "all deliberate speed" to admit the African-American students in these cases to public schools on a racially nondiscriminatory basis. And so it became the responsibility of the fifty-eight men who sat on the district and circuit courts in the Fourth and Fifth circuits to try to understand the intent of *Brown I* and *II* and to enforce them appropriately (Peltason: 1961).

The policy options we have been discussing can be summed up in Table 7.1.

Bolling v. Sharpe was the District of Columbia companion case to *Brown.* It also shed little light on the distinctions we have been considering; however, *Bolling* was useful in reiterating the view that racial classifications are suspect and must be "scrutinized with particular

Table 7.1 *Brown v. Board of Education* Policy Options

Policy	Purpose	Results—How Measured
End *de jure* segregation	to eliminate official badges of discrimination	nullification of discriminatory laws and policies
Achieve *de facto* desegregation	as above, plus improvement in the education and mental development of African-American school children by actually ending total isolation and reducing feelings of inferiority	faculty and staff assigned in a racially neutral way; some students actually attend racially neutral, integrated schools
Seek integration	as above, plus greater improvement in the educational and mental development of African-American school children	achievements of targets or goals for faculty, staff and students that reflect some mathematical measure of proportionate racial distribution

care" (*Bolling v. Sharpe*: 694). Thus, such distinctions violate due process as well as equal protection.[4] The renewed concern for racial equality that both *Brown* and *Bolling* reflect suggests that the Supreme Court was at last entering into a commitment actually to do something about racial discrimination. It is only through considering cases from the 1960s, however, that we will be able to reduce somewhat the ambiguities of *Brown I* and *Brown II*.

In the meantime, in 1956, more than one hundred senators and representatives from southern states signed a "Southern Manifesto" vowing to resist desegregation and to overturn the Supreme Court's decision in *Brown*. In 1957, a high school in Mansfield, Texas, was ordered desegregated. Before that order, Mansfield had provided no secondary education for its African-American students. Those African-American students who sought a high school education had to commute daily to nearby Fort Worth by Greyhound bus. The Mansfield policy of providing no secondary education for African-American students was much like that in Richmond County, Georgia, which had been condoned by the Supreme Court in its 1899 decision in *Cumming v. County Board of Education of Richmond County, Georgia*. In response to the federal district court's order that African-American students be admitted to Mansfield High School, the governor of Texas sent in the Texas Rangers to "preserve order" by turning away the African-American students (Griffin and Freedman: 1956). The governor's defiance worked, probably because the case attracted relatively little attention outside the region and because the federal government was fainthearted in its enforcement. Mansfield High School remained all white for another decade.

However, in Little Rock, Arkansas, that same year Governor Faubus's open defiance of a similar court order by using the Arkansas National Guard to turn away African-American students became so visible that President Eisenhower was forced to uphold the power of the federal courts. His use of armed force to integrate Central High School in Little Rock produced at least a token result. The integration of Little Rock schools was eventually upheld by the Supreme Court in *Cooper v. Aaron* (1958).

Situations like those in Mansfield or Little Rock, while nasty and even tragic for the African-American school children and their families, did not present difficult questions of law; rather, they involved tests of will and, ultimately, of force. The more difficult legal questions involved the determination of how far federal courts could go in enforcing *Brown*. Those questions were not determined until the 1960s.

ENFORCING *BROWN*

A key case in which the Supreme Court determined in part how far federal courts could go was *Goss v. Board of Education of the City of Knoxville* (1963). Two school districts in Tennessee had submitted desegregation plans that rezoned the districts (apparently in a racially neutral way) but allowed for voluntary transfers by students from schools in which they might be in a racial minority to schools in which they would be part of a racial majority. These transfer plans were approved by the district court and by the Fifth Circuit. The Supreme Court, however, found that since the transfers were improperly cognizant of race and led toward the continued segregation of students by race, they ran "counter to the admonition of [*Brown*] . . . 'to effectuate a . . . racially nondiscriminatory school system.' " The flaw in the transfer plans was that they did not provide for transfers from schools in which students were in a racial majority to ones in which they would be in a racial minority; thus they inevitably had the one-sided effect of contributing to racial segregation. The plans were held to be constitutionally defective because they allowed voluntary segregation at the student's option. From *Goss* we finally learn that Judge Parker was wrong in suggesting in his 1955 opinion in *Briggs* that voluntary segregation was permissible. Voluntary segregation was ruled unconstitutional in *Goss,* if facilitated by any sort of apparently racially neutral public policy. The segregation outlawed by *Brown* was not limited to officially mandated segregation; it also included permissive segregation.

Following the same sort of reasoning, the Supreme Court held in *Griffin v. County School Board of Prince Edward County, Virginia,* in 1964, ten years after *Brown I,* that the closing of public schools in Prince Edward County, Virginia, was racially motivated and hence unconstitutional. It is evident from that decision that the Supreme Court was intent on a purpose beyond simply requiring the demise of explicit segregation laws. It was also evident that by 1965 the Court's patience with the "all deliberate speed" mandate from *Brown II* was wearing thin when it voided a 1957 "stair-step" plan that by 1965 still allowed the last three years of high school in Fort Smith, Arkansas, to be segregated (*Rogers v. Paul*).[5]

1966: JUDGE WISDOM AND JEFFERSON COUNTY

Possibly the most important opinion since *Brown I* was that written by John Minor Wisdom of the Fifth Circuit (an Eisenhower appointee) in *United States v. Jefferson County Board of Education* (1966). There Wisdom reflected again at length on the "supposed difference" between desegregation and integration offered by Judge Parker in *Briggs* in 1955. Parker's suggestion was, you will recall, that segregation by voluntary choice was not unconstitutional. The lawyer for Alabama in one of the companion cases to *Jefferson County Board of Education* proposed a distinction much like Judge Parker's. His suggestion was that desegregation involves the elimination of compulsory segregation so as to *allow* admission of students on a nonracial basis, while integration is the "actual placing of or attendance by Negro students in schools with whites" (*United States v. Jefferson County Board of Education*: 846, footnote 5). Wisdom answered, "The only school desegregation plan that meets constitutional standards is one that works." Integration was becoming a constitutional requirement.

Because he concluded that the courts acting alone had failed to implement integration, Wisdom eagerly embraced the application of the Department of Health, Education and Welfare's[6] regulations and guidelines, which had only recently grown out of Title VI of the Civil Rights Act of 1964.[7]

In order to be eligible to receive federal assistance for education, school systems that were "working toward desegregation" had to submit plans that provided either for racially neutral attendance zones or for "free-choice" plans, under which all students would be able each year to choose a school, regardless of where they lived within a district. Free-choice plans were allowed only if it could be shown that they would produce "significant progress" toward eliminating dual schools. Progress was to be measured by reference to prior years, with the proviso that those districts that had started late "must move faster" in desegregating their schools (Blaustein and Zangrando, 1968: 591 et seq.). School districts could also qualify for federal aid by agreeing to comply with an extant federal court desegregation order. Additionally, Title VI authorized the attorney general to sue to desegregate a school or school system.

Wisdom concluded from the provisions of the 1964 Civil Rights Act that the "national policy is plain: formerly *de jure* segregated public school systems based on dual attendance zones must shift to unitary nonracial systems—with or without federal funds" (*United States v. Jefferson County Board of Education*: 850). Against challenges to the federal authority to require such outcomes, Wisdom gave the resounding endorsement of the Fifth Circuit to federal intervention, noting that while some progress had occurred during the decade since *Brown II,* it had been too slow—in part because the federal courts were ill suited to the task of developing and enforcing a comprehensive national policy of desegregation.

Judge Wisdom had before repudiated Judge Parker's gloss in *Briggs* that suggested that only the demise of formal de jure segregation was required by the Fourteenth Amendment. Now in the *Jefferson County* case he suggested that one reason for Parker's opinion in *Briggs* was a suggested distinction between providing relief for individuals and class actions providing relief for African-American students as a whole. The *Briggs* opinion, Wisdom said, treated the remedy of *Brown* as one according a "personal and present right" to be free from discriminatory school policies, while Wisdom understood *Brown* primarily as sustaining class actions to benefit African-American students as a discriminated class. "The separate school system was an integral element in the Southern State's general program to restrict Negroes as a class from participation in the life of the community, the affairs of the state, and the mainstream of American life: Negroes must keep their place" (*United States v. Jefferson County Board of Education*: 866). "Segregation is a group phenomenon, and its redress must be group wide to be adequate." Wisdom's words suggest that this was an especially impor-

tant point in the evolution of equal protection law following *Brown*. The
classwide remedy that Wisdom proposed is clearly an example of
group- or bloc-regarding equality. Its acceptance by the Supreme Court
would confirm the broadest possible application of *Brown v. Board.*

Wisdom's opinion in the *Jefferson County* case also turned the de
facto/de jure distinction around. While Wisdom would no doubt have
conceded that racial isolation in public schools (whatever its source)
contributed to the psychological harm done to African-American school
children, he concluded that when separation results from "a state policy
of apartheid" it "aggravates the harm" (*Jefferson County v. Board of Education*: 868). The state has the special responsibility to "undo the harm
it created and fostered." On the other hand, due to the state action
clause of the Fourteenth Amendment, the federal government would
not have the power to undo purely de facto segregation.

Wisdom also referred disapprovingly in his opinion to a federal district court decision involving the schools in Gary, Indiana, where the
judge found that attendance zones were based on reasonable nonracial
criteria so there was no evidence of a purpose to segregate by race. The
Seventh Circuit had affirmed that holding in 1964, saying that states do
not have an affirmative duty to provide an integrated education where
only de facto desegregation exists (*Bell v. School City of Gary, Indiana*).
Despite that ruling, Wisdom noted that the *Gary* decision had been
questioned. It was argued that insistent adherence to neighborhood
public schools, even in the face of residential patterns that clearly
would produce de facto segregation, might be problematic under equal
protection requirements.

Another federal district court opinion, this one from New York, had
also held that federal courts must consider the inadequate education
arising from de facto segregation. They should not blithely accept segregation on the grounds that it was not coerced but only accepted
(*Branche v. Board of Education of Town of Hempstead*: 153). In much the
same manner, a federal district court case from Springfield, Massachusetts, had held that a neighborhood school policy "must be abandoned
or modified when it results in segregation in fact" (*Barksdale v. Springfield School Committee*: 543).

The point that Judge Wisdom noticed was that the holding in *Brown*
implied the necessity of integrated education to improve the educational opportunity of African-American school children, regardless of
the causes of their segregation. Ironically, in the sense of securing
remedies for segregation, the South was fortunate in being in the position to avoid the de facto/de jure distinction. School districts in the

South had clearly experienced their racial segregation by and through state action. Wisdom concluded that in other parts of the country the continued use of neighborhood schools, even when they lead to "grossly imbalanced schools," presents a constitutional question "some day to be answered by the Supreme Court" (879).

Another important point in Judge Wisdom's opinion in the *Jefferson County* case is that relief for the entire class of African-American school children within a district means that the Constitution must be "both color blind and color conscious." It is color blind when equal protection is used to ensure that no further racial disadvantage is enforced against a traditionally disadvantaged group. It must be color conscious to prevent the perpetuation of discrimination based on race. Both HEW and the courts must be able to collect racial data in order to measure progress and compliance (*United States v. Jefferson County Board of Education*: 876). That is to say once again that the equality that Judge Wisdom was then seeking to enforce had become group or bloc regarding because its achievement was to be measured by the results experienced by African-Americans as a whole, rather than by individual African-American students.

If our society had neither the present intent to discriminate nor the consequences of prior discrimination in its communities and if de facto segregation caused by neighborhood patterns that reflect race or economic condition did not exist, then there would be no difference between individual-regarding and bloc-regarding equality. Students might then be distributed through the schools randomly or in a racially neutral way. But when, because of a history of de jure racial discrimination or because of the de facto segregation of neighborhoods, implementation of change necessitates an affirmative policy of integration, group- or bloc-regarding equality becomes inevitable. Such action must be taken if the fact of segregation is to be confronted, rather than merely requiring the demise of de jure segregation.

Whenever group- or bloc-regarding equality becomes the object of policy, the circumstances (some would say rights) of particular students, whether "black or white," may for a while be suspended, while group-regarding equality is accorded the groups of which they are a part. The best hope is that group-oriented outcomes will be only a transitory phenomenon, lasting only until racial discrimination in public education is in fact eradicated.

Congress, while not necessarily recognizing the distinction between individual-regarding and bloc-regarding equality, was well aware of the distinction between de jure and de facto discrimination when it enacted civil rights legislation. Neighborhood schools, at least in those districts with no history of de jure segregation, came to be the object of congressional protection. In 1966 Congress prohibited HEW from pursuing a policy of requiring busing across district lines or of placing children in schools to reduce racial imbalance produced only by de facto segregation (Congressional Quarterly Service, 1968: 93). Congress could not interfere with the constitutional power of federal courts to remedy the consequences of de jure segregation except by proposing a constitutional amendment.

Finally, whether their policies called for desegregation or integration, the federal courts that reviewed the effectiveness of school district desegregation plans, or of their own orders, eventually had to resort to numerical measurements of efficacy. Whether those be called quotas, targets, goals, or yardsticks, their purpose is to measure the progress of bloc-regarding equality. In the *Jefferson County* case, Judge Wisdom accepted the counting of the number of African-American students who attend schools with whites as a reasonable measure of progress. His opinion was eventually upheld on rehearing en banc.[8]

1968: THE SUPREME COURT BECOMES IMPATIENT

Justice Brennan wrote three opinions in 1968 that were consistent with Judge Wisdom's pro-integration bloc-regarding opinion in *Jefferson County*; by then the passage of thirteen years since *Brown II* had demonstrated what the outcomes of freedom of choice and voluntary transfer plans would be in southern communities, and they clearly had not made much difference.[9]

In a case from New Kent County, Virginia, a freedom-of-choice plan, consistent with 1966 HEW guidelines, had been adopted. The county had approximately an equal number of "blacks and whites," and there was no clear pattern of residential racial segregation in the county. In its school system of about 1,300 students, more than 700 were African-Americans. The system had one comprehensive school for blacks and one for whites, without attendance zones. Had the county been divided into two zones, with one racially neutral school in each, substantial integration would have resulted. Instead, the freedom-of-choice plan allowed students to choose either the predominantly "white" or the predominantly "black school." In three years no white child had chosen to attend the predominantly "black school," while 115 African-American children had chosen the predominantly "white school." Thus 85 percent of African-American school children continued to attend an "all-black school." While Brennan's opinion in 1968 did not hold freedom-of-choice plans always to be per se unconstitutional; he did hold that they must be measured by their effectiveness in producing an integrated school system. Freedom of choice clearly had failed in New Kent County; the school board now had the duty of formulating an effective plan (*Green v. County School Board of New Kent County, Virginia*: 1696). A free transfer plan from Jackson, Tennessee, met the same fate in 1968. It had produced no white transfers to any "black schools" and only seven African-American students enrolled in predominantly "white schools" (out of a total student enrollment of more than 7,000) (*Monroe v. Board of Commissioners of the City of Jackson, Tennessee*).

The pace of change was clearly accelerating. In 1969, one year later, the Supreme Court sustained a federal district court order of Judge Frank Johnson of Alabama,[10] which required that "in each school the ratio of white to Negro faculty members [be] substantially the same as it is throughout the system" (*United States v. Montgomery Board of Education*: 1674). A Fifth Circuit panel had modified his order to require only substantial or approximate adherence to the district ratio, but the Supreme Court reversed the panel and held in 1969 that Johnson's order "promises realistically to work, and promises realistically to work *now*" (*United States v. Montgomery Board of Education*: 1675, *emphasis added*).

Also in 1969, in an even more curt and impatient opinion, the Supreme Court held that allowance for "all deliberate speed" was over. Dual school systems were to be terminated and school boards were required to "operate now and hereafter only unitary schools." By unitary the court meant "systems within which no person is to be effectively excluded from any school because of race or color" (*Alexander v. Holmes County Board of Education*: 30). That certainly meant no more de jure racial restrictions on school attendance; whether it also meant that districts would always be required to implement positive steps toward racial integration of students was, as yet, unclear. What was clear was that the Supreme Court was on the threshold of adopting bloc- or group-regarding equality as the standard by which integration of public schools would be measured.

8

INTEGRATION, BUSING, AND GROUP-REGARDING EQUALITY

Darius Swann, an American black man working as a missionary in India, picked up a newspaper and was riveted by the photo on the front page. It showed a young black girl in a prim checkered dress, a large bow at the collar, her head erect and her eyes defiant, making her way through an angry mob.

The girl in the picture was Dorothy Counts, who had broken the color barrier at a Charlotte high school.

—Frye Gaillard, "On and Off the Bus in Charlotte"

1971: *SWANN V. CHARLOTTE-MECKLENBURG BOARD OF EDUCATION*

When the Swann family returned to Charlotte in 1964, Darius Swann, now a theology professor, remembered the photo of Dorothy Counts and decided to support the continuing efforts toward integrating the public schools of Charlotte. The suit was filed in 1965 on behalf of his son James and others bearing the Swann name (Gaillard, 1988: 22). By any measure *Swann v. Charlotte-Mecklenburg Board of Education* is the most important Supreme Court decision on school desegregation since *Brown*. The fact that it was written by Warren Burger, the man whom President Nixon nominated as chief justice, involves no little irony. Both Nixon and Gov. George Wallace of Alabama, respectively the Republican and American Independent party candidates for president, campaigned in 1968 against "forced busing" of school children for the purpose of achieving integration. Nixon vowed to appoint "strict constructionist" federal judges who wouldn't be likely to require such busing.

The parties in the *Swann* case were in agreement that in 1969 the Charlotte-Mecklenburg school system still had not achieved the unitary school system apparently required by federal court rulings.[1] However, the parties had difficulty in agreeing to a particular remedy. The board plan called for the closing of certain schools, for revised attendance zones to achieve greater racial balance, and for a voluntary majority-to-minority transfer plan. High school attendance zones were drawn like pie wedges, extending from the city center to suburban and rural areas of the county.

A plan prepared by a court-appointed expert took the board's rezoning and combined it with nine satellite, or noncontiguous, zones at the junior high level. The elementary level used zones, pairing, and grouping of schools to enhance integration. The grouping of elementary schools entailed busing between nine inner-city "black schools" and twenty-four suburban "white schools." After a number of hearings and appeals, the board reluctantly yielded to the expert's plan pending appeal to the Supreme Court.

An important factor in the *Swann* case was that in 1960 local officials had created the Charlotte-Mecklenburg School District by merging Charlotte city schools with Mecklenburg County schools. The purpose of the merger was efficiency rather than integration, but the result was a countywide school system that made a metropolitan plan for integrating public schools feasible (Schwartz, 1986: 9).[2]

Federal District Judge James McMillan, who originally ordered the plan for integrating the Charlotte-Mecklenburg schools, noted that no whites had objected when buses were used to maintain segregated schools. Only mandatory busing to achieve integration was held objectionable by Charlotte whites. Likewise, the neighborhood school principle had never been successfully invoked to permit African-American students to attend "white schools" nearest their homes. It was raised by whites only against the prospect of mandatory busing of white students. McMillan held that neighborhood schools had no standing to override constitutional requirements (*Swann v. Charlotte-Mecklenburg Board of Education* [hereafter cited as *Swann*], U.S. District Court opinion: 1369).

Chief Justice Burger eventually wrote for a unanimous Supreme Court in *Swann*. He began by noting that the objective in these cases was "to eliminate from the public schools all vestiges of state-imposed segregation" (*Swann*: 1275). In that context he identified four problem areas:

(1) to what extent racial balance or racial quotas may be used as an implement in a remedial order to correct a previously segregated system;

(2) whether every all-Negro and all-white school must be eliminated as an indispensable part of a remedial process of desegregation;

(3) what the limits are, if any, on the arrangement of school districts and attendance zones, as a remedial measure; and

(4) what the limits are, if any, on the use of transportation facilities
to correct state-enforced racial school segregation. (*Swann*: 1279)

The chief justice wrote that a systemwide ratio of 71 to 29 percent,
"white-to-black" students, in each individual school in the system was
not a fixed mathematical requirement but was a "useful starting point"
in devising a remedy for a previously segregated system. The "very
limited use of mathematical ratios was within the equitable discretion
of the District Court" (*Swann*: 1280). Even so, that was not to suggest
that no single-race schools might exist, but they were to be avoided if
possible. However, Burger recognized the tendency of people of the
same race to congregate in certain neighborhoods and required only
that single-race schools be closely scrutinized to be sure that they were
not state enforced. The use of attendance zones (including pairing,
clustering, or grouping of neighborhoods that are not contiguous) was
held to be within the remedial powers of the courts. Thus, the Supreme
Court unanimously accepted that race-conscious student assignments
might be made to counteract the effects of past de jure school segregation. The corollary was that at least while remedies for past de jure
segregation were sought, racially neutral assignments to schools might
be insufficient. Finally, the Court accepted that the enforcement order
in *Swann* would require the mandatory busing of school children that
"averaged seven miles" and that "would not take over 35 minutes at the
most" (*Swann*: 1283). However, the limits of busing might come when
the time or distance required were so great as to constitute a health risk
or to interfere with the educational process. To require all these measures would be within the sound discretion of a district judge whose
purpose it was to eliminate "all vestiges of state-imposed segregation."
It is important to note that the Supreme Court did not address in *Swann*
any form of segregation save that resulting from a prior de jure system
of racially segregated schools.

Swann clearly represents the Supreme Court's acceptance, however
reluctant, of the objective of group- or bloc-regarding equality articu-
lated earlier in Judge Wisdom's opinion in *Jefferson County* and in Judge
Johnson's order in the *Montgomery* case. The only concession to indi-

vidual-regarding equality in *Swann* was one that Judge Wisdom also allowed—the individual option of transferring from a school in which a student is part of a racial majority to one in which he or she would be in a minority. This was seen as an "indispensable remedy," even if the transfer would require the support of free transportation and the assurance of a space for all those who chose to transfer (*Swann*: 1281).

Several scholars have noted that Chief Justice Burger was for a long time a holdout against the majority in *Swann*. He nonetheless assigned himself the writing of the opinion for the Court. At first he sought to affirm the circuit court, which had imposed constraints on Judge McMillan's district court order. However, the eventual unanimous opinion (after six redrafts) affirmed Judge McMillan. Chief Justice Burger had reluctantly conceded to other members of the Court. His final draft contained language from the drafts of several of the more "liberal" justices.[3]

The chief justice's reservations about *Swann* were supposedly reflected about a year later in *Winston-Salem/Forsyth County Board of Education v. Scott.* The argument runs that Burger went out of his way in the *Winston-Salem* case to "personally paint on *Swann* a conservative gloss" (Wilkinson, 1979: 149; Schwartz, 1986: 188 et seq.). However, the chief justice mostly seemed to reaffirm in the *Winston-Salem* case what the *Swann* opinion ultimately said: that fixed quotas by race are not required but that mathematical ratios are acceptable as a means toward achieving integration; that busing within limits is also within the discretion of a federal trial judge, and that single-race schools require close scrutiny but are not absolutely forbidden. The fact remains that under any interpretation of *Swann,* the Supreme Court embraced group- or bloc-regarding equality as its objective. Whatever *Brown v. Board* may have meant or intended in 1955, by 1971 in *Swann* the Supreme Court clearly had embraced an understanding of equality that measured achievement of a unitary school system by examining the degree to which racial proportions in individual schools matched the racial proportions in a school district as a whole. To do that is to require group-regarding equality.

1973: THE DENVER SCHOOL CASE

Two years after *Swann* in the Denver school case, *Keyes v. School District No. 1, Denver,* Justice Powell's concurring opinion referred to what we have identified as group- or bloc-regarding equality as the "affirmative duty" concept, that is, the duty to take whatever steps may be necessary to create a unitary school system. Powell argued that, while the language in *Brown I* was expansive, its precise ruling was negative. It forbade de jure segregation. Powell concluded that *Brown* eventually was transformed. The transformation, he found, had begun with the keystone case of *Green v. County School Board of New Kent County, Virginia,* in 1968. In *Green,* you will recall, a school system in a rural Virginia county was placed under the affirmative obligation to operate a unitary school system, rather than being allowed to maintain segregation through a "voluntary transfer" policy. Powell agreed that the unanimous Court in *Swann* fully embraced the "affirmative duty" to integrate, but he believed the source of that duty had been misplaced. The majority's premise in *Swann* was that the duty flowed from "a long history of officially imposed segregation." Powell thought that was mistaken. He suggested that in fact the segregation of the Charlotte-Mecklenburg schools probably had complex multiple causation, including "segregated residential and migratory patterns the impact of which on the racial composition of our schools was often perpetuated and rarely ameliorated by action of public school authorities." He went on to say, "Segregation is a national, not a southern phenomenon" (*Keyes v. School District No. 1, Denver* [hereafter cited as *Keyes*]: 2704). Powell, who himself once had served on the Richmond, Virginia, School Board, wrote that "where segregated public schools exist within a school district, . . . there is a *prima facie*[4] case that the duly constituted authorities . . . are sufficiently responsible to warrant imposing on them a nationally applicable burden to demonstrate that they nevertheless are operating a genuinely integrated school system" (*Keyes*: 2705).

Failing to rebut prima facie discrimination, what should school authorities be required to do? Powell would have preferred a policy of individual-regarding equality. He certainly viewed large-scale, long-distance busing with distaste, and he also viewed mathematical ratios with suspicion. Instead, he would have required that faculty assignments, attendance zones, school construction, school closings, and consolidations be done at least in a racially neutral way, and, where possible, to enhance integration. But he placed great value on the neighborhood school, hence his conclusion, "The single most disruptive element in education today is the widespread use of compulsory transportation, especially at elementary grade levels" (*Keyes*: 2719).

Powell was indeed prescient in suggesting that the demise of the neighborhood school (in significant part due to busing orders) would "hasten an exodus to private schools," encourage the "movement from inner city to suburb," and "further geographical separation of the races" (*Keyes*: 2718). The unpleasant realities he foresaw were evident in the 1974 Detroit school case.

It was a harsh reality that the court confronted in almost all the school desegregation cases outside of the South—how could the federal courts, even with pervasive power over discriminatory public school systems, devise an effective remedy for tacit societal racism, or for that matter, for the vestiges of explicit de jure racism? The requirement of group- or bloc-regarding equality in public education seems inevitably to involve policies and programs that have taxed the capacities of courts. Group-regarding equality necessarily involves the federal courts in assessing the impact of policies on groups, while courts often have had difficulty enough in providing proper justice for the individuals who stand before them. This is not to suggest that individual cases do not produce general principles of constitutional law, but that is quite a different matter from expecting courts on their own to develop full-scale ameliorative programs.

Unlike Justice Powell, the majority in the Denver case was prepared to sustain a broad desegregation order once a finding had been made of some sort of de jure segregation, thereby creating a presumption of discrimination that affected the entire school system. Justice Brennan's majority opinion held that a finding of "intentionally segregative board actions" in a "meaningful portion of the school system" raised a presumption that other segregated schooling was not "adventitious." The remedies called for in the desegregation order, which included busing, were, however, contingent on the finding that the school district's purposive acts had contributed to racially segregated schools. That was the decisional basis that Justice Powell had sought to avoid. The manifold causes of racial segregation made the de jure/de facto distinction, in his view, not only a narrow legalism but also infused a strong regional bias into school desegregation cases.

1974: THE METROPOLITAN DETROIT SCHOOL CASE

The necessity of basing a comprehensive integration remedy on a finding of some sort of de jure discrimination reached its almost inevitable natural limits in *Milliken v. Bradley* (referred to as *Milliken I* and *Milliken II*), the metropolitan Detroit school case. In *Milliken* Justice Powell was a silent member of a five-justice majority. Chief Justice Burger wrote for the majority, and the constraints on court-ordered integration contained in his opinion were ultimately based on the boundary lines that circumscribe a school district.

Contributions to de jure segregation were found by the lower court on the part of the Detroit Board of Education and to some degree on the part of various entities of the State of Michigan. There were no such findings as to the fifty-three school districts that surrounded the city of Detroit and lay within the three-county metropolitan desegregation area. According to Chief Justice Burger, to fashion a metropolitan remedy the districts that are part of the remedy must themselves have contributed in some manner to the de jure segregation that the courts seek to redress. The record in *Milliken* revealed de jure segregation in the Detroit schools. It was clear, on the other hand, that the remedies available within the Detroit system were at best illusory. Nothing better than token integration was possible in a district where almost 70 percent of the students in 1973 were African-American. However, by including the suburbs it was possible to create a metropolitan school district that was almost three-quarters white (Wilkinson, 1979: 219). For the chief justice and the five-member majority, the boundary lines, coupled with the tradition of local control of schools, were decisive. The majority held that with no finding of de jure discrimination on the part of the suburban school districts, they should be protected by their boundaries and allowed to run their own systems.

It is particularly interesting that the prima facie rebuttable presumption of discrimination suggested by Justice Powell in the Denver case was not reasserted in the Detroit case. Given the presence of fifty-three predominantly white suburbs surrounding Detroit, could not a prima facie presumption of discrimination have been the starting point, with each of the suburban districts having the burden of proving they were in fact operating unitary and nondiscriminatory systems? Justice Powell was silent. For Chief Justice Burger, however, the "scope of the remedy was determined by the nature and extent of the constitutional violation" (*Milliken I*: 3127). If no violation were proved, then no remedy would be possible!

The conflict between the majority and the minority in *Milliken* in part had to do with different ways of defining the domain to be accorded equality. The plaintiffs in the Detroit case wanted group-regarding equality to be applied as a domain of account that included the entire metropolitan area. The majority adhered tenaciously to the legal boundaries of school districts as the proper domain of allocation for applying bloc-regarding equality between African-American and white students. They would cross those boundaries and expand the domain only when some complicity in de jure discrimination was proven. The minority was willing to expand the domain to include all the students within the metropolitan area. The domain of account would thus be defined primarily by the nature of the problem and the efficacy of the remedy, rather than by the location of de jure discrimination. The minority was also willing to look beyond local boundaries because they saw some complicity in discrimination on the part of the Michigan state government (see Rae, 1981: chapter 3 on domains of account and allocation).

Unless it can be shown that district boundary lines were created or gerrymandered for discriminatory purposes, the majority opinion left the specification of the relevant domain of allocation up to the state or local authority that had power to draw boundary lines. The dissenters were much more willing to have the domain for equality defined by the extent of segregation. The majority position is logical in requiring a clear connection between prior wrongdoing and present remedy before allowing a domain to be enlarged. However, the majority met a practical "Waterloo" in any situation that was similar to that in Detroit. Under the majority position in the Detroit case, the Supreme Court no longer had any effective remedy for integrating the Detroit public schools. Of course, given the reality of white flight and the choice of private education, there might well have been no effective remedy even had the four-member minority position in *Milliken* prevailed. Even so, it is easy to agree with Justice Marshall's dissent, which noted that after twenty years of "small, often difficult steps" toward desegregation, the majority in *Milliken* took "a giant step backward" (*Milliken I*: 3145).

When the *Milliken* case was returned to the federal district court, the judge ordered the submission of a plan that was limited to the Detroit school system. The plan ultimately implemented called for student reassignments, for magnet schools, and for remedial programs for students, teachers, and administrators The *Milliken* case came back to the Supreme Court in 1977, when the revised Detroit plan was sustained in a unanimous opinion by Chief Justice Burger (*Milliken II*).

While the Detroit case revealed the limits of the Court's zeal for enforcing metropolitan integration, the Boston school case revealed the intensity of the opposition to busing in a relatively compact northern city. The Boston suit was filed in 1972. Judge Garrity, the federal judge assigned to the case, conducted a fifteen-day trial and received over 1,000 exhibits. The ratio of "white-to-black" students in the Boston schools was 61 percent to 21 percent, but that ratio was rarely represented in specific schools. Racial imbalance in the Boston schools was clearly established, but the question of who or what had caused it remained. Judge Garrity found that with respect to the building of schools and the utilization of facilities the Boston School Committee had intentionally created or maintained segregation. The committee had also consistently rejected proposals to redraw attendance zones to reduce racial imbalance. The school committee, on the other hand, admitted the fact of racial imbalance but argued that it simply reflected a city with considerable de facto segregation. The schools had been operated without the system taking "affirmative action to counteract that de facto segregation" (*Morgan v. Kerrigan*: [Circuit opinion] 584). The First Circuit opinion rejected the argument that school authorities in a northern city, which had never had a statutory dual school system, therefore cannot be guilty of a constitutional violation. Under the *Keyes* test, it was sufficient that the Boston authorities had engaged in policies or practices that had the effect of creating or maintaining segregation. The First Circuit opinion reviewed the long and complicated trial record and found vivid and ample support for Judge Garrity's conclusion that Boston school authorities had engaged in practices that had the effect of perpetuating racial imbalance. The entire school system of Boston therefore was unconstitutionally segregated. Judge Garrity ordered a comprehensive plan of desegregation to begin implementation in September 1974. The plan eventually implemented included mandatory busing. In the fall of 1974, the first bus from Roxbury, a predominantly "black" neighborhood, arrived at South Boston High School and riots broke out. Between 1974 and 1977, Boston was a much-publicized arena for conflict over the integration of its schools. However, the Supreme Court consistently refused to review Judge Garrity's orders, so it made no explicit contribution to the Boston case (Metcalf, 1983: 197 et seq.).

The fact that a majority of the Supreme Court was no longer at the cutting edge of enforcing school integration was also evident in *Pasadena City Board of Education v. Spangler* in 1976, two years after the Boston desegregation order. In *Swann* the unanimous opinion of the court had said in its last paragraph that neither school authorities nor federal district judges were required to adjust the racial composition of the schools each year, once the affirmative duty to operate a unitary school system had been met. In the *Pasadena* case the last paragraph of *Swann* became the rule of the case. Once Pasadena had achieved a unitary school system, the power of a federal judge to order year-by-year adjustments to the racial composition of particular schools was exhausted (*Pasadena City Board of Education v. Spanger*: 2705). Only Marshall and Brennan dissented. They argued that so long as the compliance of the Pasadena School Board with the federal court's order was incomplete, the federal judge ought to have continuing enforcement powers.

Writing for the majority, Justice Rehnquist freed the school board of responsibility for resegregation caused by population migration. He found that a unitary school system had been achieved in Pasadena, measured by the absence of any school in which minority students were in a majority. Having once achieved that condition, the schools were under no continuing obligation to readjust the schools to take white flight into account.

Also in 1976, the Supreme Court overturned a decision of the Fifth Circuit and remanded the Austin, Texas, school case for a determination of "segregative intent." The Circuit Court had apparently inferred segregative intent from the school district's insistence on a neighborhood school assignment policy. (*Austin Independent School District v. United States*: 517). Burger and Rehnquist joined in a concurring opinion by Justice Powell that was critical of the extent of busing required by the lower courts.[5]

In 1977, one year later, Justice Rehnquist again wrote for the court's majority, but now with only brief concurring opinions by Stevens and Brennan (Marshall did not participate). The majority opinion held that three allegedly isolated instances of discrimination in Dayton, Ohio, did not warrant the imposition by a federal district court of an extensive systemwide desegregation plan (*Dayton Board of Education v. Brinkman* [hereafter cited as *Dayton I*]: 2774 et seq.).[6]

It seems safe to conclude that by 1977, only 23 years after *Brown I,* the Supreme Court was quite reluctant to lead the offensive against racially segregated public education in America. Indeed, as others have noted, it was only during the five years between 1968 (*Green v. County School Board of New Kent County, Virginia*) and 1974 (*Milliken v. Bradley*) that the U.S. Supreme Court aggressively pursued a policy of integration.

By 1980, others were clearly more aggressive than the U.S. Supreme Court in seeking integration. Two cases from the early 1980s involved local initiatives in Seattle and Los Angeles, both seeking to eradicate de facto segregation in their public schools. Those efforts produced angry and aggressive local opposition. In Seattle, the school board had voluntarily prepared the "Seattle Plan," which called for mandatory busing to rectify de facto segregation. Local opponents campaigned successfully for a statewide initiative that prohibited local school boards from implementing mandatory busing to remedy de facto segregation. The initiative did allow mandatory busing in a variety of other instances, including court-ordered busing required by the Fourteenth Amendment (*Washington v. Seattle School District No. 1*, 1982: 3191). Justice Blackmun wrote an opinion for a five-member majority. He concluded that the initiative against busing violated the Equal Protection Clause because "it uses the racial nature of an issue to define the governmental decision-making structure, and thus imposes substantial and unique burdens on racial minorities" (*Washington v. Seattle School District No. 1*: 3195). The key point was that the single instance in which the power to mandate busing was denied local school authorities was that of remedying de facto racial segregation.

The Los Angeles case, also in 1982, went the other way. Powell wrote for the majority, but with only Marshall dissenting. The case began in California state courts. Enforcing the Equal Protection Clause of the California state constitution, the California supreme court ordered the preparation of a desegregation plan for Los Angeles that would have required substantial mandatory student assignment and busing, because both de facto and de jure segregation were held to violate the state constitution. Local opposition led eventually to the ratification of a state constitutional amendment that limited mandatory busing to situations in which a federal court "would be permitted under federal decisional law to do so to remedy a violation of the Equal Protection Clause of the Fourteenth Amendment to the Federal Constitution" (*Crawford v. Board of Education of the City of Los Angeles*: 3213). Justice Powell wrote that nothing requires the State of California to do more than the Fourteenth Amendment requires or for it to continue a higher standard previously required. Even Blackmun and Brennan agreed that this was different from the Seattle situation, for the people of California were in theory responsible both for the original state constitution and for its amendment, while in the Seattle case a statewide initiative had reached out to limit the voluntary policies of local school authorities in the single instance of mandatory busing.

In 1983, despite the efforts of the Reagan administration to urge reconsideration of an order including busing, the Supreme Court refused to hear the Nashville school case, thereby leaving in place a court-ordered busing plan (*Metropolitan County Board of Education of Nashville and Davidson County, Tennessee v. Kelly*). It was not until 1991 that the Supreme Court spoke again. In the past several years, school districts have increasingly sought declarations that they have achieved unitary status and thus are to be released from federal court oversight. In September 1988, the journal *Black Enterprise* reported that the U.S. Department of Justice intended to "close out" 200 school desegregation orders in six southern and western states because "unitary status" had been achieved. That move was opposed by the NAACP but favored by those who saw busing as a failure. In May 1989, the Fifth Circuit sustained a district court's findings that the schools in Oxford, Mississippi, did not discriminate in their achievement groupings, disciplinary practices, and one-race extracurricular activities. The school desegregation case that had begun in Oxford in 1969 was finally dismissed, and unitary status was declared twenty years after its filing (*Quarles v. Oxford Municipal Separate School District*).

Finally, in January 1991, the Supreme Court spoke on the question of unitary status, and thus on the termination of a federal desegregation order, in the Oklahoma City school case. By this time, however, only Blackmun and Stevens remained to join in Justice Marshall's dissent. The five-member majority spoke through Chief Justice Rehnquist's opinion.

The Oklahoma City school case had been filed in 1961. In 1963 the federal district court found that Oklahoma City had engaged in de jure segregation of its schools. By 1972 the district court found that previous efforts to desegregate the Oklahoma City schools had not worked, and it ordered the school authorities to implement a plan that called for extensive busing, beginning with kindergarten. In 1977, after five years under the busing plan, the school district moved to close the case, on the grounds that it had complied with the court's previous orders and was successfully operating under the required plan. The court found that unitary status had been achieved and that jurisdiction could be terminated, in part because it had no reason to find that termination of judicial supervision would result in the "dismantlement of the Plan." But by 1984 circumstances (including the patterns of integrated and de facto segregated neighborhoods) had changed sufficiently that school authorities stopped busing for kindergarten through fourth grade, thus allowing a number of single-race neighborhood schools. It continued to allow for voluntary transfers. Because of that decision, in 1985 plaintiffs moved to reopen the case in federal court.

The federal district court refused to reopen the case, chiefly because it viewed its prior finding of unitary status as binding and found no current de jure segregation. The Tenth Circuit Court reversed, however, holding that while the prior termination order was binding, the termination did not release the school district from the duty to enforce the previously ordered injunctive order for desegregation. But on remand the district judge found that local school authorities "had done nothing for 25 years to promote residential segregation, and that the school district had bused students for more than a decade in good-faith compliance with the court's orders." The district judge also found that the present neighborhood segregation was "the result of private decisionmaking and economics" and was "too attenuated to be a vestige of former school segregation" (*Board of Education of Oklahoma City v. Dowell*: 634–35). On appeal the Tenth Circuit reversed again, however, holding that the school authorities continued under an "affirmative duty" to do nothing that would seriously impede previous efforts to produce a unitary system. The Supreme Court granted review, and thus the stage was set for it to speak on school desegregation for the first time since 1982.

The majority led by Rehnquist reversed the Tenth Circuit but, rather than ruling outright, decided in favor of a remand to the district court, but with certain guidelines. The district court was directed to consider whether a sufficient showing had been made to allow the court's previously ordered plan to be dissolved. In deciding whether unitary status had been achieved sufficiently to terminate its previous injunction, the district court was directed to examine "every facet" of school operations. If the trial court found that its injunction should have been terminated, it then should consider again whether the school authorities were engaging in any form of de jure segregation, subject to the following admonition:

A school district which has been released from an injunction imposing a desegregation plan no longer requires court authority for the promulgation of policies and rules regulating matters such as assignment of students and the like, but it of course remains subject to the mandate of the Equal Protection Clause of the Fourteenth Amendment. (*Board of Education of Oklahoma City v. Dowell*: 638)

To that Justice Marshall in dissent replied:

The practical question now before us is whether, 13 years after [the] injunction was imposed, the same School Board should have been allowed to return many of its elementary schools to their former one-race status. The majority today suggest that 13 years of desegregation was enough. (*Board of Education of Oklahoma City v. Dowell*: 639)

Whether or not Justice Marshall is entirely right, there is, to be sure, little in the *Oklahoma City* case to encourage those who seek the continuation of vigorous federal judicial enforcement. These days the best that can be hoped for is the continuation of magnet schools and other attractive "choice" programs within districts (Armor, 1989).

With respect to urban public school integration, the efforts to achieve group-regarding equality must in the end be judged a failure. However, the failure was not due to the impropriety of a group-regarding understanding of equality but to court-imposed constraints on the domain in which it would be applied. In multidistrict metropolitan areas the Supreme Court judged domain (the school district boundaries) to be more important than the achievement of group-regarding equality. And in the end it chose not to confront de facto segregation.

9

AFFIRMATIVE ACTION PROGRAMS IN HIGHER EDUCATION AND EMPLOYMENT

I feel compelled to pursue a further course of action. . . . Applicants chosen to be our doctors should be those presenting the best qualifications, both academic and personal. . . . I am convinced a significant fraction . . . is judged by a separate criterion. I am referring to quotas, open or covert, for racial minorities. . . . I realize that the rationale for these quotas is that they attempt to atone for past discrimination. But instituting a new racial bias, in favor of minorities is not a just solution.
> —Alan Bakke's letter to Dr. George Lowery, chairman of the Admissions Committee of the Medical School of the University of California at Davis, as quoted in Sindler, *Bakke, DeFunis and Minority Admissions*

Almost everything written in the preceding chapters about the integration of public primary and secondary schools would apply equally to public higher education, with the key and obvious difference that public higher education does not involve the volatile issues of the neighborhood school or of bus transportation from home to school and back again. Instead, issues about admission criteria, rarely important in primary and secondary education, become the focus of concern, most often in questions about admission to graduate professional programs. Landmark cases involving admissions to graduate programs in both law and medicine reached the Supreme Court of the United States in the 1970s.

DISCRIMINATION IN GRADUATE PROFESSIONAL PROGRAMS

A great deal has been written about the 1978 case of *Regents of the University of California v. Bakke* (hereafter cited as *Bakke*), which involved admission to medical school, as well as its putative precursor in 1974, *DeFunis v. Odegaard,* the law school admission case. Examining each of these cases in the context of the equality issues that have already been raised should especially clarify the key distinction between individual-regarding and bloc-regarding equality.

Bernard Schwartz's book on *Bakke* reveals that at the Court's conference on the *DeFunis* case, Brennan, White, Marshall, and Powell were in agreement that race was not per se an inadmissible consideration in admissions decisions, but Justice Stewart strongly asserted that the case was moot and should not be decided (Schwartz, 1988: 33).[1]

Only Justice Douglas's dissent in *DeFunis* contains any discussion of the merits of the case, because the balance of the court considered only the question of mootness. Douglas came out strongly in favor of individual-regarding equality. Using race as a factor in admissions, he wrote, "introduces a capricious and irrelevant factor working an invidious discrimination" (*DeFunis v. Odegaard*: 1714). Instead, he said several times, applications must be "considered in a racially neutral way" (*DeFunis v. Odegaard*: 1717). What had the University of Washington actually done?

Excepting Asian-Americans, all the minority applicants who eventually were admitted to the University of Washington's law school were below the "automatic reject" index score of 74.5.[2] All of them had index scores below that of Defunis. They almost certainly would have been rejected but for their minority status, so Justice Douglas's requirement of racial neutrality was on point. However, he did not intend to suggest that the index scores used by the University of Washington represented the last word in either neutrality or objectivity. Douglas would willingly have jettisoned the lot of standardized tests in favor of some better means of assessing the "motivation, perseverance and ability" related to success in law school (*DeFunis v. Odegaard*: 1713).

The most interesting aspect of Douglas's opinion was that he was willing, given the reality of the LSAT, to have racial minorities considered as a separate group to make sure that "racial factors do not militate against an applicant or on his behalf" (*DeFunis v. Odegaard*: 1715). Still, he required that this be done in a "racially neutral way" so that the individual merits of candidates were fairly assessed.[3] Douglas distinguished this from the racial ratios accepted by the Court in *Swann v. Charlotte-Mecklenburg Board of Education* because in *Swann* no one was excluded from school and because "no one ha[d] a right to attend a segregated public school" (*DeFunis v. Odegaard*: footnote 18, 1715). Thus, he believed that no one suffered a disadvantage because of the racial ratios used to measure the success of integration in *Swann*. He concluded, however, that DeFunis had suffered a significant disadvantage in his rejection by the law school of the University of Washington.

Douglas rejected group- or bloc-regarding equality in the form of racial quotas in such decisions, citing cases that had previously rejected racial ratios in jury selection as well as proportionate hiring requirements. He saw no end to the potential of group claims once a principal of "proportional representation" (that is, group-regarding equality) was accepted, nor did he see how conflicts between competing group claims would be avoidable or soluble (*DeFunis v. Odegaard*: 1716 et seq.). His apprehensions, expressed about the implications of group-regarding equality in April 1974, did not have long to wait for further consideration, for in June 1974, Alan Bakke filed suit seeking admission to the University of California at Davis Medical School.

At the time of his first application for admission, Alan Bakke was a thirty-one-year-old former Marine officer and an employed mechanical engineer with a desire to study medicine "more than anything else in the world" (Sindler, 1978: 75). For the 1973 admissions year, almost 2,500 applicants competed for the 100 places in the entering class of the University of California at Davis Medical School. Actually, almost 2,200 of them competed for 84 places. The remaining 16 places were held for 291 "disadvantaged minority applicants." Admissions criteria included the Medical College Admissions Test (MCAT) score, undergraduate grade point average, undergraduate science grade point average, and a score based on an evaluation of a candidate's interview with an admissions representative. An interview was required of all those candidates who passed initial screening. These factors were combined to give each candidate a benchmark score.[4]

Bakke's scores were markedly above the minority "special" admittees, although a spokesperson for the medical school was careful to note that even the special admittees, though possessed of lower benchmark scores than either Bakke or the "regular" admittees, were sufficiently well qualified to succeed in medical school.

Within the several opinions in *Bakke* there appear some clear implications for the distinction between individual-regarding and group- or bloc-regarding equality. However, most of the pages were spent considering the question of which standard of equal protection review ought to be applied.[5] The decisive vote and opinion of Justice Powell held that racial distinctions "of any sort" were suspect and required the "most exacting judicial scrutiny" (*Bakke*: 2748). The University of California argued against that position, and eventually four members of the Court concurred that discrimination against members of the white majority could, under certain circumstances, be viewed as benign and thus be subjected to less exacting review.

Justice Powell wrote, however, that if the Equal Protection Clause protected all individuals against classifications based on race or ethnic background (rather than protecting only those who are members of a particular group that traditionally has been the object of discrimination) then the constitutional safeguards must be applied consistently (*Bakke*: 2753). Thus, when a policy impinges upon a person because of his ethnic background, there should be only one standard for assessing whether the "burden he is asked to bear on that basis is tailored to serve a compelling governmental interest." The apparent exceptions, Powell wrote, were no exceptions at all; they merely involved remedies for the vindication of constitutionally protected rights, as in instances of segregated public education (*Swann*) or employment discrimination (*Albemarle Paper Co. v. Moody,* 1975). Adherence to some mathematical ratio for no other reason than racial preference, Powell wrote, was a purpose that was not only "insubstantial," it was "facially invalid" (*Bakke*: 2757).

Powell nonetheless saw a way out. Attainment of a diverse student body was a permissible objective for public higher education, albeit one that could not be pursued to the extent of setting aside a certain number of seats for minority students. Thus, "No such facial infirmity exists in an admissions program where race or ethnic background is simply one element to be weighed fairly against the other elements—in the selection process" (*Bakke*: 2763). Powell used the example of Harvard as an admissions program in which race was considered as a positive factor but in which quotas were not used.

Brennan, White, Marshall, and Blackmun concurred with Powell that racial considerations in admissions were not absolutely prohibited either by federal civil rights legislation or by the Fourteenth Amendment, but they agreed with the University of California that racial preferences and even quotas could be "benign" when remediation of discrimination was the policy objective. A memo prepared by Brennan during the court's deliberations argued "that we are just deluding ourselves if we think there is a meaningful, judicially enforceable distinction between setting aside a reasonable number of places for qualified minorities and a process that accomplishes the same end by taking race into account of one of several admissions factors" (Schwartz, 1988: 92). For the four justices who supported the University of California's position, to hold that the Constitution must be entirely "color blind" was a position that entailed a view of society that was an "aspiration rather than ... [a] description of reality" (*Bakke*: 2767). Since these justices held that race could be taken into account under certain circumstances, the question again arose as to what standard of review ought to be applied. To pass constitutional review, the four held that remedial racial classifications "must serve important governmental objectives and must be substantially" related to "achievement of those objectives" (*Bakke*: 2783).[6] The University of California's purpose of remedying the effects of past societal discrimination was "sufficiently important to justify the use of race-conscious admissions programs where there is a sound basis for concluding that minority underrepresentation is substantial and chronic, and that the handicap of past discrimination is impeding access of minorities to the Medical School" (*Bakke*: 2784). The university's program was approved whether its purpose was to redress the institution's own history of discrimination or "that of society at large" (*Bakke*: 2788). At the final court conference on Bakke, Justice Marshall said, "This is not a quota to keep someone out, it's a quota to get someone in" (Schwartz, 1988: 96).

Justice Blackmun, who because of illness had missed some of the deliberations of the Court, was the last to join with Brennan, Marshall, and White in voting to uphold the use of quotas. It was not until the last conference of the court's 1977–78 term that Blackmun circulated a memo with his views on the merits. He wrote, "It is the unconstitutional use of race that is prohibited, not the constitutional use" (Schwartz, 1988: 134).

In the final opinions, Brennan, White, Marshall, and Blackmun asked "whether the . . . program stigmatizes any discrete group or individual and whether race is reasonably used in light of the program's objectives." They found that it did not stigmatize and that the set-aside of sixteen places was reasonable (*Bakke*: 2791). Bakke, they concluded, was unlikely to be affected by his rejection in the same way as "black school children" had been affected before *Brown*. Justice Marshall was particularly eloquent in describing the difference:

> The position of the Negro today in America is the tragic but inevitable consequence of centuries of unequal treatment. Measured by any benchmark of comfort or achievement, meaningful equality remains a distant dream for the Negro. (*Bakke*: 2801)
>
> In light of the sorry history of discrimination and its devastating impact on the lives of Negroes, bringing the Negro into the mainstream of American life should be a state interest of the highest order. To fail to do so is to ensure that America will forever remain a divided society. (*Bakke*: 2802)

The four remaining justices, Stevens, Burger, Stewart, and Rehnquist, didn't reach the level of constitutional review at all. They simply held that Title VI of the 1964 Civil Rights Act prohibited race-conscious remedial programs such as that of the University of California.

The factor that may have sorted the justices in *Bakke* into two groups of four, with Powell having the decisive vote between them, was their different understandings of equality. The group led by Marshall and Brennan accepted group- or bloc-regarding equality in varying degrees. The strongest foundation for their position, and the way most consistent with *Swann,* is once again to accept group-regarding equality as a form of compensatory justice directed toward the remediation of previous and specific individual, group, or societal discrimination. Usually, such reluctant acceptance of group-regarding equality is coupled with the hope that the need for it will disappear soon (see, for example, Blackmun's separate opinion in *Bakke*: 2895).

The more traditional judicial view of equality in a case such as *Bakke* is clearly that of individual-regarding equality. Indeed, as O'Neill has suggested, individual-regarding equality is part of the liberal democratic tradition of "radical individualism of basic needs and rights" (O'Neill, 1981: 630). Group-regarding equality represents what Sindler has called an "alternate view," which stresses groups and group outcomes (Sindler, 1978: 14), and what O'Neill views as "radically redistributive group rights" (O'Neill, 1981: 627).

Sindler argues that departures from individual-regarding equality are seen by their proponents as a means of achieving individual equality in the long run. Because it is slow and uncertain to promote upward mobility of minorities through strict "meritocratic" processes, "The most direct way to eliminate this uncertainty and unreliability was to predetermine what proportion of wins should go to minorities and then to achieve that proportion by some form of preferential selection of minority candidates" (Sindler, 1978: 14).

Curiously, the notion of "group proportionality of results" was not specifically raised by any of the briefs that supported the position of the University of California (Sindler, 1978: 264; O'Neill, 1981: 627). That Brennan, White, Marshall, and Blackmun accepted group-regarding equality is best indicated by their agreement that neither minority applicants nor the University of California need themselves be the objects or source of any particular prior acts of discrimination. It is minority applicants as a group, rather than any particular victims, that are the objects of remediation, and, while the University of California might be motivated to remediate by its own history of discrimination, it may just as well seek to redress societal discrimination, in which it might have had only a very tenuous and indirect part. In Rae's terms the university was prepared to use its domain of allocation to compensate in part for discrimination outside its own domain. The university was pursuing compensatory equality.

O'Neill's essay on the "language of constitutional equality" helps us appreciate the possibility of thinking about rights from a group rather than strictly from an individual perspective. He pointed out that during the last half of the nineteenth century lawyers and judges had no particular difficulty in learning to think of corporations as legal "persons" whose rights were protected by the Fourteenth Amendment.[7] There may be no reason, save for habit and the limitations of our concepts, for continuing to think of rights as being due to individuals only. O'Neill argued that the individualistic approach is distributive only and produces only incremental results, while group-regarding equality is "radically redistributive"; it has the potential for rapidly shifting resources to a traditionally deprived group (O'Neill, 1981: 627). That is also a point considered by Amy Gutmann in her book *Democratic Education*.

Gutmann cited an article by Richard Wasserstrom (1980), which argued that racial quotas are attractive since they offer a relatively effective and expedient means for moving toward the ideal of a racially neutral society. This consequentialist case for group-regarding equality persuaded Wasserstrom, but Gutmann continued to have doubts.

Gutmann was correct in suggesting that there are several pitfalls in the uses of group-regarding equality. For one thing, groups have no consciousness and do not themselves live and experience either discrimination or advantage. Only individuals can do that. That, of course, is true as well with the corporations that *are* recognized as legal individuals, but in certain circumstances particular corporate entities clearly can be the direct objects of discrimination. That is not so with respect to groups in admissions decisions in higher education. In admissions decisions only an actual person can experience discrimination, and that reality may suggest that only individuals should count in that context. This point gets very close to Dworkin's consideration of when a person has a right to be treated as an equal (Dworkin, 1977: 227) or its opposite, when a person has a right not to be treated with contempt (Dworkin, 1977: 44). Both the positive and negative versions imply human consciousness of one's treatment by others.

There is also a problem with competing group claims, as Douglas noted in his opinion in *DeFunis*. If only one group claims its proportionate share, there may be no great difficulty, but as the number of groups that make claims increases, there may be no easy resolution of their claims—a point acknowledged by Douglas Rae as well (Rae, 1981: 37–38).

It is also the case that the achievement of group-regarding equality in one context may serve to divert attention from malignant inequalities in another. It is possible, even likely, that the achievement of group-regarding equality in one domain (such as proportionate representation of African-Americans in the legal profession) might do little to improve the lot of African-Americans as a whole. Even the achievement of group-regarding equality with respect to earned incomes (so that the average incomes of African-Americans and whites would be the same) might have little to do with whether incomes among African-Americans and whites are fairly distributed.

Another legitimate concern is whether group-regarding remedies such as racial quotas, while at the outset clearly remedial and temporary in nature, may eventually be viewed by potential recipients as matters of right or entitlement rather than as remediation. One of the best examples is that of employment preferences for veterans of World War II, a policy in force long after it had finished serving its original purpose (Gutmann, 1987: 210). Another example is offered by the continuation of remedial measures for certain castes in India—to the point where they are eventually considered by some to be entitlements (as we will see Chapter 12).

The choices between individual-regarding and group-regarding equality are indeed difficult ones. One important question is whether group-regarding equality inevitably involves the use of quotas. Gutmann argues that while equal protection clearly excludes discrimination against African-Americans, it should not be taken to preclude *all* forms of discrimination in their favor. For her, the key rationale for prohibiting discrimination against African-Americans in admissions decisions is the gatekeeping function that universities perform in selecting individuals for highly desired careers. Whether that should justify preferential treatment of African-American applicants raises some difficult issues for her.

Gutmann argues that as long as all the students who are admitted are academically qualified, there is nothing that necessarily demands that the "most qualified" be admitted. With Justice Douglas, she would have the credentials of all qualified candidates reviewed to determine whether any students possess special qualities that ought to be taken into account. Athletes, for example, might be admitted because of their special talents—assuming that they possess the minimum academic qualifications. Her problem is with the question of whether being "black" represents a special qualification. Justice Powell answered in *Bakke* that it might be, because a school could reasonably choose to seek a diverse student body, and Gutmann accepts that as a reasonable but not necessary position.

Setting up a racial quota and setting aside a special admissions process (again assuming that those who are admitted through the special process are nonetheless academically qualified) is for her another matter. The consequentialist justification for quotas is that they will be more likely to produce substantial results than will a policy that merely takes race into account as one factor among several. Her clear preference is for the thorough evaluation of individual qualifications. The objective would be to identify applicants for admission who might be overlooked by rigid adherence to quantified measures such as standardized test scores (Gutmann, 1987: 211), similar to the distance-travelled concept proposed in the conclusion of this book. It is also worth remembering that in his *Bakke* deliberations, Justice Brennan thought that the distinction between quotas, on the one hand, and race considered positively as one factor among several, on the other, was illusory.

It is one thing to consider such policies under the premise that all candidates who are admitted are academically qualified. Compensatory programs for those who have below standard qualifications, present even more difficult issues. While those issues certainly do arise within higher education, they also can be illustrated by cases involving compensatory employment practices.

RACIAL DISCRIMINATION IN EMPLOYMENT

Apart from public education, the most frequent case context for racial discrimination is in employment, which includes questions of hiring, promotion, retention, and retirement. While Title VII of the Civil Rights Act of 1964, as well as the Fourteenth Amendment, figures prominently in employment cases, whether statutory or constitutional the issues are essentially the same.

Griggs v. Duke Power Co. (1971) is an important case interpreting the meaning of Title VII.[8] It allowed employers to use ability tests in hiring decisions, provided the tests were not designed, intended, or used to discriminate on racial lines. Equal Employment Opportunity Commission guidelines that were written to implement Title VII, however, required such tests to be demonstrably job related. Duke Power Company, having a proven history of prior racial discrimination, still chose to require a high school degree and certain standardized tests as criteria for several of its positions. The standardized tests were in fact instituted on the day Title VII came into effect. Neither the high school diploma nor the standardized tests were shown to have any relationship to actual job performance, although they did have the effect of disproportionately excluding African-American applicants.

The eight justices participating in *Griggs* were unanimous in sustaining the EEOC guidelines and in holding that the diploma requirement and the standardized tests were barred by Title VII. The *Griggs* opinion contains an interesting summary statement of the purposes of Title VII:

> In short, the Act does not command that any person be hired simply because he was formerly the subject of discrimination, or because he is a member of a minority group. Discriminatory preference for any group is precisely and only what Congress has proscribed. What is required by Congress is the removal of artificial, arbitrary and unnecessary barriers to employment when the barriers operate invidiously to discriminate on the basis of racial or other impermissible classification. (*Griggs v. Duke Power Co.*: 853)

Four years later in *Albemarle Paper Co. v. Moody* the Supreme Court sustained the rigorous standards for test validation that had been issued as part of EEOC Guidelines.[9] The tests that were used were required to evidence *"a high degree of utility."*

Together, *Griggs* and *Albemarle* erected some significant barriers under Title VII against discriminatory employment tests. The next question was whether these same stringent standards might be adopted as constitutional requirements under the Fourteenth Amendment.

Washington v. Davis (1976) was the constitutional case, but the majority of the court proved reluctant to extend *Griggs* and *Albemarle*. The complainants in *Davis* were African-Americans whose applications to become District of Columbia police officers had been rejected, chiefly because of a test used as a screening device. At the trial it was shown that the test had a racially disproportionate tendency to exclude African-American applicants and that it had not been validated as to its relationship with actual job performance. The test was supposed to measure "verbal ability, vocabulary, reading and comprehension" (*Washington v.*

Davis: 2045). According to the court's majority, the test was validated only for its relevancy in selecting applicants who would be able to cope with the police recruit training program.

The key difference between *Davis* and *Griggs/Albemarle* is that *Davis* was brought under the due process clause of the Fifth Amendment.[10] At the time of filing suit, Title VII did not apply to the government of the District of Columbia, and while Title VII was later amended to apply, the complaint in *Davis* was never amended to raise Title VII issues. The complaint had to be judged by constitutional principles of equality. For the majority, Justice White refused to extend Title VII rules as constitutional requirements:

> However [Title VII review] proceeds, it involves a more probing judicial review of, and less deference to, the seemingly reasonable acts of administrators and executive than is appropriate under the Constitution where special racial impact, without discriminatory purpose is claimed. We are not disposed to adopt this more rigorous standard for the purposes of applying the Fifth and Fourteenth Amendments in cases such as this. (*Washington v. Davis*: 2051)

Justice White went on to adopt the reasoning of the district court that the relationship of the test to the training program was a sufficient answer to the challenge that the test was racially discriminatory in outcome, if not in purpose. The key notion was that minimal verbal and communication skills, as reflected by the test, would be "useful, if not essential to satisfactory progress in the training regimen" (*Washington v. Davis*: 2052).

Even more important is the majority's treatment of discriminatory impact versus discriminatory intent. While Title VII shifts the burden of test validation to the employer, once discriminatory impact is shown, the majority in *Davis* required some sort of showing of discriminatory purpose as well. Quoting from *Keyes* (the Denver school integration case) that the "differentiating factor between *de jure* segregation and so-called *de facto* segregation is the *purpose or intent* to segregate," Justice White held that disproportionate racial impact does not by itself trigger the strict constitutional scrutiny required of explicit racial classifications (*Washington v. Davis*: 2048 et seq.). In the instance of a job test that is facially neutral, White agreed that disproportionate racial impact required some limited scrutiny, but he accepted the conclusion of the trial judge that the efforts of the D.C. Metropolitan Police to recruit African-

American officers and their increasing numbers in recruit classes provided sufficient answers to charges of discrimination.

The majority's distinction between Title VII and equal protection standards was clearly important three years later in *United Steelworkers v. Weber* (1979). In *Weber,* a collective bargaining agreement that called for the reservation of 50 percent of the openings in a plant craft training program (until the percentage of "black craft workers" was equivalent to the percentage of African-Americans in the local labor force) was challenged by a white employee. As a voluntary private agreement, the Equal Protection Clause was inapplicable, so only Title VII could be invoked, which Weber did, claiming that the 50 percent set aside for African-Americans violated Title VII's prohibition against racial discrimination.

For the majority, Justice Brennan held that Title VII does not prohibit all voluntary race-conscious affirmative action plans. Rather, the purpose of Title VII was to remediate "the plight of the Negro in our economy" (*United Steelworkers v. Weber:* 2727). The particular plan agreed to in *Weber* was acceptable for two reasons: (1) its impact on white employees was limited—no one was to be fired and the training program was not closed to whites, who were allocated 50 percent of the openings; and (2) it was a temporary measure, one designed to eliminate an existing racial imbalance, rather than a permanent one designed to maintain racial proportionality. Brennan accepted, as he had in *Bakke,* the possibility of group-regarding equality as a constitutional and lawful outcome.

Rehnquist was caustic in dissent. He invoked the imagery of "newspeak" from George Orwell's *1984* against the majority's interpretation of the "plain language" of Title VII. Rehnquist held tenaciously to an individual-regarding understanding of equality. Title VII, he wrote, "prohibits all racial discrimination in employment" (*United Steelworkers v. Weber:* 2736). Both Rehnquist's and Brennan's positions are tenable; they simply represent different understandings of equality. Another key confrontation between Rehnquist's views and Brennan's came five years later in 1984.

Firefighters Local Union No. 1784 v. Stotts (1984) presents with extraordinary clarity the conflicting views of members of the court. By 1984, only Brennan, Marshall, and Blackmun were consistent supporters of group-regarding equality. Justice White, who had refused to elevate Title VII requirements to constitutional status in *Washington v. Davis,* wrote for the majority in *Stotts.*

The case began as a class action brought by *Stotts,* who alleged that
the Memphis Fire Department had discriminated in hiring on the basis
of race in violation of Title VII. A consent decree was eventually entered
that provided for relief to certain individuals but also adopted a goal of
increasing minority representation in each job classification within the
department. One provision of the consent decree was that 20 percent
of the promotions within each job classification would be given to
"blacks." A year later, the city of Memphis, then facing a deficit, began
a policy of layoffs, based on seniority. At Stotts's request, however, the
district court entered an order barring the city from applying its seniority system so that the percentage of African-Americans within certain
classifications would be decreased. To comply with that policy, some
whites with greater seniority than "black" employees were laid off or
demoted.

For the majority, Justice White held to a statutory interpretation that
Title VII allowed the continuance of seniority systems as long as there
was no proof of discrimination. Even with such proof, the remedy was to
grant relief to those who had proven themselves to be the victims of
discrimination by awarding compensatory seniority. Thus, in White's
view, it was the individual victims of discrimination who were required
to prove their cases and claim their compensation. Just as in *Washington
v. Davis,* it was necessary to prove an intent to discriminate and to
demonstrate specific consequences in order to claim relief.

Writing for the three dissenters, Justice Blackmun argued that White
had failed to distinguish between a suit claiming individual relief and a
class action, such as that brought by Stotts.[11] In Title VII class action
suits, race-conscious affirmative action relief was appropriate and:

> The purpose of such relief is not to make whole any particular
> individual, but rather to remedy the present class-wide effects of
> past discrimination or to prevent similar discrimination in the fu-
> ture. Because the discrimination sought to be alleviated by race-
> conscious relief is the class-wide effects of past discrimination,
> rather than discrimination against identified members of the class,
> such relief is provided to the class as a whole rather than to its
> individual members. (*Firefighters Local Union No. 1884 v. Stotts*:
> 2606)

Thus we see a stark contrast between individual-regarding and group-
regarding equality. Fallon and Weiler contrast these as the "model of

individual justice" and the "model of group justice," which are, for all practical purposes, the same as Rae's two versions of equality. Fallon and Weiler suggest that the model of individual justice has at its center a principle disfavoring classification—that is, the prohibition of all race-conscious classifications. This principle is also highly individualistic and rests on the invisible hand of the market (Fallon and Weiler, 1985: 12 et seq.). The "group justice model" views the Fourteenth Amendment as a provision dedicated to the protection of disadvantaged groups, especially African-Americans. It rests on the fact of historical and institutional racism and on the consequent culture of poverty and deprivation passed on from one generation to the next. As we saw in the dissenting views in *Washington v. Davis,* this model rests on the presumptive illegality of disparate group outcomes. According to Fallon and Weiler, a weaker version of this understanding is found in *Griggs,* where the disparate outcomes of employment tests merely shift the burden of justification to the employer. The stronger version, they say, indicates the understanding that the group is an important and independent unit of analysis. In support of their position, they cite an article by Owen Fiss (Fiss, 1976) which suggests that group recognition in this context be based on long-standing group identity and on psychological and perceptive interdependence. Also, group justice is supposed to be contingent on past societal discrimination, which warrants remedial treatment, possibly even to the detriment of innocent individual members of a dominant majority (Fallon and Weiler, 1985: 18 et seq.).

Nonetheless, a majority of the Supreme Court continued to reject group-regarding equality, no matter what conditions might be attached. Thus the chief justice joined Powell and Rehnquist in the 1986 decision in *Wygant v. Jackson Board of Education.* With the separate concurrence of O'Connor and White, they held that preferential protection against layoffs for minority employees, contained in a collective bargaining agreement between a local Michigan school district and a teachers' union, violated the Equal Protection Clause. In a deceptively simple opinion, the majority simply held that racial preferences were subject to "searching examination," that they "must be justified by a compelling governmental interest," and that the means used by the state must be "narrowly tailored" toward the achievement of its goal (*Wygant v. Jackson Board of Education*: 1846). Moreover, a plurality of the justices in *Wygant* held that a preference required some showing of prior discrimination by the governmental unit involved. Preferences against layoffs, they held, were "too intrusive"—they impose the "entire burden of achieving racial equality on particular individuals, often resulting in serious disruption of their lives" (*Wygant v. Jackson Board of Education*: 1851).

The four dissenters would have confirmed the right of the local school board and the union to develop a race-conscious layoff policy. Stevens's separate dissent was especially clear in saying, "In our present society race is not always irrelevant to sound governmental decisionmaking." He concluded that the decision to include more minority teachers in the Jackson, Michigan, school system served a valid public purpose, that it was adopted with fair procedures and given a narrow breadth, that it transcended the harm to petitioners, and that it was a step toward that ultimate goal of eliminating entirely from governmental decisionmaking such irrelevant factors as a human being's race (*Wygant v. Jackson Board of Education*: 1867 et seq.).

Also in 1986, *Local 28 of Sheet Metal Workers v. EEOC* and *Local 93, International Association of Firefighters v. City of Cleveland* represented outcomes opposite to *Wygant* and in favor of racial preference, but ones decided by a badly divided court. The opinions by Brennan were variously joined or concurred in by Marshall, Blackmun, Stevens, O'Connor, and Powell, at least in parts. White, Rehnquist, and Burger were the only unambiguous dissenters. The Sheet Metal Workers local had been found guilty of racial discrimination in violation of Title VII, so the question before the court was whether the remedial provisions of Title VII allowed a federal district judge to order race-conscious relief, even when those who would benefit from the order might not themselves have been the victims of discrimination. The relief that was ordered involved a minority membership goal of about 29 percent (roughly the percentage of nonwhites in the New York City labor pool). Six justices agreed that a district judge may, "in appropriate circumstances, order preferential relief benefiting individuals who are not the actual victims of discrimination as a remedy for violations of Title VII" (*Local 28 of Sheet Metal Workers v. EEOC*: 3054).

The *Firefighters* case was different because it involved a consent decree that had been entered providing for race-conscious relief against a union local that had been charged with discrimination on the basis of both race and national origin. Again, the relief benefited some who had not been the actual victims of discriminatory practices, and a majority of the court sustained the consent decree, its voluntary nature being a key factor.

Rehnquist and Burger continued to view all such instances of race-conscious relief as being barred by Title VII. White was not quite so preemptive but held that the relief granted was not justifiable under the particular facts of the case. All three dissenters were bothered by the implication of awarding relief to those who had not been personally injured, to the detriment of other employees who had not themselves been the perpetrators of discrimination. Again, the conflict was between viewing individuals or groups as the most relevant units of analysis. It is a characteristic of group-regarding equality that the provision of relief is an award to the group as a whole, rather than the rectification of a specific discriminatory act directed toward a particular person.

By 1987, Warren Burger had retired as chief justice. Rehnquist replaced him and Rehnquist in turn had been replaced as associate justice by Antonin Scalia. In *United States v. Paradise,* decided in February of that year, Rehnquist, Scalia, O'Connor, and White were together in dissent. The five-member majority upheld a 50 percent set-aside of promotions to the rank of corporal in the Alabama Department of Public Safety. That set-aside was based on a finding in 1972 of "almost four decades" of discrimination against the hiring of "blacks" as troopers, on a failed 1979 consent decree, and on subsequent remedial court orders (*United States v. Paradise*: 1057, et seq.). The majority was persuaded that the occasion warranted the remedy, but the dissenters concluded that a more narrowly tailored remedy was possible and that a 50 percent quota was not "manifestly necessary." It is only fair to note that all members of the court found the actions of the Alabama Department of Public Safety to be "pervasive, systematic and obstinate discriminatory conduct" (*United States v. Paradise*: 1080). Apparently all members of the court would have accepted race-conscious relief of some sort under certain extreme circumstances. The justices disagreed over assessing the necessity of specific measures and in the breadth and pace of the remedy to be fashioned.

Little more than a year later, the court was again badly divided over a Title VII suit brought by an African-American woman against a Texas bank. She charged racial discrimination in the bank's repeated rejection of her application for promotion to a supervisory position. The promotion decisions had been made by white supervisors who made subjective judgments of the candidates for promotion. Justice O'Connor wrote the principal opinion in *Watson v. Fort Worth Bank and Trust* (1988), but it was divided into several parts, with most of the justices variously concurring or dissenting in different parts. Newly confirmed Justice Kennedy (Justice Powell's replacement) did not participate, and the remaining eight members concurred in that part of Justice O'Connor's opinion that held that the plaintiff should have been allowed to use statistical evidence to demonstrate the disparate impact of an employment practice.

The lower courts had held that the plaintiff must show disparate treatment. Under that requirement, the burden of proving that the employer intentionally discriminated remains at all times with the plaintiff. Watson argued that disparate impact analysis,[12] much like that employed in *Griggs v. Duke Power Co.,* ought to be applied. The novel question before the court was whether disparate impact analysis may be applied to a "subjective or discretionary promotion system," and all the participating justices agreed that it may.

Members of the court divided, however, over the implications of disparate impact. O'Connor, joined by Rehnquist, White, and Scalia, was concerned that employers' responses to statistically based disparate impact cases would be to adopt racial quotas. This, they reminded, was contrary to the expressed intent of Congress (*Watson v. Fort Worth Bank and Trust:* 2787 et seq.). They were also careful to note that no employer need introduce validation studies in order to sustain otherwise subjective evaluations. Employers could show "business necessity" in a variety of ways. O'Connor's opinion suggested that the burden of proving discrimination remains with the plaintiff at all times (*Watson v. Fort Worth Bank and Trust:* 2790).

Justice Stevens agreed that disparate impact analysis ought to be applied but wanted to defer further judgment until the trial court could make finding of fact both about the prima facie evidence of discrimination and about the bank's justification of its subjective practices. Thus, there was no majority on the court except on the holding that disparate impact analysis was in some way applicable.

Blackmun, Brennan, and Marshall were chiefly concerned about O'Connor's reluctance to shift the burden of proof to the employer once the plaintiff was able to make a prima facie case of discrimination through statistical evidence. They rejected any implication that employers ought to have an easier time justifying subjective practices than they would with standardized employment tests (*Watson v. Fort Worth Bank and Trust:* 2792 et seq.). Watson's victory would indeed be illusory, they argued, if employers could readily escape the burden of demonstrating the job-relatedness of their subjective evaluations of employees. The dissenters' conclusion that the majority of the court was *not* intent on expanding the protection against racial discrimination for employees was sustained in the next term of the Court.

During the 1988–89 term of the Supreme Court, a solidified conservative majority left Marshall, Brennan, and Blackmun consistently in dissent on racial affirmative action cases, joined by Stevens in two cases.[13] The majority of the court was apparently intent on confining affirmative action precedents. One of Stevens's dissents from that purpose came in the first case from the 1988–89 term that we will consider. It actually came late in the term, but it contained the next verse of the Title VII issues represented by the *Watson* case above.

Wards Cove Packing Co., Inc. v. Antonio, decided in June 1989, continued the controversy over disparate impact analysis raised in Clara Watson's case. Justice White wrote for the five-member majority, which now included Justice Kennedy, who had not participated in the *Watson* case. He wrote that the circuit court had misperceived the proper application of statistical evidence. It had held that a prima facie disparate impact case had been made by the showing that cannery workers who worked on the line in a salmon-canning factory tended to be disproportionately minority, while workers who worked away from the line and in higher-paying positions tended to be disproportionately white. Justice White held that the proper comparison was not between the two job categories at the cannery but with the "composition of the qualified persons in the labor market," or, in certain instances, with the composition of "otherwise qualified applicants" for the preferred jobs within the factory (*Wards Cove Packing Co., Inc. v. Antonio*: 2121).

White's principal justification for his position was that the absence of minority employees in higher-paying positions might be due to the "dearth of qualified non-white applicants" rather than to the employer's employment practices. The concern expressed earlier by the plurality in *Watson* that an employer's response to a prima facie finding of discrimination might simply be the use of racial quotas was suggested again as an unacceptable outcome. Also, as before in *Watson,* the majority required that the plaintiff show that particular hiring practices were causally related to racial disparity. A showing of disparate outcomes, coupled with a complaint about specific practices (here nepotism, separate hiring channels for cannery line and higher paying jobs, and seasonal rehire preferences) would not be sufficient to shift the burden of justification to the employer, according to the majority (*Wards Cove Packing Co., Inc. v. Antonio*: 2125). Instead:

> The touchstone of this inquiry is a reasoned review of the employer's justification for his use of the challenged practice. A mere insubstantial justification will not suffice, because such a low standard of review would permit discrimination to be practiced through the use of spurious, seemingly neutral employment practices. At

the same time, though, there is no requirement that the challenged practice be "essential" or "indispensable" to the employer's business for it to pass muster. (*Wards Cove Packing Co., Inc. v. Antonio*: 2126)

Stevens's dissent in *Wards Cove Packing* was an expression that approached outrage: "Turning a blind eye to the meaning and purpose of Title VII, the majority's opinion perfunctorily rejects a long-standing rule of law and underestimates the probative value of evidence of a racially stratified work force. I cannot join this latest sojourn into judicial activism" (*Wards Cove Packing Co., Inc. v. Antonio*: 2127).

The majority's "reformulation" of the order and burden of proof raised for Stevens an unanswerable question: "Why the Court undertakes these unwise changes in elementary and eminently fair rules is a mystery to me" (*Wards Cove Packing Co., Inc. v. Antonio*: 2136).

Writing a short separate dissent, Justice Blackmun asked another troubling question about the majority, "One wonders whether the majority still believes that race discrimination—or, more accurately, race discrimination against non-whites—is a problem in our society, or even remembers that it ever was" (*Wards Cove Packing Co., Inc. v. Antonio*: 2136).

To be fair, the majority did express a quite legitimate concern. If one's understanding of equality of job opportunity is based strictly on racially neutral individual-regarding equality, then for the Court to encourage the use of racial quotas by employers, however inadvertent, was to be avoided at all costs.

The majority's concern for the preservation of individual-regarding equality was revealed again one week after the *Wards Cove Packing* case was announced, when the same five-member majority that had prevailed there came together again in *Martin v. Wilks.* This time the five decided that white Birmingham firefighters, who had not been parties to a 1974 lawsuit that had led (in 1981) to consent decrees that provided race-conscious remedies for "black firefighters," could challenge those decrees in a subsequent lawsuit. The lawsuit filed by the white firefighters alleged that they were being denied promotions in favor of less qualified African-American candidates. The majority ruled that since *these* firefighters had not been parties to the lawsuit, they were not bound by it; in effect the majority's ruling allowed the issues resolved by the consent decree to be tried repeatedly.

Stevens's dissent, joined predictably by Brennan, Marshall, and Blackmun, agreed that the white firefighters who had not been parties to the lawsuit were not absolutely bound by it but concluded that the consent decrees would nonetheless be subject only to collateral attack.[14] The appropriate distinction in Stevens's view was that while the nonparties were not personally bound by the prior consent decree, that does not mean that they had been deprived of legal rights. The consent decrees might thus produce changes in the terms and conditions of employment that would have an impact on the nonparty firefighters, but that did not mean that they were denied any legally protected right (*Martin v. Wilks*: 2189).

Martin v. Wilks chiefly involved technical points on judgments and collateral attacks that distinguished it from the issues that occupy the center stage of most racial preference cases. Its consequence, however, was to make affirmative action orders and consent decrees unusually vulnerable to subsequent attack by disgruntled applicants or employees who perceive themselves as victims of "reverse discrimination." In support of the majority position, however, is the view that race-conscious affirmative action remedies are supposed to be temporary measures designed to overcome the results of prior discrimination. By allowing the propriety of race-conscious measures to be challenged again by those who were not parties to the original action, the opportunity to withdraw those measures, once they have fulfilled their purpose, is provided.

We have considered ten Supreme Court decisions that followed the landmark Title VII decisions in *Griggs* and *Albemarle*. It should be helpful now briefly to review those decisions and to analyze the trends they may reflect.

Table 9.1 reveals, on a case-by-case basis, the issues involved and the divisions into blocs that usually have characterized the court in these cases. That is even more vividly portrayed in summary version in Table 9.2.

Even recognizing the short tenure of Scalia and Kennedy, the summary in Table 9.2 clearly presents the sharp division that separates Rehnquist, O'Connor, White—and (in his day) Burger—from Blackmun, Brennan, and Marshall. If, in addition to their votes, we take account of the substance of their opinions, Scalia and Kennedy are securely in the conservative bloc as well. Only Powell can be counted as a swing vote. Stevens occasionally crosses over to vote against affirmative action claims, but his vote is no longer essential to the pro-individual-regarding equality majority.

Of course, it is not possible to conclude that it is strictly their commitments to individual-regarding or to group-regarding equality, respec-

Table 9.1 Summary of Justices' Votes in Racial Preference Cases

Against Minority Claimant	In Favor of Minority Claimant

1. *Washington v. Davis* (1976)—D.C. police officer screening tests

White (majority opinion)	Brennan
Burger	Marshall
Blackmun	
Powell	
Rehnquist	
Stevens	
Stewart	

2. *United Steelworkers v. Weber* (1979)—minority hiring target
(50 percent of openings) in collective bargaining agreement

Burger	Brennan (majority opinion)
Rehnquist	Blackmun
	Marshall
	Stewart
	White

(Powell and Stevens not participating)

3. *Firefighters Local 1784 v. Stotts* (1984)—seniority rules vis-à-vis
preservation of affirmative action gains in layoffs

White (majority opinion)	Blackmun
Burger	Brennan
O'Connor (replacing Stewart)	Marshall
Powell	
Rehnquist	
Stevens	

4. *Wygant v. Jackson Board of Education* (1986)—seniority rules vis-à-vis
protection of affirmative action gains in layoffs
(complex multipart decision)

Powell (announced the	Blackmun
judgment of the Court—	Brennan
no majority opinion)	Marshall
Burger	Stevens
O'Connor	
Rehnquist	
White	

5. *Local No. 28, Sheet Metal Workers v. EEOC* (1986)—Court ordered
race-conscious remedies vis-à-vis Title VII (complex multipart decision)

Burger	Brennan (majority opinion)
Rehnquist	Blackmun
White (but expresses agreement	Marshall
with certain aspects of the	Powell
majority opinion)	Stevens
O'Connor (but concurs in part)	

Table 9.1 (Continued)

Against Minority Claimant	In Favor of Minority Claimant

6. *Local No. 93, International Association of Firefighters v. City of Cleveland* (1986)—race-conscious remedies in consent decree

Burger	Brennan (majority opinion)
Rehnquist	Blackmun
White	Marshall
	O'Connor
	Powell
	Stevens

7. *United States v. Paradise* (1987)—promotion quota for "black corporals" in Alabama Department of Public Safety

O'Connor	Brennan (majority opinion)
Rehnquist (chief justice replacing Burger)	Blackmun
	Marshall
Scalia (replacing Rehnquist)	Powell
White	Stevens

8. *Watson v. Fort Worth Bank and Trust* (1988)—application of disparate impact analysis to subjective promotion criteria

Parts I, II-A, II-B, III

	O'Connor (majority opinion)
	Blackmun (separate opinion)
	Brennan (separate opinion)
	Marshall (separate opinion)
	Rehnquist
	Scalia
	White
	Stevens (concurs)

Parts II-C, II-D

O'Connor (plurality opinion)	Blackmun
Rehnquist	Brennan
Scalia	Marshall
White	
Kennedy not participating (replacing Powell)	

9. *Wards Cove Packing Co., Inc., v. Antonio* (1989)—burden of proof in Title VII disparate impact cases

White (majority opinion)	Blackmun
Kennedy	Brennan
O'Connor	Marshall
Rehnquist	Stevens
Scalia	

Table 9.1 (Continued)

Against Minority Claimant	In Favor of Minority Claimant

10. *Martin v. Wilks* (1989)—subsequent challenge to consent decree providing for promotion preferences for "black firefighters"

Rehnquist (majority opinion)	Blackmun
Kennedy	Brennan
O'Connor	Marshall
Scalia	Stevens
White	

Table 9.2 Summary of the Justices' Votes

	Against Minority Claimant		In Favor of Minority Claimant	
	%	n	%	n
Burger	100.0	6	0.0	0
Kennedy	100.0	2	0.0[a]	0
Rehnquist	95.0	9½	5.0	½
White	85.0	8½	15.0	1½
Scalia	70.0	3½	30.0	½
O'Connor	68.7	5½	31.3	1½
Stewart	50.0	1	50.0	1
Powell	50.0	3	50.0[a]	3
Stevens	22.3	2	77.7[a]	7
Blackmun	10.0	1	90.0	9
Brennan	0.0	0	100.0	10
Marshall	0.0	0	100.0	10

All of the votes counted as ½ here come from the *Watson* case, in which there was a unanimous holding that disparate impact analysis was applicable to subjective promotion criteria. Counting that part of the Watson case as a ½ vote in favor of the minority claimant may give it undue credit, but it is at least applied consistently in this summary.

[a]Indicates a justice then on the bench who did not participate in deciding a case.

tively, that separate the two blocs of justices, but it is clear from their opinions that their different perspectives on the proper understanding of equality are quite important.

Former Chief Justice Burger may now rue the day that he wrote for the majority and upheld mandatory busing and racial proportionality in the *Swann* case, although he might yet maintain that his formulation of a specific wrong–specific remedy for school integration was quite different from the race-conscious relief upheld by Blackmun, Brennan, and Marshall in employment cases.

The employment cases clearly are part of a process through which the court explicates its understanding of equality of opportunity in America. In a simple case, equality of opportunity would be achieved if each competitor had an equal chance of success. An example of what Rae calls *prospect-regarding equality of opportunity* exemplified in chapter 1 was a fairly run lottery in which each participant has one equal chance.

You will recall that the other version of equality of opportunity—which Rae calls *means-regarding equality of opportunity*—is achieved when competitors compete in an arena with fair rules and with the same equipment. This was exemplified in chapter 2 by a footrace or by a fairly conducted boxing match in which each boxer has gloves of the same weight. In this second version, the unequal abilities of the competitors are supposed to determine the outcome. Rae refers to this as a contest in which there are "legitimately unequal prospects of success" (Rae, 1981: 64 et seq.).

Ordinarily we think only of the second version, that is, of means-regarding equality of opportunity, in employment situations. This represents a way of arguing for "meritocracy" rather than for selection based on nepotism or race or sex, none of which ordinarily would have anything to do with job-related criteria.

Means-regarding equality of opportunity, however, usually involves only marginal equality, which is to say that the barriers of race may be removed in employment, while leaving other obstacles (socioeconomic background or education) in place. To the extent that such obstacles have been caused (altogether or in part) by past racial discrimination, then that discrimination continues to contribute to ill-distributed outcomes even when means-regarding equality of opportunity is apparently achieved by the removal of explicit racial barriers (Rae, 1981: 74; Fishkin, 1983). In fact, even if we are able to achieve perfect means-regarding equality by the removal of all de jure or de facto racial barriers, we will still have with us the effects of past discrimination. The present achievement of means-regarding equality will do nothing to compensate for the effects of past discrimination. A group that has been the subject of past discrimination must in the present achieve results at a rate absolutely greater than a previously advantaged group in order to lessen the gap between the groups. (Dorn, 1979: 120). For African-Americans to achieve the same results as whites will thus not lessen "black-white" differences, although it will keep those differences from becoming even greater. The answer is simple, though, as we have seen, controversial:

What this suggests is that lessening the "black/white" employment differential requires more than merely reducing overall unemployment and ensuring equal opportunity. Rather it requires
hiring blacks at a faster rate than whites during periods of rapid
growth, and laying them off at a slower rate during periods of
economic slowdown. This is exactly the opposite of past and current practices. As a result of bias and of seniority systems that tend
to perpetuate the effects of past discrimination, blacks continue to
suffer disproportionately during periods of layoff and are the last to
benefit from growth. (Dorn, 1979: 122–23)

Dorn's analysis leads to the conclusion that group-regarding equality
is a necessity, at least in the short run, if our object is to move toward
overall equality of employment between "blacks and whites" as groups.

The conflict between individual and group equality that we saw vividly in *Stotts* and several other employment cases is thus the precise
focus of controversy. Blackmun, Brennan, and Marshall were willing to
accept the cost of race-conscious relief to achieve the vision of racial justice that group-regarding equality entails. These three justices
were also willing to accept the use of a domain of allocation of any
employer to compensate for discrimination in the larger society. Rehnquist, O'Connor, White, and probably Scalia, and Kennedy, were not.

Fallon and Weiler would confine group-regarding race-conscious relief to those instances of "group-based subordination" that have been
"aided and abetted by government and by law." They would accept it
where historic discrimination has "had an enduring impact, measurable
now in economic and social disparities between racial groups." They
would accept it where historic discrimination has produced a group
identity—the identity of being "black" in the United States, for example.
With the convergence of these three elements, they hold that a "Model
of Social Justice" warrants "affirmative discrimination" (Fallon and
Weiler, 1985: 35 et seq.). Blackmun, Brennan, and Marshall no doubt
would agree.

We have come a long way from *Brown v. Board* in 1954. Whether one
looks at *Swann* and its denouement in the *Milliken* case, or at *Bakke* and
its rejection of explicit racial quotas, or at the competing understandings of equality of opportunity represented by the employment cases, it
is clear that casual citizen observers of *Brown v. Board,* if transported
from 1954 to 1991, might be mystified by what they would see. Only
among a small community of scholars, lawyers, and judges is there any
in-depth understanding of the competing claims of individual-regarding

and group-regarding equality. Yet issues involving racism, neighborhood schools, busing, quotas, equality of opportunity, affirmative action, or reverse discrimination (pick whichever value-laden label you prefer) have contributed considerable heat and strife to American political life in the past thirty-five years. Such emotive contributions are likely to continue. In 1990 the Democratic-controlled Congress passed a civil rights bill whose purpose it was to overrule the majority in both *Wards Cove* and *Martin v. Wilks*. President Bush vetoed the bill, expressing his belief that it would make employers resort to "quotas" to avoid employment discrimination suits. The Senate failed by a single vote to override his veto. The struggle continued in 1991 with renewed efforts of Democrats to enact a remedial civil rights act against the consistent opposition of the Bush administration. Moderate Republican Senator Danforth of Missouri offered a compromise that would have prohibited the use of credential requirements (a high school diploma, for example) unless it could be shown that the credential bore a "manifest relationship to the employment in question" (*Congressional Quarterly Weekly Report,* June 29, 1991: 1760). Even that compromise was rejected by President Bush, this time on the grounds that such a prohibition of educational credentials would detract from his administration's commitment to education (*Congressional Quarterly Weekly Report,* August 3, 1991: 2170).

Eventually other events made it impossible for President Bush to withhold his consent to compromise civil rights legislation. The embarrassment resulting from the hearings on the nomination of Clarence Thomas coupled with the rising visibility of David Duke as a Republican candidate, first for governor of Louisiana, then for the Republican nomination for the presidency, created the prospect of a president and a party publicly identified as being hostile to civil rights both of women and of African-Americans. This led Bush in late October 1991 to endorse a compromise measure that varied little in substance from the versions he previously had threatened to veto. On November 21, 1991, President Bush signed the Civil Rights Act of 1991. It had the effect of overturning, or at least seriously restricting, the Supreme Court's anti-affirmative action decisions of 1989.

10

EQUAL PROTECTION AND
SEX DISCRIMINATION

Although the Union Law College in Chicago, Illinois conferred its first law degree upon a woman in 1870,[1] the Illinois state court was not nearly so progressive. In August of 1870, Myra Bradwell passed the bar examination but was denied admission to the practice of law based solely on her sex by the state Supreme Court. She appealed this decision to the U.S. Supreme Court. There the Justices concluded that Illinois possessed the sole right to set standards for admission to practice in its state courts independent of federal supervision. Expanding on the majority opinion, Justice Bradley went so far as to remark that "proper timidity and delicacy . . . evidently unfits [women] for many of the occupations of civil life."
—McGlen and O'Connor, *Women's Rights*

Myra Bradwell's was the first case that challenged a sex-based distinction under the Fourteenth Amendment. That amendment had been ratified only four years earlier, and the U.S. Supreme Court's opinion in Myra Bradwell's case was delivered only one day after the Court's decision in the *Slaughter-House Cases,* the first judicial interpretation of the Fourteenth Amendment (see chapter 4).

Admission to the practice of law, the Court held in *Bradwell v. Illinois,* is not one of the privileges or immunities belonging to citizens of the United States. In his opinion in *Bradwell,* Justice Miller referred to the *Slaughter-House* decision for a discussion of those privileges or immunities and for the first discussion of the meaning of equal protection. The *Slaughter-House* opinion said only, "We doubt very much whether any action of a state not directed by way of discrimination against the negroes as a class, or on account of their race, will ever be held to come within the purview of this provision" (*Slaughter-House Cases*: 407).

It was only Justice Bradley who went beyond the outright rejection of Myra Bradwell's petition to comment on the fitness of women for the practice of law: "Man is, or should be, woman's protector and defender. The natural and proper timidity and delicacy which belongs to the female sex evidently unfits it for many of the occupations of civil life. . . .

The paramount destiny and mission of woman are to fulfill the noble and benign offices of wife and mother. This is the law of the Creator" (*Bradwell v. Illinois*: 446).

During the exchange that took place between Thaddeus Stevens and Congressman Hale of New York during the 1866 debates on the wording of the Fourteenth Amendment, Stevens hastily contradicted the suggestion by Hale that the Equal Protection Clause might require that married women and single women be treated alike, much less that women might be treated as the equals of men (see chapter 3). So at least one key proponent of the Fourteenth Amendment clearly did not have women in mind for equal protection. Justice Bradley's frank assertion of male dominance and of female submission seven years later probably fairly represented the predominant male views of that time.[2]

However, the women who had been among the leaders of the abolitionist movement had already recognized their kinship in oppression with the slaves they were working to free. The first Women's Rights Convention was held in Seneca Falls, New York, in 1848, yet the American Anti-Slavery Association was unwilling in 1866 to unite the causes of slaves and women. Thereafter, antislavery women joined with men who supported their cause to form the American Equal Rights Association, whose purpose was universal suffrage for "blacks and women." Even that association eventually separated the interests of African-Americans and women to support ratification of the Fourteenth Amendment. Thus it was in 1869, one year after the ratification of the Fourteenth Amendment, that Elizabeth Cady Stanton and Susan B. Anthony founded the National Woman Suffrage Association (McGlen and O'Connor, 1983: 45–46).

Actually, there were demands for women's suffrage as far back as 1648, and women were sometimes accepted as qualified voters in the colonies and in the fledgling American states during the sixteenth and seventeenth centuries. Women's voting largely came to an end, however, in the early part of the nineteenth century (Goldstein, 1988: 73–74). The suffrage movement that was formed in 1869 was thus a revival rather than a new idea.

Virginia Minor, president of the Missouri Woman Suffrage Association, was one of 149 suffragists who sought to vote in the presidential election of 1872. Minor was refused registration by the Saint Louis voting registrar, and her attorney husband brought suit on her behalf (Goldstein, 1988: 76). Minor's case came before the Supreme Court in 1875. Chief Justice Waite had no difficulty in ruling that women were indeed citizens, but he held that the privileges or immunities of citizenship did not necessarily include the right to vote. Whether women were to be accorded the right to vote was held to be a matter for the states (*Minor v. Happersett*). This decision, along with *Bradwell v. Illinois* and the narrow interpretation of the Fourteenth Amendment in the *Slaughter-House Cases,* exhausted the potential of the privileges or immunities clause. The Equal Protection Clause yet seemed to be a possibility, but its potential was not to be realized for another one hundred years.

The National Woman Suffrage Association had at its beginning sought full equality for women, but after 1875 it, and other women's organizations, experienced a relative decline. Nonetheless, it continued to lobby the Congress for the right to vote, while a sister organization, the American Woman Suffrage Association, lobbied the states for that right. When the two women's organizations merged in 1893 to create the National American Woman Suffrage Association, the movement focused almost exclusively on the national suffrage amendment (McGlen and O'Connor, 1983: 16 et seq.; Goldstein, 1988: 83 et seq.).

Even after the ratification of the Nineteenth Amendment had offered women the prospect of greater political influence, equal protection of women through the Fourteenth Amendment was still a faint hope. In *Muller v. Oregon* in 1909, Justice Brewer conceded the power to the states to treat women differently than men by protecting women through maximum work hours legislation because:

History discloses the fact that woman has always been dependent upon man. He established his control at the outset by superior physical strength, and this control in various forms, with diminishing intensity, has continued to the present. . . . Education was long denied her, and while now the doors of the schoolroom are opened and her opportunities for acquiring knowledge are great, yet even with that and the consequent increase of capacity for business affairs it is still true that in the struggle for subsistence she is not an equal contributor with her brother. (*Muller v. Oregon*: 326–27)

The consequence of woman's vulnerability was that it was deemed appropriate to place women in a separate class from men and to provide for their protection, even if that protection was not seen as necessary for men. Three years after *Muller v. Oregon,* Justice Holmes confirmed that a state might prefer women to men in its policies because "the Fourteenth Amendment does not interfere by creating a fictitious equality when there is a real difference" (*Quong Wing v. Kirkendall,* 1912: 193).

The key difficulty in these early cases is that the then-exclusive fraternity of male judges saw the different treatment of men and women, and especially the protection of women, as natural and unexceptionable. Sex-based classifications were thus subjected only to minimal review. For most purposes, such classifications were presumed valid, and anyone who attacked them had the burden of showing that they were arbitrary and utterly without any reasonable basis in fact.

The presumed validity of sex-based classifications continued in some instances into the 1960s. The most frequently cited recent examples of such sexist U.S. Supreme Court decisions are from 1948 and 1961. In *Goesaert v. Cleary,* the 1948 decision, the Supreme Court sustained a Michigan law that prohibited women from serving as barmaids unless they were the wives or daughters of the bar owner. Justice Frankfurter deferred to the judgment of the Michigan legislature, writing that the state may take "preventive measures" against the "moral and social problems" that might result from unsupervised women working as barmaids (*Goesaert v. Cleary:* 200). To be sure, Frankfurter's deference to legislative decision-making was consistent with his avowed judicial philosophy, but even in that light, his lack of sensitivity to the issue of sexual equality was strident.

Hoyt v. Florida (1961) was another in a series of decisions holding that women could be excluded from service on juries, or allowed to serve, but on different conditions than applied to men. The earliest suggestion about the propriety of excluding women came from an 1880 case that held that "blacks" could not be excluded from jury service by law (*Strauder v. West Virginia*). The special treatment of women for jury duty was affirmed in *Fay v. New York* in 1947 and upheld again in *Hoyt* in 1961. This statement is the clearest evidence of Justice Harlan's "progress" in *Hoyt* relative to Justice Bradley's view of women in *Bradwell v. Illinois*:

Despite the enlightened emancipation of women from the restrictions and protections of bygone years, and their entry into many parts of community life formerly considered to be reserved to men, woman is still regarded as the center of home and family life. We cannot say that it is constitutionally impermissible for a State, acting in pursuit of the general welfare, to conclude that a woman should be relieved from the civic duty of jury service unless she herself determines that such service is consistent with her own special responsibilities. (*Hoyt v. Florida*: 162)

The Supreme Court took no exception to the exclusion of women from service on state grand juries in *Alexander v. Louisiana* in 1972, and it was not until *Taylor v. Louisiana* in 1975 that the Court held women to approximately the same standard of jury duty as men. It was only in 1971 that the Supreme Court began to take equality between men and women somewhat more seriously. Even then, sex-based distinctions were not treated the same as racial distinctions.[3]

HEIGHTENED SCRUTINY OF SEX-BASED CLASSIFICATIONS

An amendment to the U.S. Constitution, which would have established equal rights for women, was first proposed by the National Woman's party in 1923.[4] This Equal Rights Amendment (ERA) was introduced in each session of Congress between 1923 and 1971, but it was not until the early 1970s, with the renewal of the women's movement, that it was considered seriously. It was eventually proposed to the states for ratification in 1972. By January 1973, twenty-eight states had ratified the amendment (McGlen and O'Connor, 1983: 366 et seq.). The popular momentum that propelled the ERA was no doubt also responsible for renewed litigation seeking equal rights for women.

Leslie Goldstein, the author/editor of one of the principal casebooks on the rights of women, has suggested that the concept of women's rights has three different usages. The first is the idea that women ought to be treated as the equals of men. This usage is consistent with individual-regarding equality, in which all human beings regardless of sex are treated as a single category. The second meaning refers to the right to be favored or "protected" by law for some reason. When a definable group, in this case women, is specially protected, this is a form of segmental equality. In the instance of affirmative action programs for women, this usage may also be broadly consistent with group- or bloc-regarding equality, just as we have seen in the instance of race-conscious affirmative action. The third meaning is one that is applicable to sex-based distinctions, but not to racial ones. It involves the recognition of the real biological differences between men and women. When such differences are relevant, as in instances of birth control or abortion, pregnancy, and childbearing, then it may be appropriate to recognize them in public policies (Goldstein, 1988: xii).

The first significant case to reach the U.S. Supreme Court arising under a renewed examination of sex-based distinctions was *Reed v. Reed,* decided by the court in 1971. Chief Justice Burger wrote for a unanimous court in the *Reed* case. The case involved a minor who had died in Idaho without a will. His adoptive parents, who had separated prior to his death, each sought appointment as administrator of their son's estate. Idaho law provided that whenever two members of the same entitlement class (here the mother and father) are considered for appointment as the administrator of an estate, "males must be preferred to females." The Idaho judge made no attempt to determine the relative competencies of the parents but considered himself bound by the requirement that he give preference to the male. The Idaho Supreme Court sustained the mandatory preference for males against a challenge brought by Sally Reed, the boy's mother, under the Equal Protection Clause of the Fourteenth Amendment.

The U.S. Supreme Court applied the rational purpose test, but for the first time found the preference established by Idaho law to be "arbitrary." A classification, Chief Justice Burger wrote, "must be reasonable, not arbitrary, and must rest on some ground or difference having a fair and substantial relation to the object of the legislation, so that all persons similarly circumstanced shall be treated alike" (*Reed v. Reed*: 254). The purpose cited by the state in support of the preference was that of reducing the workload of probate courts by eliminating one source of conflict, but the Supreme Court held that the preference did not advance that purpose in a manner consistent with the requirement of equal protection. The mandatory preference to members of one sex over the other was instead an "arbitrary legislative choice" (*Reed v. Reed*: 254). Chief Justice Burger's opinion is terse, and nowhere does it reflect a new perspective or standard of review of sex-based distinctions. The result, however, was quite different from the presumptive validity reflected in the 1948 *Goesaert* case (allowing restrictions on women serving as barmaids) or in the 1961 *Hoyt* case (allowing states to excuse women from jury service on different grounds than men).

A year later the Supreme Court was no longer unanimous concerning a sex-based distinction. In the 1972 opinion in *Stanley v. Illinois,* Justice White wrote for the court, and Chief Justice Burger joined in Justice Blackmun's dissent. The case involved a provision of Illinois law by which the children of unwed fathers become wards of the state on the death of their mother.

Peter Stanley had lived with Joan Stanley "intermittently" for eighteen years, and they had three children together. Upon the death of Joan, the children were taken from Peter and placed with court-appointed guardians. The question before the court was whether "a presumption that distinguishes and burdens all unwed fathers [is] constitutionally repugnant?" (*Stanley v. Illinois*: 1211). That question was much the same as the presumption in favor of males which the court rejected in *Reed*.

It was held to be a denial of equal protection to deny unwed father Peter Stanley a hearing on his fitness as a parent, while allowing all other parents a fitness hearing. Justice White wrote:

> Procedure by presumption is always cheaper and easier than individualized determination. But when, as here, the procedure forecloses the determinative issues of competence and care, when it explicitly disdains present realities in deference to past formalities, it needlessly risks running roughshod over the important interests of both parent and child. It therefore cannot stand. (*Stanley v. Illinois*: 1215)

If we generalize from Justice White's words, then our facile traditional stereotypes about the supposed differences in the inherent nature and qualities of both men and women, as well as their attributed social roles, must be scrutinized from the perspective of equal protection.

The development of the Supreme Court's understanding of what might constitute sex-based discrimination was by then proceeding at a quick pace. In 1973 in *Frontiero v. Richardson,* the Supreme Court reached what today may still be the height of its skepticism about the use of sex-based distinctions. Justice Brennan wrote for a four-member plurality in *Frontiero.* Only Justice Rehnquist dissented, but Burger, Blackmun, Powell, and Stewart, who agreed with Brennan on the outcome, did not agree with Brennan's analysis. A fifth vote would have rendered sex-based distinctions suspect and subject to about the same strict scrutiny that was then applied to racial distinctions.

Frontiero involved a female member of the U.S. Air Force who sought allowances for her "dependent" husband. Benefits would automatically have been granted for the wife of a male serviceman, but Sharron Frontiero was required by statute to demonstrate that her husband was in fact dependent on her for more than one-half of his support. Her objections were twofold: (1) she challenged the procedure by which she was required to demonstrate her husband's dependency, while a serviceman husband would not be required to demonstrate the dependency of his wife; and (2) she and her husband would be entitled to benefits only if he was dependent for more than one-half of his support, while there was no such limitation for a wife.

At the federal trial level, a three-judge federal court "surmised" that Congress could reasonably have concluded that men are so pervasively the breadwinners in our society and women so commonly dependent on their husbands that it would make administrative sense to indulge a presumption of dependency when male servicemen were involved.[5]

Brennan and the three justices who joined his opinion held that sex-based classifications are "inherently suspect and must therefore be subjected to close judicial scrutiny" (*Frontiero v. Richardson*: 1768). They found "implicit support" for that position in *Reed v. Reed,* which they saw as a departure from the traditional rational-basis analysis of sex-based distinctions: "There can be no doubt that our Nation has had a long and unfortunate history of sex discrimination. Traditionally, such discrimination was rationalized by an attitude of 'romantic paternalism' which, in practical effect, put women not on a pedestal, but in a cage" (*Frontiero v. Richardson*: 1769).

To confirm that observation, Brennan then cited with disapproval the words of Justice Bradley in *Bradwell v. Illinois* that we reviewed at the outset of this chapter. It seemed especially important to Brennan that sex, like race or national origin, is an "immutable characteristic determined solely by the accident of birth" (*Frontiero v. Richardson*: 1770). He also saw sex as being different than "nonsuspect statuses such as intelligence or physical disability" because sex frequently "bears no relationship to ability to perform or to contribute to society" (*Frontiero v. Richardson*: 1770).

According to Brennan the only purpose served by the presumption was "administrative convenience," but the government had offered no evidence to satisfy the requirements of strict scrutiny that it was in fact less expensive for the government to indulge the presumption that all wives were dependent on their military husbands than it would be to require proof of that dependence. Instead, there was substantial evidence in the record that many wives would be unable to demonstrate their dependency.

Justice Stewart simply concurred with the outcome without giving his reasons, but Powell, joined by Burger and Blackmun, found it unnecessary to characterize sex as a suspect classification. He thought

the rule in *Reed v. Reed* against procedure by presumption was sufficient. Moreover, he noted that the Equal Rights Amendment, then before the states for ratification, would, if ratified, make the characterization of sex as a suspect classification moot.

The next sex discrimination case was an anomaly relative to *Reed* and
Frontiero. Kahn v. Shevin (1974) involved a $500 Florida property tax
exemption for widows.[6] Kahn, a widower, applied for an exemption but
was denied because he was a male. The tax exemption was eventually
upheld by the Florida Supreme Court. The opinion of the U.S. Supreme
Court was written by Justice Douglas. Despite the fact that he had been
among the four justices who would have held sex to be a suspect classification in *Frontiero,* he now found that the State of Florida had a fair
and reasonable basis for determining that the "financial difficulties confronting the lone woman in Florida or in any other State exceed those
facing a man" (*Kahn v. Shevin*: 1736).

Florida's determination was not just for administrative convenience;
it recognized financial inequity and sought to compensate for it—at
least so Justice Douglas found. The problem with his position is that
just as in *Reed* and *Frontiero,* the proffered distinction between men and
women is not universally valid, and it *may* be based once again on a
presumption of dependence resulting from a stigmatizing stereotype
of women. Conversely, it *may* be an example of an effort to confer
a benefit on women to compensate for manifest economic disadvantage. Whether it is perceived as one or the other is a matter of profound
difference.

In reviewing the sex discrimination cases from this period, Judith
Baer has attempted to distinguish between "invidious and benign" policies. This distinction represents a special problem with policies directed toward women, for some policies that were planned and implemented by men as benign have actually proved to be invidious. This
was often the case with the sort of restrictive or "protective legislation"
that was designed to remove women from the workplace and keep them
in the home to safeguard the "integrity" of the family. In seeking an
acceptable justification for compensatory affirmative action programs
that would actually benefit women, she sought to distinguish between
those that actually compensate for "prejudice and oppression" and
those that may harm rather than help. A third outcome represented her
"discard" category, reserved for those policies that may appear to have
a benign purpose but accomplish virtually nothing. Baer put *Kahn v.
Shevin,* with its annual tax benefit of $15, in this category.

Cleveland Board of Education v. LaFleur (1974) presented an easier issue, for it involved a clear disadvantage that could only be applied to women. The existence of real physiological differences between men and women makes sex discrimination different from racial discrimination. Women have an inescapable monopoly over pregnancy and childbirth, while differences in race confer no equivalent monopoly. Nonetheless, the Supreme Court had to decide in *LaFleur* whether a school board's policy toward pregnancy was appropriate. The Cleveland school board required pregnant teachers to take an unpaid leave five months prior to expected childbirth and not to return until the semester that began after their baby was three months old. The justification for the policy was to ensure "continuity of instruction" and to keep physically incapacitated teachers out of the classroom.

Justice Stewart wrote for the court over the dissent of Justice Rehnquist. He found the cutoff dates a violation of due process because they were arbitrary and had no "rational relationship to the valid state interest of preserving continuity of instruction" (*Cleveland Board of Education v. LaFleur*: 798). As in *Reed* and *Stanley*, a majority of the court continued to reject irrebuttable presumptions based on sex, but here on grounds of due process. The ability to work while pregnant was seen as an individual matter, to which a single presumptive cutoff date was ill suited. Hence, the Cleveland school board's policy was held to be arbitrary and irrational.

In dissent, Rehnquist was provoked by Stewart's use of Fourteenth Amendment due process, rather than sex discrimination, to strike down the policy of the Cleveland board. He suggested that many statutes draw lines with a fixed date or age as the active rule. He saw no basis for holding the particular line drawn by the Cleveland school board invalid. The important difference between the majority's and Rehnquist's perspective is that the majority position required the assessment of actual people and conditions (just as it did in *Reed* and *Stanley*), while Rehnquist's position would have allowed a cutoff to be applied to all pregnant women regardless of their particular condition.

We should note that a similar provision of Utah law, by which women were presumed to be incapacitated from work for purposes of unemployment compensation for a period beginning twelve weeks prior to birth and continuing for six weeks after birth, was also held unconstitutional in *Turner v. Department of Employment Security* in 1975. The per curiam opinion noted that such presumptions must yield to "more individualized means" of determination when "basic human liberties are at stake" (*Turner v. Department of Employment Security*: 251).

In the 1974 case of *Geduldig v. Aiello*, we encounter yet another policy that seems to rest on a real physiological difference between men and women. *Geduldig* involved a California state disability insurance program that did not cover pregnancy. Since only women can get pregnant, this seems an obvious example of sex-based discrimination, that is, unless the state could offer some reasonable justification for their exclusion. Nonetheless, Stewart's opinion found an interesting way out: "There is no risk from which men are protected and women are not. Likewise, there is no risk from which women are protected and men are not" (*Geduldig v. Aiello*: 2492). In other words, the two relevant classes here were pregnant women and nonpregnant persons (male and female). Hence there was no sex discrimination.

Brennan was not persuaded. He wrote in dissent that while pregnancy was excluded, men were fully covered for treatments or conditions that primarily or exclusively apply to them (prostate surgery, circumcision, hemophilia, and gout) (*Geduldig v. Aiello*: 2494). Stewart's acceptance of the California exclusion was thus seen as a retreat from the heightened scrutiny of sex-based distinctions applied by the court in *Reed, Frontiero,* and subsequent cases.

Schlesinger v. Ballard (1975) involved an "up or out" rule for male U.S. Navy officers after nine years of active service. For female naval officers the "up or out" rule applied only after thirteen years service. Judith Baer assigned *Schlesinger* to her "discard category" (like *Kahn v. Shevin* above), because the benefit it appeared to offer women was illusory. But in *Schlesinger* Justice Stewart upheld the navy's policy because women deserved more time than men, since their exclusion from sea, combat, or aircraft duty made it more difficult for women to achieve promotion. In dissent, however, Brennan suggested that exclusions from these forms of duty were also questionable restrictions on the opportunities open to female officers. Such an illusory benefit as additional years of service should not survive close judicial scrutiny. Instead female officers were, in Brennan's view, systematically disadvantaged by navy policy.

In *Weinberger v. Wiesenfeld* (1975) Stephen Wiesenfeld challenged the provision of Social Security survivor benefits for widows and minor children, while widowers received survivor benefits for their children but not for themselves. Justice Brennan also found this policy to contain a number of problems. It represented stereotypical generalizations about men and women; as in *Frontiero,* men were seen as providers and women as their dependents. This "denigrated" the work of women who contribute significantly to their families' support. Moreover, the purpose of enabling "the widow to remain at home and care for the chil-

dren" of the marriage ignored the possibility that it was "no less important for a child to be cared for by its sole surviving parent when that
parent is male rather than female" (*Weinberger v. Wiesenfeld*: 1235). Finally, the policy ignored the fact that working women pay Social Security taxes just as males, but their surviving spouses would receive no
benefits. As Baer noticed, what were offered as benefits turned out to
be burdens (Baer, 1983: 144). It was evident that sexual stereotypes
were finally seriously questioned by the Supreme Court.[7]

Only a month later, Justice Blackmun appeared to be as offended by
sexual stereotypes as Brennan had been in the *Wiesenfeld* case. His
opinion in *Stanton v. Stanton* set aside a Utah statute that, in cases
concerning child support, set the age for majority for males at twenty-
one, while the age for women was eighteen. This distinction as to age of
majority, he held, could not pass any equal protection test, "compelling
state interest or rational basis, or something in between" (*Stanton v.
Stanton*: 1379). Utah's justification of the difference was that males
needed to complete their education, while women did not.[8] The Utah
Supreme Court had observed, "It is the man's primary responsibility to
provide a home and that it is salutary for him to have education and
training before he assumes that responsibility" (*Stanton v. Stanton*:
1378). Women, on the other hand, mature earlier and tend to marry
earlier than males, Utah argued. Blackmun aggressively attacked this
as a stereotype:

> No longer is the female destined solely for the home and the rear-
> ing of the family, and only the male for the marketplace and the
> world of ideas. . . . Women's activities and responsibilities are in-
> creasing and expanding. Coeducation is a fact, not a rarity. The
> presence of women in business, in the professions, in government,
> and, indeed, in all walks of life where education is a desirable, if not
> always a necessary, antecedent is apparent and a proper subject of
> judicial notices. (*Stanton v. Stanton*: 1378)

Only Justice Rehnquist dissented. The court had come a long way from
its cavalier rejection of Myra Bradwell's petition in 1873, and it clearly
confirmed its willingness to engage in heightened scrutiny of sex-based
distinctions in 1976 in *Craig v. Boren.*

Craig v. Boren arose from a provision of Oklahoma law that made it a
crime to sell 3.2 percent beer to males under the age of twenty-one or to
females under the age of eighteen. Following in the tradition of *Reed v.
Reed,* the majority opinion by Justice Brennan concluded that "classifi-

cations by gender must serve important governmental objectives and must be substantially related to the achievement of those objectives" (*Craig v. Boren*: 457). To meet those requirements, the state offered statistical evidence to show that the incidence of alcohol-related automobile accidents was higher for males than for females. Brennan was unmoved. "Even were this statistical evidence accepted as accurate," he wrote, "it nevertheless offers only a weak answer to the equal protection questions presented here." The DWI arrest rate for males was 2 percent, while the rate for females was 0.18 percent (*Craig v. Boren*: 459). Even while this difference might not be trivial in the statistical sense, Brennan found that it could not form the basis for using the gender line as a classifying device. "Archaic and overbroad generalizations," "outdated misconceptions," "loose-fitting characterizations," and now statistics with an "unduly tenuous fit" simply cannot survive the sort of heightened scrutiny required by the majority opinion in *Craig v. Boren*.

In a concurring opinion in *Craig v. Boren,* Justice Powell was concerned about the appropriate standard for reviewing gender-based distinctions. Brennan's opinion, he wrote, would be viewed as creating a "middle-tier" approach. While he disliked the notion of three tiers of equal protection analysis, Powell did concede that the relatively deferential "rational basis" standard of review "takes on a sharper focus" when gender-based classifications are involved. Stevens concurred separately and argued that a single standard of review ought to be applied, one in which the offensiveness or objectionable character of the gender-based classification is weighed against the state's justification for its use. He believed gender-based distinctions to be objectionable, at a minimum, because they were based on an accident of birth. Only Burger and Rehnquist held to the line that only the "rational basis" test need be applied. And under that standard they would have held the Oklahoma law constitutional.

Having brought gender-based distinctions under "heightened scrutiny," it is interesting to observe a gender-based distinction that successfully survived such scrutiny only a year later. Judith Baer classes *Califano v. Webster* (1977) as an apt example of *present* benign discrimination, designed to compensate women for *past* economic discrimination (Baer, 1983: 148). In *Califano* a male recipient of Social Security benefits challenged the constitutionality of a provision that allowed female Social Security applicants to exclude more low-earning years in computing benefits than were allowed to male applicants. The per curiam opinion of the Supreme Court noted that improving the economic imbalance between men and women caused by "the long history of discrimination has been recognized as an important governmental objective" (*Califano v. Webster.* 1194). A statute that operates to compensate women for past economic discrimination is not the accidental by-product of archaic views of women. It is not based on a stereotypical notion of the dependency of women on men but on the reality of the traditionally lower wages and salaries paid to women. Like *Bakke,* it is an example of bloc- or group-regarding equality. Benign discrimination in favor of women does not stigmatize males, even though they do not receive the same benefit. Such statutory provisions for compensatory measures, and for equal employment opportunity of female workers, have been relatively recent developments. The Supreme Court's interpretation of federal statutes on sex discrimination has at its core much the same sort of conceptualization as that in racial equal protection cases.

With *Orr v. Orr* (1979), we return to terrain very much like that in *Reed v. Reed* in 1971. *Orr v. Orr* involved a provision of Alabama law that husbands, but not wives, may be required to pay alimony upon divorce. The only justifications that Alabama could offer were that the wife usually continues to be dependent on the husband or to treat sex as a "proxy for need." Since a divorce case requires a hearing at which the financial position of both husband and wife can readily be determined, there is no need for such a proxy. The unconstitutionality of the provision was thus clearly covered by the *Reed* precedent.

Califano v. Westcott (1979) involved the federal Aid to Families with Dependent Children, Unemployed Father (AFDC-UF) program. An amendment enacted in 1968 provided welfare benefits for families with an unemployed father, but none when the mother was unemployed. Twenty-six states participated in this program of federal assistance, which was separate from the general AFDC program. The Westcotts were a family in which the mother had been the wage earner. The father could not qualify for benefits because he had not been previously employed for a period of time sufficient to qualify. The mother, however, was unemployed and had the employment record to qualify for benefits. The Court unanimously held this program to be discriminatory.

Parham v. Hughes (1979) involved a Georgia statute under which the mother of an illegitimate child could sue for the wrongful death of that child. A father who had legitimated a child could also sue, but only if there were no mother, while a father who had not legitimated a child could not sue for its wrongful death. This was not the first case to raise an equal protection issue involving the rights of the father of an illegitite child. The Court's 1972 decision in *Stanley v. Illinois* required that an unwed father be granted a hearing on his fitness as a guardian, rather then being presumed to be unfit. Only a year before the *Parham* decision, Justice Marshall had written a unanimous opinion in *Quilloin v. Walcott* (1978) holding that Georgia could require a father to legitimate an illegitimate child before he could claim the right to void an adoption. Now in *Parham v. Hughes,* Justice Stewart, writing for a four-member plurality, concluded that the Georgia wrongful death statute did not discriminate against the father because he was a male, but because the mothers and fathers of illegitimate children are in fact not similarly situated. Under Georgia law, only a father can legitimate a child by voluntary unilateral action. The Georgia wrongful death statute simply reflects that reality and protects the rights of those who have elected to legitimate their children.

Powell concurred separately, chiefly because Georgia had provided an illegitimate father a convenient mechanism for overcoming his disability by acknowledging his child. White, in a dissent for himself, Blackmun, Brennan, and Marshall, wrote that the "plain facts of the matter are that the statute . . . discriminates between unmarried mothers and unmarried fathers" (*Parham v. Hughes*: 1751). He found it an "incredible presumption that fathers (but not mothers) of illegitimate children suffer no injury when they lose their children" (*Parham v. Hughes*: 1754).

Parham was decided on April 24, 1979. *Caban v. Mohammed* was decided on the same day. While Stewart wrote the plurality opinion for himself, Stevens, Burger, and Rehnquist in *Parham,* the same four joined in Stevens's dissent in *Caban*. Powell provided the fifth vote for the majority in *Caban* and wrote the majority opinion. These divisions are important because the issues in the two cases have much in common.

The New York statute at issue in *Caban* permitted an unwed mother, but not an unwed father, to block the adoption of a child by simply withholding consent. Powell's opinion in *Caban* held the New York statute to contain an unconstitutionally broad overgeneralization:

The effect of New York's classification is to discriminate against unwed fathers even when their identity is known and they have manifested a significant paternal interest in the child. . . . We conclude that this undifferentiated distinction between unwed mothers and unwed fathers . . . does not bear a substantial relationship to the State's asserted interests. (*Caban v. Mohammed*: 1769)

Stewart's dissent turns on the interest asserted by the state of protecting the child's status by requiring only the consent of the mother to adoption. When the father had custody, his consent was required as well. Mostly, Stewart was convinced that unwed mothers and fathers are not similarly situated with respect to their children. The State of New York, he wrote, gives the mother custody of her illegitimate children, "precisely because it is she who bears the child and because the vast majority of unwed fathers have been unknown, unavailable or simply uninterested" (*Caban v. Mohammed*: 1771).[9]

Sometimes procedural points, rather than substantive principles, determine the outcome of cases. The question of who should have the burden of proving a claim is an important example of that, as we have seen previously in instances of racial discrimination. One case from 1979 raised important issues regarding the burden of proof assumed by those who would bring sex discrimination cases. *Personnel Administrator of Massachusetts v. Feeney* (1979), challenged the Massachusetts civil service veterans' preference on the grounds that it discriminated against women.

The difficulty in *Feeney* was that the preference statute was facially neutral, meaning that it made no reference to sex, and in itself manifested no sex-based distinction. Did the preference have a discriminatory result or effect? It did in practice because veterans were overwhelmingly males. Nevertheless, the Court in *Feeney* was unanimous in holding that an intent to discriminate must be shown when a statute is facially neutral but has a sexually disparate result. The majority of seven, joining in an opinion by Justice Stewart, placed the burden of proving discriminatory intent on the plaintiff and found no such intent. Marshall and Brennan in dissent placed the burden of proof on Massachusetts and thus found discriminatory intent.

The resolution of discrimination claims by placing a heavy burden of proof on those who allege such discrimination has offered a way for the federal courts in the 1980s to reject the claims without having to repudiate entirely substantive discrimination precedents from the 1970s. We shall see even more evidence of that outcome in the cases from the late 1980s at the end of this chapter.

Kirchberg v. Feenstra (1981), however, involved such an obvious instance of sexual stereotyping that the Supreme Court unanimously rejected it. In *Kirchberg,* a Louisiana statute gave the husband as the "head and master" of the property jointly owned with his wife the unilateral right to dispose of the property without the wife's consent. The Court held that Louisiana had "failed absolutely" to offer any persuasive justification for its statute. Only Rehnquist and Stewart felt it necessary to express any separate view, and their concern was only to reject any implication of retroactive application of the ruling.[10]

Now we come to two 1981 cases that seem to represent a retreat from the development of the law on sex discrimination that followed logically from the 1971 cornerstone case of *Reed v. Reed.* As we have seen, the ten years that followed the *Reed* case contained the court's flirtation with strict scrutiny in *Frontiero* in 1973, its acceptance of heightened scrutiny in *Craig v. Boren* in 1976, and its frequent rejection of "archaic and overbroad stereotypical generalizations" about women. By 1981, a generalization that *any* policy distinction between men and women that rested *solely* on an unsubstantiated social stereotype would be held unconstitutional seemed to be well-supported by precedent. In 1981, *Michael M. v. Superior Court of Sonoma County* and *Rostker v. Goldberg,* however, seem to represent a different view. The fact that the majority opinion in both cases was written by Justice Rehnquist suggests a new direction, or at least a new majority. Rehnquist had joined in the unanimous opinion in *Reed v. Reed,* but he usually had been a dissenter (and not infrequently alone) when a majority of the court found that women had been the victims of discrimination. It may also be pertinent that popular support for the Equal Rights Amendment had reached its lowest point in 1980, and the eventual failure of its ratification was evident by 1981 (McGlen and O'Connor, 1983: 379).[11]

Michael M. v. Superior Court was a 5 to 4 outcome, with Brennan, Marshall, Stevens, and White in dissent. The case involved the provision of the California Penal Code that defined unlawful sexual intercourse as "an act of sexual intercourse accomplished with a female not the wife of the perpetrator, where the female is under the age of 18." Thus, men alone could commit the offense. Why shouldn't a woman who had an act of sexual intercourse with a male under the age of 18 (who was not her husband) also be guilty of a crime? A gender-neutral law would make both men and women criminally responsible, especially when the sexual act was committed by an adult with a minor, and would apparently serve the state's interest as well, or better. In *Michael M.,* for example, the male was seventeen and one-half while the female was sixteen and one-half, yet only he was held culpable. Rehnquist's answer to the suggestion that a gender-neutral law would be preferable was that the key justification for the California statute was the prevention of illegitimate teenage pregnancies. He considered this to be an important interest because "only women may become pregnant, and they suffer disproportionately the profound physical, emotional and psychological consequences of sexual activity" (*Michael M. v. Superior Court*: 1205). Of course, the possibility of pregnancy is a physiological reality, but even so, was Rehnquist's perception of pregnancy grounded on sexual stereotypes? Perhaps, for while he readily upheld the protection of women, he found nothing to suggest that men are in need of the special solicitude of the courts, because of "past discrimination or peculiar disadvantages" (*Michael M. v. Superior Court*: 1208).

Brennan's dissent acknowledged the importance of the state's purpose in preventing teenage pregnancies but argued that the Court's majority had failed to apply the second part of the heightened scrutiny test. Is the statute substantially related to the achievement of its intended purpose? In Brennan's view, the California provision had two flaws. The first was demonstrated by the fact that "at least 37 states have enacted gender-neutral statutory rape laws." The second was California's failure to demonstrate that a gender-neutral law would be a less effective means for achieving its purpose (*Michael M. v. Superior Court*: 1216). Indeed, he argued, it is possible that a gender-neutral law would be even a greater deterrent.

Conceding Rehnquist's point that *Michael M.* rests, at least in part, on a physiological difference between men and women, his opinion in *Rostker v. Goldberg,* the draft registration case, does not seem to have even that justification. The ERA, which might itself have required draft registration of both men and women, was defeated by the time *Rostker v. Goldberg* reached the Supreme Court. Moreover, the provision in federal law that women were to be excluded from combat was not questioned by the six-member majority in *Rostker;* hence the decision to exclude women from draft registration could be based on the statutory premise that the draft was chiefly for the purpose of securing combat troops.

Is the due process clause of the Fifth Amendment violated by requiring males, but not females, to register for the draft?[12] Rehnquist reviewed at length the authority of Congress over national defense and military affairs. That authority, he wrote, demanded "a healthy deference to legislative and executive judgments in military affairs" (*Rostker v. Goldberg*: 2652). It cannot be denied, he continued, that the interest of the government in raising and supporting an army is an important one. Since Congress has exempted women from combat roles (and the draft, should it be renewed, would be chiefly for the purpose of securing combat troops), the decision to exempt women from draft registration was not only "sufficiently but also closely related to Congress' purpose in authorizing registration" (*Rostker v. Goldberg*: 2659). Rehnquist's logic is apparently irrefutable if it is legitimate to exclude women from combat, and also if it is true that the draft's principal purpose would be to secure combat troops.

White's dissent assumed that the exclusion of women from combat roles is constitutional, but he challenged the premise that the draft is for the purpose of securing combat troops. He cited Department of Defense figures that seemed to indicate a need for a large number (at least 80,000) of noncombatant positions that could be filled by women and that would free males for combat roles. Thus, he found no justification for excluding women.

Marshall's dissent scorned Rehnquist's opinion, which, he said, "places its imprimatur on one of the most potent remaining public expressions of 'ancient canards about the proper role of women'" (*Rostker v. Goldberg*: 2662). To pass heightened scrutiny, the government should instead be required "to show that registering women would substantially impede its efforts" to prepare for the draft. The government cannot meet this burden, he concluded, "without showing that a gender-neutral statute would be a less effective means of attaining this end" (*Rostker v. Goldberg*: 2666). This could not be done, for even the Defense Department said that fully one-third of the demand for induction would be for noncombat skills.

The litigants in *Rostker* took the position that the exclusion of women from combat was irrelevant to their case; consequently, that issue was not raised, and none of the opinions questioned that exclusion. However, even the exclusion of women from combat must sometimes rest on social preference rather than on any relevant physiological difference between men and women. That is especially true in these days of high technology armaments. Fighting ships, tanks, and combat aircraft may involve a number of aptitudes these days, but size and physical strength often are not the most important ones. The contributions of women both in the seizure of Noriega in Panama and in the Persian Gulf War clearly sustain that conclusion.

Judith Baer has taken the position that the decision in *Rostker* will have a practical effect but little impact on doctrine (Baer, 1983: 125). That is a fond wish, even if decisions since *Rostker* so far have borne her out. Nonetheless, the majority's willing acceptance in *Rostker* of what must be, in large measure, a socially determined distinction between men and women may yet have doctrinal implications for the future. The next equal protection case of the Supreme Court came out strongly against a sex-based distinction. however.

Justice Sandra Day O'Connor's opinion in the 1982 case of *Mississippi*

University for Women v. Hogan seems irrefutable, even though it was decided in the face of dissents by Burger, Blackmun, Powell, and Rehnquist. Hogan sued because he had been denied admission to the baccalaureate nursing program of Mississippi University for Women. The university's justification was that its exclusion of men was compensatory for discrimination against women, but Justice O'Connor was not persuaded that the exclusion of men from a nursing program rested on anything more than archaic and stereotypical notions about appropriate careers for men and women. The fact that the university allowed men to audit classes but not to receive actual credit also belied the alleged compensatory purpose of the statute.

Among the several dissents, Powell's was an impassioned plea for preservation of the single-sex college,[13] and it is true that a case can be made for the special opportunities for intellectual and social leadership that are open to women in women's colleges simply because of the absence of males. Still, that case presupposes that women will not be capable of competing effectively with men in coeducational institutions.[14] The contemporary success of women in achieving parity with men in coeducational law schools provides one answer to Powell's passion for the preservation of women's colleges. Another answer is that since there are yet ample opportunities for women in private women's colleges, there is no compelling state need for single-sex colleges.[15]

In *Wimberly v. Labor and Industrial Relations Commission of Missouri* (1987) the Court was unanimous in upholding a Missouri statute that disqualified any unemployment compensation applicant who had left work for reasons causally unrelated to the employer. Linda Wimberly had left work on pregnancy leave under a company policy that provided for rehiring her only if a position was available when she was ready to return. When she was ready, there was no position. She then filed for unemployment benefits but was denied under Missouri's statutory exclusion. Federal unemployment law provided that no state that participates in the federally assisted compensation program shall deny any compensation "solely on the basis of pregnancy or termination of pregnancy" (*Wimberly v. Labor and Industrial Relations Commission of Missouri*: 824).

Justice O'Connor wrote for a unanimous Court, holding that the generality of the state statute, which applied to all persons who left employment for reasons not causally related to the work or to the employer, meant that compensation was not being denied "solely on the basis of pregnancy."

Within three months the Supreme Court upheld voluntary policy preferences for women, but by a 5 to 4 vote. Brennan wrote for the five-member majority in *Johnson v. Transportation Agency, Santa Clara County* (1987). The Santa Clara County Transportation Agency had adopted an affirmative action plan that applied to women. In selecting from the applicants for the position of road dispatcher, it passed over Paul Johnson, a male employee, and promoted a female. The question in the case was whether the promotion was a violation of Title VII.

The agency's affirmative action plan took into account the under-representation of women in a variety of positions. For example, none of the 238 skilled craft worker positions were held by women. No quota was included, but the plan authorized the consideration of both ethnicity and sex when evaluating applicants, when such groups were poorly represented (as women were in the instance of road dispatchers). Both Johnson and the female who was promoted were deemed qualified for the job (*Johnson v. Transportation Agency, Santa Clara County*: 1448).

Brennan found the program to be much like the "Harvard Plan," which was noted with approval by Justice Powell in the *Bakke* case. Johnson had no absolute right to the dispatcher's position. He was still employed by the agency. The agency only took sex into account as one factor in determining that the female should be promoted. The promotion:

> was made pursuant to an affirmative action plan that represents a moderate, flexible, case-by-case approach to effectuate a gradual improvement in the representation of minorities and women in the Agency's work force. Such a plan is fully consistent with Title VII, for it embodies the contribution that voluntary employer action can make in eliminating the vestiges of discrimination in the workplace. (*Johnson v. Transportation Agency, Santa Clara County*: 1457)

Justice Scalia wrote the key dissent. He was concerned that the affirmative action plan of the agency was not based on a finding of previous purposeful discrimination, but only on manifest imbalance in the work force. He also opposed the use of a domain of allocation for compensatory purposes, when the discrimination occurred outside the immediate agency. Once again, the conflict on the Supreme Court was between those who adopted individual-regarding equality as the single acceptable understanding of equality and those who were willing to include the alternative goal of bloc- or group-regarding equality for compensatory purposes. Scalia was quite clear on that. He wrote that, "Ever so subtly . . . we effectively replace the goal of a discrimination free society with the quite incompatible goal of proportionate representation by race and sex in the workplace" (*Johnson v. Transportation Agency, Santa Clara County*: 1566).

Recent cases on sex discrimination concerned the burden of proof for those who bring complaints. Thus, they are related to *Personnel Administrator of Massachusetts v. Feeney* (1979) and to *Texas Department of Community Affairs v. Burdine* (1981) reviewed earlier in this chapter. The 1988 decision in *Watson v. Fort Worth Bank and Trust* (see chapter 9) involved whether statistical evidence reflecting the exclusion of a particular group, through application of largely subjective promotion criteria, was sufficient to invoke disparate impact analysis. You will recall that Justice O'Connor's answer for the Court was that a complainant might offer "statistical evidence of a kind and degree sufficient to show that the practice in question has caused the exclusion of applicants for job or promotions because of their membership in a protected group" (*Watson v. Fort Worth Bank and Trust*: 2788). However, much of what was apparently given in *Watson* was taken away in 1989 in *Wards Cove Packing Co., Inc. v. Antonio* (also reviewed in chapter 9).

A more recent case on sex discrimination is somewhat more friendly to the complainant. In *Price Waterhouse v. Hopkins* (1989) Blackmun, Marshall, and Stevens joined Brennan in a plurality opinion favoring a woman who had been denied a partnership in a major accounting firm. White and O'Connor concurred separately, leaving Rehnquist and Scalia joined in a dissent written by the newly fledged Justice Kennedy. It is interesting to note that an allegation of sex discrimination was also involved in the 1984 Supreme Court decision in *Hishon v. King & Spaulding*. That case had only involved the question of whether the decision on partnership (in this instance in a law firm) was covered by the provisions against sex-based discrimination in Title VII. The Court, in an opinion by Chief Justice Burger, unanimously held that the partnership decision was subject to Title VII, thus paving the way for the 1989 *Price Waterhouse* decision.

Ann Hopkins's case against Price Waterhouse involved a burden of proof issue. She proved that her sex was involved in a "mixture of motives" involving the partnership decision. Brennan held that Price Waterhouse then had the burden of showing that it would have denied her partnership even had it not taken her sex into account. Among other things she had been advised by a Price Waterhouse partner to "walk more femininely, talk more femininely, dress more femininely, wear make-up, have her hair styled, and wear jewelry" (*Price Waterhouse v. Hopkins*: 1782). Also, a witness for Hopkins had testified at trial that Price Waterhouse had probably been influenced by sex stereotyping.

Both the trial and circuit courts had held Price Waterhouse to the burden of showing by "clear and convincing evidence" that it would have made the same decision without taking Hopkins's sex into account. Brennan held that standard of proof to be too severe; proof by a preponderance of the evidence was sufficient. Even that burden was a departure, especially in the view of the dissenters, from the rule in the 1981 *Burdine* case. *Burdine* had held that once the employer showed a nondiscriminatory reason for its decision, the burden of proof was placed on the plaintiff to show that the nondiscriminatory reason was not the real one. Justice O'Connor in her concurring opinion agreed that the *Price Waterhouse* case was a departure from the *Burdine* rule, but it was an acceptable one suitable to the situation in which both discriminatory and acceptable reasons were mixed.

The intricacies of the evidentiary rules regarding the burden of proof in discrimination cases are clearly beyond the scope of this chapter, but we must nonetheless be aware of the fact that the court recently has often used burden of proof questions, rather than substantive conclusions, to dispose of controversial issues of race or sex discrimination.

The most recent sex discrimination case, again involving a burden of proof issue, was decided in March 1991 in *International Union, UAW v. Johnson Controls*. In an unusual unanimous opinion by Justice Blackmun (White, Rehnquist, Kennedy, and Scalia concurred separately) the Supreme Court held facially discriminatory an employer's policy barring all women (excepting only those whose infertility was medically proven) from jobs involving exposure to lead above the level permitted by the Occupational Safety and Health Administration (OSHA) standard. The court held that the employer failed to demonstrate that the sexual exclusion was a bona fide occupational qualification (BFOQ). The court's unanimity was probably due to the fact that the case turned on the proper interpretation of the Pregnancy Discrimination Act, which forbids sex-specific policies unless the employer can show that a woman's "reproductive potential" prevents her from adequately doing her job. This the employer could not do, for the potential danger to a fetus due to lead exposure in no way impaired a woman's capacity to perform her job.

But for Blackmun probably the key objection was that the Johnson Controls' policy was not gender neutral, because it did not apply to men but applied to women regardless of the practical prospect of pregnancy. Thus, sexually inactive single women and women likely to be past childbearing age were covered by the policy unless affirmative steps were taken by them to demonstrate actual infertility. The concurrence of White, Rehnquist, and Kennedy reserved the possibility for an employer to justify a sex-specific fetal protection policy in some instances, for example, by proving its necessity as a means for avoiding tort liability. Scalia's concurrence mostly was intended to limit the case strictly to one of statutory interpretation.

CONCLUSION

It is difficult to generalize these days about the Supreme Court's recent decisions on gender discrimination. The Court's decisions overturning instances of "archaic and stereotypical generalizations" about sex are to some degree muted by the majority decisions in *Michael M.* on statutory rape and in *Rostker* on draft registration. Still, a majority of the Court continues to overturn the most patent instances of sexual stereotyping. As is the case with racial affirmative action programs, the Court is badly divided over affirmative action for women in employment cases. A bare majority endorses group- or bloc-regarding equality and thus accepts affirmative action as a means of achieving gender equality. Still, affirmative action policies have been accepted only occasionally, and even then reluctantly.

A tally of the votes and outcomes of the cases reviewed here will give a good indication of the direction of the Court's justices over the twenty years since their first modern sex discrimination decision in *Reed v. Reed* (1971) (Table 10.1). The justices who have been involved in ten or more cases since 1971 are arrayed in Table 10.2 in the order of their support for claims that invoke gender equality. We have recorded as pro equality votes those that support either a claim of individual-regarding equality for men or women, or when group- or bloc-regarding equality for women in affirmative action cases is accepted.

It is evident that Powell's reputation as an occasional swing voter during his tenure on the Court is sustained by his votes on gender equality cases. Apart from that, Burger's and Rehnquist's have clearly been the dissonant voices on these cases. The rest of the court has largely been supportive of sex-based discrimination claims, although Marshall and Brennan stand out for their consistent support.

When we examine the forty cases (including Title VII cases) by identifying a male or a female complainant and counting the won-lost record, we find that men invoked equality in eighteen cases and won

Table 10.1 Sex Discrimination Cases from 1971 through the October 1990 Term of the Supreme Court

Case (Date of decision)	Gender of Claimant	Won/Lost	Burger	Blackmun	Brennan	Douglas	Marshall	White	Stewart	Powell	Rehnquist	Stevens	O'Connor	Scalia	Kennedy	Souter
Reed v. Reed (11/22/71)	F	W	P	P	P	P	P	P	P	ns	ns					
Stanley v. Illinois (4/3/72)	M	W	C	C	P	P	P	P	P	np	np					
Frontiero v. Richardson (5/14/73)	F	W	P	P	$\bar{P}$	$\bar{P}$	$\bar{P}$	$\bar{P}$	P	P	C					
Cleveland Board of Education v. LaFleur (1/21/74)	F	W	C	P	P	P	P	P	P	P	C					
Kahn v. Shevin (4/24/74)	M	L	C	C	P	C	P	P	C	C	C					
Corning Glass Works v. Brennan (6/3/74)	F[3]	W	C	C	P	P	P	P	np	P	C					
Geduldig v. Aiello (6/16/74)	F	L	C	C	P	P	P	C	C	C	C					
Schlesinger v. Ballard (1/15/75)	M	L	C	C	P	P	P	P	C	C	C					
Weinberger v. Wiesenfeld (3/19/75)	M	W	P	P	P	np	P	P	P	P	P					
Stanton v. Stanton (4/15/75)	F	W	P	P	P	P	P	P	P	P	P					
Turner v. Dept. of Employment Security (11/17/75)	F	W	P[3]	P[3]	P	np	P	P	P	P	C					
General Electric v. Gilbert (12/7/76)	F	L	C	C	P		P	C	C	C	C	P				
Craig v. Boren (12/20/76)	M	W	C	P	P		P	P	P	P	C	P				
Califano v. Goldfarb (3/2/77)	M	W	C	C	P		P	P	C	P	C	P				

Case	Sex	Decision									
Califano v. Webster (3/21/77)[4]	M	L	C	C	C	C	C	C	C	C	C
Dothard v. Rawlinson (6/27/77)	F	W/L	P[5]	P	P	P	P[5]	P	P	P	P
Nashville Gas v. Satty (12/6/77)	F	W/L[6]	P	P	P	P	P	P	P	P	P
Quilloin v. Walcott (1/10/78)[5]	M	L[7]	C	C	C	C	C	C	C	C	C
City of Los Angeles v. Manhart (4/25/78)[8]	F	W	P	P	P	P	P	P	P	C	P
Orr v. Orr (3/5/79)	M	W	P	P	P	P	P	C	C	C	P
Parham v. Hughes (4/24/79)	M	L[9]	P	P	P	P	C	C	C	C	C
Caban v. Mohammed (4/24/79)	M	W[9]	P	P	C	C	C	C	C	C	C
Personnel Administrator of Massachusetts v. Feeney (6/5/79)	F	L	P	C	C	C	C	C	C	C	C
Califano v. Westcott (6/25/79)	F	W	P	P[10]	P[10]	P[10]	P	P	P[10]	P	P
Wengler v. Druggists Mutual Insurance Company (4/22/80)	M	W	P	P	P	P	P	P	C	P	P
Kirchberg v. Feenstra (3/23/81)	F	W	P	P	P	P	P	P	P	P	P
Michael M. v. Superior Court of Sonoma County (3/23/81)	M	L	C	P	C	C	C	C	C	C	P
County of Washington v. Gunther (6/8/81)	F	W	P	C	C	C	C	C	P	C	P
Rostker v. Goldberg (6/25/81)	M	L	C	C	C	P	P	P	C	C	C
Mississippi University for Women v. Hogan (7/1/82)	M	W	C	C	C	C	C	P	C	P	P	P

(Continued)

Table 10.1 (Continued)

Case (Date of decision)	Gender of Claimant	Won/Lost	Burger	Blackmun	Brennan	Douglas	Marshall	White	Stewart	Powell	Rehnquist	Stevens	O'Connor	Scalia	Kennedy	Souter
Newport News Shipbuilding & Dry Dock Co. v. EEOC (6/20/83)[11]	M	W	P	P	P		P	P		C	C	P	P			
Lehr v. Robertson (6/27/83)[12]	M	L	C	P	C		P	P		C	C	C	C			
Arizona Governing Committee v. Norris (6/27/83)	F	W	P[13]	P[13]	P		P	P		P[13]	P[13]	P	P			
Hishon v. King & Spaulding (5/22/84)[14]	F	W	P	P	P		P	P		P	P	P	P			
California Federal Savings and Loan v. Guerra (1/13/87)	F[15]	W		P	P		P	C		P	C	P	P	P		
Wimberly v. Labor and Industrial Relations (1/21/87)[16]	F	L		np	C		C	C		C	C	C	C	C		
Johnson v. Transportation Agency, Santa Clara County California (3/25/87)[15]	M	L		C	C		C	P		C	P	C	C	P		
Watson v. Fort Worth Bank and Trust (1/29/88)[17]	F	W		P	P		P	P			P	P	P	P	np	
Price Waterhouse v. Hopkins (5/1/89)[17]	F	W		P	P		P	P			C	P	P	C	C	
International Union, UAW v. Johnson Controls (3/20/91)[18]	F	W		P			P	P			P	P	P	P	P	P

P= pro on the issue of gender equality raised;

C = con;

ns = not yet serving;

np = not participating

[1]Denotes the four justices who voted in *Frontiero* for the application of the strict scrutiny standard.

[2]Suit was brought by a federal agency on behalf of a female complainant.

[3]Burger and Blackmun would have granted certiorari and had full argument.

[4]While the equality claim is rejected here, this case must be categorized as one in which compensatory equality for women is sustained.

[5]While the objection to height and weight criteria is sustained by the Court, Justices Brennan and Marshall alone dissent to the majority's acceptance of gender-based work assignments to male and female prison guards.

[6]The opinion by Justice Rehnquist restrictively remanded one issue to the trial court.

[7]Case involves the interest of an unwed father in the adoption of his illegitimate child.

[8]Class action brought on behalf of women to challenge a gender-based distinction.

[9]Case involves the interests of the father of an illegitimate child.

[10]Held the challenged provision discriminatory but did not agree with the majority's disposition of the case.

[11]Suit brought by the EEOC on behalf of a male complainant.

[12]These cases perhaps would be better classified as ones involving a distinction between married and unmarried fathers, but the laws involved also distinguished between males and females.

[13]Opinions express differences as to the calculation of benefits.

[14]Overrules the dismissal of a case, holding that the complaint states a cause of action under Title VII. Does not involve a decision on the merits of the case.

[15]This is an affirmative action case. The pro votes are in favor of affirmative action relative to female employees.

[16]Holds only that the Pregnancy Discrimination Act does not *require* preferential treatment.

[17]Cases turn chiefly on questions involving burden of proof.

[18]A class action.

Table 10.2. Justices' Percentage Support for Sexual Equality Claims

Justice	Percentage of Support	(Number of cases)
Marshall	92	(40 cases)
Brennan	90	(39 cases)
O'Connor	82	(11 cases)
White	77	(40 cases)
Stevens	72	(29 cases)
Blackmun	66	(38 cases)
Stewart	57	(29 cases)
Powell	54	(36 cases)
Burger	34	(32 cases)
Rehnquist	26	(37 cases)

The tally includes several Title VII sex discrimination cases not explicitly re-viewed in this chapter. The list here excludes Douglas (9 cases), Scalia (7 cases), and Kennedy (2 cases). Douglas voted in favor of equality in all but one of the cases in which he participated. Scalia's record is 4–3 in favor of findings of discrimination. Kennedy's two votes have been against the equality claim in *Price Waterhouse v. Hopkins* and in favor of equality in *International Union, UAW v. Johnson Controls.*

half of them. Women invoked equality, including affirmative action claims, in twenty-two cases and clearly won sixteen of them (73 percent). Thus while equal protection doctrine in gender equality cases is to some degree in a continuing state of confusion, women have by and large been the winners in the past twenty years of litigation. However, given the recent divisions on the Court, the resignation of Justice Brennan (and his replacement by the still enigmatic Justice Souter), and the resignation of Justice Marshall (and his replacement by Judge Thomas) the future is at best uncertain.

11

BREAKING NEW GROUND FOR
CATEGORICAL DISCRIMINATION

*But mere negative attitudes, or fear, unsubstantiated by factors which are
properly cognizable in a zoning proceeding, are not permissible bases for
treating a home for the mentally retarded differently from apartment
houses, multiple dwellings, and the like. It is plain that the electorate as a
whole, whether by referendum or otherwise, could not order city action
violative of the Equal Protection Clause.*
—*City of Cleburne, Texas v. Cleburne Living Center*

In each instance of possible discrimination, the fundamental question
is whether those who are subject to some sort of distinctive treatment
ought, instead, to be treated like everyone else. Inclusionary individual-
regarding presumes that all individuals ought to be treated alike unless
there is some reasonable reason for differential treatment. We have
seen that race has most clearly and most often been identified in Supreme Court cases as a suspect classification, so that any use of a racial
category for special treatment requires an especially compelling justification. While sex has not progressed to that point, we have seen that
under *Craig v. Boren* a sexual distinction must serve important governmental objectives and must be substantially related to the achievement
of those objectives in order to justify such treatment. Now we go beyond race and sex to review other forms of categorical discrimination.

ALIENS

Apart from race, one of the earliest subjects of scrutiny under the
Equal Protection Clause was the treatment of aliens under the law.
Indeed, we touched on the subject of alienage briefly in our consider-
ation of early interpretations of equal protection in chapter 4.

The 1886 opinion of the Supreme Court in *Yick Wo v. Hopkins* contained the first judicial consideration of alienage under the Fourteenth

Amendment.[1] While Justice Matthews's opinion in *Yick Wo* rested in part on a treaty between the United States and China that placed an obligation on the U.S. government to protect and secure for Chinese nationals the same rights and privileges that were then accorded the citizens of the "most favored nation," he noted as well that the Fourteenth Amendment was not "confined to the protection of citizens" and that its provisions were "universal in their application." Thus, the Supreme Court found that the Equal Protection Clause was violated when a San Francisco ordinance gave its officials such unbridled discretion that they could deny permission to Chinese to run a laundry (except when located in buildings of brick or stone) while permitting others to have laundries in wooden buildings.[2] The narrow point involving the economic right to operate a laundry is trivial, at least in retrospect, but the Supreme Court's willingness to protect the rights of Chinese aliens, roughly in the same manner as the rights of U.S. citizens, remains a landmark even today.

However, in 1893, seven years after *Yick Wo,* the Supreme Court had no difficulty in sustaining the power of the federal government to provide for immigration, naturalization, expulsion, or exclusion of aliens under processes that probably were logically inconsistent even with the then limited due process of law that the Fifth and Fourteenth amendments would have required for citizens. The Supreme Court held that the federal government was specially empowered to deal with alienage, even while aliens were protected against arbitrary discrimination by the states (*Fong Yue Ting v. United States*). In 1896, however, even the federal government was constrained by the protection the Bill of Rights afforded aliens, when it sought not merely to expel or exclude aliens but to punish them at hard labor for their violation of immigration laws (*Wong Wing v. United States*). Public property rights, however, were another matter; they could be reserved for state citizens.

In 1877, for example, the Supreme Court sustained Virginia's power to reserve to its own citizens the raising of oysters within the tidewaters of that state and to exclude from that enterprise even U.S. citizens of sister states (*McCready v. Virginia*). From that decision the power to prohibit the killing of wild birds "by any foreign born person" and to make it unlawful for any "such person to possess a shotgun or rifle" was inferred in 1914, on the grounds that a state may preserve wild game for its own citizens (*Patsone v. Pennsylvania*). Still, outcomes that sustained the exclusion of aliens were not without exception.

In 1915 in *Truax v. Raich,* the Supreme Court held unconstitutional an Arizona statute that prohibited any employer of more than five persons from hiring aliens as more than 20 percent of its work force. To deny aliens the opportunity to work was held to be tantamount to the right to deny them "entrance and abode, for in ordinary cases they cannot live where they cannot work" (*Truax v. Raich*: 11). No "special public interest," such as the Court found above in *McCready* and *Patsone* (and which involved the public domain or common property of the citizens of a state) was shown. Nor did the Arizona law protect the "devolution of real property" or involve public works or the expenditure of public monies, all of which might occasion such a "special public interest" that exclusion of aliens might be sustained. These points were illustrated in two cases decided only a few weeks later.

In *Heim v. McCall* and *Crane v. New York* (1915) the Supreme Court sustained a New York law that restricted employment in public works to citizens of the United States. The conclusion that the Equal Protection Clause of the Fourteenth Amendment did not forbid *all* distinctions involving aliens was affirmed by additional holdings in 1923 that states could forbid aliens to own land (*Terrace v. Thompson* and *Porterfield v. Webb*).[3] All these decisions came under the "special public interest" rule, a doctrine that, though upheld by the Supreme Court, reached beyond its plausible implications in 1927. In that year the Court sustained a state law that excluded aliens from operating pool and billiard rooms on the grounds that they were so often the meeting places of "idle and vicious law-breakers and other undesirable persons" that it was reasonable for Ohio to require citizens to manage them because citizens would be more familiar with the laws and customs of this country than would aliens (*State of Ohio v. Deckebach*: 630).

The "special public interest" doctrine was effectively curbed in 1947 in *Takahashi v. Fish and Game Commission,* when the Supreme Court overturned a state law that prohibited resident aliens from commercial fishing within the three-mile offshore limit. *Takahashi* rested, to a large degree, on federal legislation enacted under the Fourteenth Amendment that guaranteed to all, including aliens, "the full and equal benefit of all laws and proceeding for the security of persons and property" (8 United States Code, sec. 41) but even apart from that statute, the "special public interest" of the state over fishing grounds was viewed skeptically by the Court. *Takahashi's* negative implications for the "special public interest doctrine" were affirmed in *Graham v. Richardson* (1971), a decision that at the time seemed to establish an "Alien Bill of Rights," but one that lasted only a few years.

Graham v. Richardson was profoundly affected by the holding in *Shapiro v. Thompson* (1969) that states could not discriminate against newcomers from sister states by requiring an unreasonably long residency period prior to qualifying for welfare benefits. In *Graham,* state laws that denied welfare benefits to resident aliens were thus struck down. The key language in the case describes alienage as a *suspect classification,* which like nationality or race, is "inherently suspect and subject to close judicial scrutiny." Aliens were also described as a "prime example" of a "discrete and insular minority" (*United States v. Carolene Products Co.,* 1938) that requires the special solicitude of the federal courts.

Nonetheless, the status of aliens as a "discrete and insular minority" has sometimes been questioned. The qualifications for that condition may include "an immutable characteristic determined solely by the accident of birth" (*Frontiero v. Richardson,* 1973), which obviously is not the case with aliens, who ordinarily can become citizens (Tribe, 1988: 1545). Yet aliens undeniably have often been a disadvantaged minority and thus the object of discriminatory legislation. Judith Baer noted correctly that Justice Brennan's language in *Frontiero* and Justice Blackmun's opinion in *Graham* simply pose two different definitions of a suspect classification. Whether a suspect classification is based on an "immutable characteristic" or on a "history of treatment as a disadvantaged minority" is, in either instance, a matter of judicial construction (Baer, 1983: 120).

The Court's judgment of whether aliens ought to be held a suspect classification again involves a question of what Rae calls inclusionary equality. Should everyone within the United States be treated alike without regard to citizenship, or should the status of lawful resident aliens be recognized as different from citizens (in certain respects) for public policy reasons? The right to vote is the most obvious example. To make alienage a suspect classification requires a compelling justification for any such differential treatment, even though certain exclusions of aliens (voting again being the best example) continue to be sustained.

Following *Graham* in 1971, the Supreme Court also struck down a state law excluding aliens from the competitive state civil service (*Sugarman v. Dougall,* 1973), from admission to the practice of law (*In re Griffiths,* 1973), from admission to the federal competitive civil service (*Hampton v. Mow Sun Wong,* 1976) and from licensure as civil engineers (*Examining Board v. Otero,* 1976).

Yet by the time *Nyquist v. Mauclet* was decided in 1977, the majority that once favored treating alienage as a suspect classification had shrunk to five members. Burger, Powell, Rehnquist, and Stewart dissented from the decision in *Nyquist* that held unconstitutional a New York law that excluded resident aliens from state financial aid for higher education. The dissenters were persuaded that New York's classification was different from the exclusions of aliens that the Court had struck down before because aid *was* made available to aliens who had applied for citizenship or who affirmed the intent to become citizens as soon as they were eligible (*Nyquist v. Mauclet*: 2130 et seq.). However, even that distinction was effectively jettisoned a year later when the Court in an opinion by Chief Justice Burger came very close to reviving the "special public interest" doctrine to sustain the exclusion of aliens from appointment to the New York State Police (*Foley v. Connelie,* 1978). This time only Brennan, Marshall, and Stevens dissented. Burger's opinion suggested that the state need only show some rational justification for its policy of exclusion when it acted on matters "firmly within [its] constitutional prerogative" (*Foley v. Connelie*: 1070).

The chief justice's short list of subjects falling within a state's constitutional prerogatives included exclusion of aliens from voting, from running for or holding elective office, from jury service or, as in *Foley,* from service as police officers. This short list of permissible exclusions soon grew, however. By 1979 it included exclusion of aliens from teaching in public schools (*Ambach v. Norwick*) and, by 1982, from serving as probation officers in California (*Cabell v. Chavez-Salido*). Both times Justice Blackmun joined the three dissenters from *Foley* in opposing these outcomes, so the Supreme Court was once again divided 5 to 4.

Yet even a state's "constitutional prerogative" did not sustain all exclusions. In 1982, Justice Brennan once again wrote for a majority, this time to overturn Maryland's policy of denying in-state tuition status to certain domiciled nonimmigrant aliens. The case turned, however, not on Fourteenth Amendment protection but on the Supremacy Clause[4] of the Constitution which, he concluded, prevented the states from imposing burdens against aliens beyond those contemplated by Congress (*Toll v. Moreno*: 2983). Only Burger and Rehnquist dissented.

The last key alienage decision involved the right to public education *Plyler v. Doe* (1982). Both Texas state law and the policies of certain local school districts denied access to free public education to the children of undocumented illegal aliens. The Supreme Court held 5 to 4 that even illegal aliens were protected by the Fourteenth Amendment. For the dissenters the question was not one of whether illegal aliens were entitled to any protection under equal protection review, but rather how much latitude ought to be accorded the states in their policy judgments.

Justice Brennan wrote for the majority that, while neither undocumented aliens nor their children could be treated as a suspect class (because of the relevance of their illegal status in this country) and while public education is not a constitutionally guaranteed right, Texas policy nonetheless "imposes a lifetime hardship on a discrete class of children not accountable for their disabling status" (*Plyler v. Doe*: 2398). In Brennan's opinion the hardship of the children was real and enduring, but Texas achieved no substantial state interest to offset these costs. The *Plyler* opinion may well have been result oriented, rather than being grounded on any solid standard of equal protection review, but at least we know that if the hardship is great and if the gain to the state is slight, even the children of strangers—that is, of illegal aliens may be protected by the Equal Protection Clause.

VOTING AND ELECTIONS

After its famous threshold decision in *Baker v. Carr* (1962), the Supreme Court opened the electoral process to equal protection review. The Court held voting to be a fundamental right, so that federal or state laws that restricted access to the ballot or that diluted the value of a vote were accorded strict scrutiny. *Reynolds v. Sims* (1964) sets forth this basic approach, "Since the right to exercise the franchise in a free and unimpaired manner is preservative of other basic civil and political rights, any alleged infringement of the right of citizens to vote must be carefully and meticulously scrutinized" (*Reynolds v. Sims*: 1381).[5]

These "fundamental rights" cases are conceptually distinct from those invoking categorical discrimination. Rather than asking whether all people ought to be treated alike (individual-regarding equality) or whether there is some compelling basis for a particular categorical distinction, the fundamental rights cases urge that certain rights are so fundamental that no one ought to be excluded from them without some especially compelling justification. The results, however, have been much the same as in suspect classification cases. For example, a provision of the Texas constitution that excluded all servicemen from voting in that state, regardless of the length of their residency, was thus overruled in *Carrington v. Rash* (1965); state poll taxes were struck down under that standard of review in *Harper v. Virginia State Board of Elections* (1966); and a New York provision that limited the franchise in public school elections to parents or guardians of enrolled school children, or to taxpayers residing within the district, met the same fate

(*Kramer v. Union Free School District,* 1969).[6] General state exclusions of nonproperty owners from voting in bond elections were overturned in *Cipriano v. City of Houma* (1969) and *City of Phoenix v. Kolodziejski* (1970).

In *Rosario v. Rockefeller* (1973) a New York closed-primary law required enrollment in a political party at least 30 days prior to the general election in order to vote in the next party primary. The effect of this rule was to require enrollment about eight months before a presidential primary and almost a year before a nonpresidential primary. It was upheld in an opinion by Justice Stewart over the dissents of four justices, led by Powell. Stewart was persuaded by New York's assertion that its motive was to inhibit party crossover voting whereby members of one party can attempt to influence the outcome of another party's primary. This goal was held to be legitimate, even though Justice Powell protested that the cutoff of eight months or twelve months before a primary was much too severe. The exclusion in New York would have applied even to those voters who never before had declared a party preference, for whom the possibility of party "raiding" was inapplicable. The majority's deference to New York, Powell wrote, in effect reduced its review of voting cases to the "rational basis" test.[7]

An apt illustration of justices' different perceptions of the degree of deference that ought to be accorded state laws is found in *O'Brien v. Skinner* (1974). In *O'Brien* another New York law allowed inmates in a jail in a county other than that of their own residence to register and to vote absentee, while jail inmates in their own county's jail were not allowed either to register or to vote absentee. The Court's opinion by Chief Justice Burger expressed no difficulty in finding this to be a purely arbitrary distinction but did so without specifying the level or review that he was applying. Marshall, Douglas, and Brennan concurred but felt it necessary to add that since New York's provision involved the denial of the right to vote, strict scrutiny ought to be applied, and New York clearly had no compelling justification for its policy. In dissent, Blackmun and Rehnquist would have deferred even to this provision. Blackmun wrote, "These are inequalities, but they are the incidental inequalities of life, and I do not regard them as unconstitutional" (*O'Brien v. Skinner*: 747).

A year later a majority again struck down a state law, this time a Texas provision that called for a "dual election box procedure." That required voters who had rendered taxable property, and therefore were on the tax rolls, to vote in a separate box from other registered voters. A bond issue could be passed only by a majority of the votes cast in each of the separate boxes. The majority held that in an election of general interest to the public (this was a bond election, in which the proceeds of the bonds would be used to construct a library) no restrictions on voting other than residence, age, and citizenship can be used unless the state can demonstrate a compelling interest (*Hill v. Stone,* 1975). This time Rehnquist, Burger, and Stewart dissented. They found the rendering requirement of Texas law to be a minimal intrusion. Almost anyone could become a rendering taxpayer by reporting to the local tax assessor a list of their real or personal property that was legally subject to local property taxes.

The Court reached one of its rare unanimous decisions regarding elections in 1979 in *Illinois State Board of Elections v. Socialist Workers Party.* Illinois law required that independent candidates or new parties gather only 25,000 signatures in order to gain access to the statewide ballot, while local elections required signatures for independents or new party candidates equal to 5 percent of the ballots cast in the previous local election. The result in Chicago was that it required substantially more signatures to get on a local ballot than on the statewide one. There was no compelling justification offered for the difference, and all the justices agreed to strike it down (though for somewhat different reasons).

The most interesting recent case raises the possibility that federal courts may examine partisan political gerrymandering using an approach similar to that initiated in *Baker v. Carr. Davis v. Bandemer* (1986) suggested that legislative apportionment by Indiana's Republican-controlled legislature presented a justiciable question of the dilution of Democratic votes. However, the Supreme Court imposed a heavy burden of proof on plaintiffs who would raise questions of partisan gerrymandering. They would be required to show that the electoral system substantially disadvantaged certain voters for partisan political advantage. Further, the finding of partisan disadvantage would have to be supported by evidence of the "continued frustration of a majority of state voters" or the "effective denial to a minority of voters of a fair chance to influence the political process" (*Davis v. Bandemer.* 2810 et seq.). While this stipulation is not an impossible burden, the Supreme Court was clearly trying to reserve federal intervention for the most egregious instances of partisan gerrymandering.

The cases on voting and elections have in common only their relationship to the process for selecting public officeholders. The rhetorical differences among the justices as to the proper standard of review bear no clear, constant, or demonstrable relationship to the actual outcomes of the cases. In the end, it seems to have mattered only whether five members of the Court found the enacted exclusion to be intelligible and sensible—on the one hand—or arbitrary and invidious—on the other. These essentially are differences about how inclusionary equality ought to be in the context of voting. Should all individuals equally have the right to vote? What exclusions from the right to vote are defensible? What standard should be used for judging such exclusions? There is no consistency and therefore no clarity from the Supreme Court on these questions.

STATE RESIDENCY REQUIREMENTS

Shapiro v. Thompson (1969) is the landmark case on discriminatory residency requirements. Marie Thompson was a nineteen-year-old unwed mother of one child, and pregnant with her second, when she moved from Massachusetts to Connecticut to live with her mother in June 1966. She moved to her own place in Hartford two months later. Her application for AFDC (Aid to Families with Dependent Children) payments was denied because she had not lived in the state for one year prior to her application. The waiting period was justified as a measure to preserve the "fiscal integrity" of state public assistance programs.

If people can be deterred from entering the state by such a residency requirement, the welfare burden on the state would not be increased by the "influx of indigent newcomers," the state argued (*Shapiro v. Thompson*: 1328). While such a residency requirement indeed might have worked as planned, the Supreme Court held that the state's classification was not acceptable and that it was not based on a compelling governmental interest. The Connecticut residency requirement also violated the fundamental right to move from state to state, "a right so elementary [that it] was conceived from the beginning [of the Republic] to be a necessary concomitant of the stronger Union the Constitution created" (*Shapiro v. Thompson*: 1329).[8]

Laurence Tribe has commented that *Shapiro* constitutes the first major statement of the "'fundamental rights strand' of equal protection strict scrutiny" as well as a classic instance of state interference with the right "to travel throughout the length and breadth of our land" (Tribe, 1988: 1455). It is probably more accurate to say that the fundamental rights approach flows from the right to vote cases such as *Baker v. Carr* (1962) and *Reynolds v. Sims* (1964) and was voiced as early as 1942 in *Skinner v. Oklahoma*. In any event, the "fundamental rights strand" has usually been sustained by the cases that have followed *Shapiro,* but there have been notable exceptions.

The early state residency cases were consistent with *Shapiro. Dunn v. Blumstein* (1972) overturned a Tennessee durational residency requirement for voting (one year residency within the state and three months within the county). In *Vlandis v. Kline* (1973) the Court overturned a Connecticut statute that created an irrebuttable presumption against out-of-state students becoming Connecticut residents for university tuition purposes during the course of their studies within the state. The Court proclaimed, as it had done before in a number of cases, including *Stanley v. Illinois,*[9] that irrebuttable presumptions are suspect. There was no good reason, Justice Stewart wrote, why bona fide claims of residence could not be determined on a case-by-case basis, even though that would impose a modest burden on the state.

Memorial Hospital v. Maricopa County (1974) involved an Arizona statute that required one-year residency in the county as a condition to receiving nonemergency care in a county hospital. Marshall wrote the Court's opinion, which followed closely the reasoning in *Shapiro.* As before, the right to interstate travel being deemed fundamental, the state was required to show a compelling public interest in support of its policy. On its part, Arizona could only claim fiscal responsibility, the need to deter immigration, and the need for budgetary planning. The Court held that the state had not met its heavy burden of justification, while it had imposed a severe penalty on newcomers who consequently might not secure proper medical care. Only Rehnquist dissented.

Rehnquist wrote for a majority in *Sosna v. Iowa* (1975), however, in upholding an Iowa one-year durational residency requirement for filing divorce actions. He found that Iowa's residency requirement for divorce was not founded on budgetary considerations or on mere administrative convenience, as was arguably the case in *Shapiro, Dunn,* and *Memorial Hospital.* Instead, he concluded that Iowa had a legitimate state interest in requiring that divorce litigants be "genuinely attached to the State," as well as a desire to protect its divorce decrees from collateral attacks in sister states. In dissent, Marshall and Brennan would have continued the line of authorities that *Shapiro* began.

Zobel v. Williams (1982) involved the singular instance of Alaska residents receiving dividend distributions from state mineral income. Not surprisingly, Alaska enacted a preferential distribution for long-term residents. Each adult resident was to receive one dividend unit for each year of actual residency since 1959, the year in which Alaska became a state. Among Alaska's policy objectives, the only one that was even plausible was its effort to reward its residents for their past contributions to the state. That objective, however, was held not to be a legitimate state purpose. Chief Justice Burger noted that that argument had been made and rejected in *Shapiro* (*Zobel v. Williams*: 2314). Again, only Rehnquist dissented. The degree of deference he was willing to accord state economic regulations was enough to encompass Alaska's preferential distribution.

Martinez v. Bynum (1983) involved a Texas statute that allowed a school district to deny free education to a minor who lived apart from parents or guardian, if his or her chief purpose was to attend a particular public school. Roberto Morales, the student in question, had left his parents' home in Mexico to live with his sister in Texas for the purpose of attending public school. Justice Powell's opinion sustained the law, in part because it did not involve a durational element. A bona fide residency requirement, without presumptive or durational barriers to becoming a resident, was legitimate according to Powell. The only persons excluded from free public education under the Texas provision were those minors who came to a school district for the sole purpose of attending school and who intended to leave when school was completed.

Marshall's dissent protested that the majority opinion had in effect rewritten the Texas statute. Before Powell's revision, Marshall suggested that it provided only that free tuition could be denied to any minor who, while living apart from parent or guardian, moved to a school district for the primary purpose of attending school, regardless of any intent to become a permanent resident. The important point of the case is that, like the Iowa's residency requirement for divorce, not all residential requirements are rejected by the Court.

Finally, two cases on voting rights involve state efforts to confer a special benefit on Vietnam veterans but to limit the benefit to those who were state residents as of a particular date. In *Hooper v. Bernalillo County Assessor* (1985), a New Mexico statute that granted a tax exemption to Vietnam veterans who had resided within the state before May 8, 1976, was held unconstitutional. In *Attorney General of New York v. Soto-Lopez* (1986), a New York statute that granted a veterans' preference for public employment to veterans who had entered the military service while living in New York was overturned.

The only important difference in the cases is that Brennan's opinion in *Soto-Lopez* noted that in both *Hooper v. Bernalillo County Assessor* and in *Zobel v. Williams,* the time-limited state preferences had failed even to pass rational basis scrutiny. New York's veterans' preference in *Soto-*

Lopez was sufficiently well grounded to have a rational basis, but it nonetheless did not meet the state's "heavy burden of proving that it has selected a means of pursuing a compelling state interest which does not impinge unnecessarily on constitutionally protected interests" (*Soto-Lopez*: 2325).

The case outcomes on residency are unusually clear. States may have residency requirements, but they cannot impose unreasonable barriers against claims of residency. They may require reasonable connections to the state for certain policy purposes, but they cannot confer an economic advantage for long-term residents while denying the same to newcomers. In effect, all lawful state residents must be treated alike. For most purposes state residents are entitled to individual-regarding equality.

MARRIAGE

In a case involving an unusual state law, the Supreme Court upheld the right to marry as a fundamental right, the denial of which would require "critical examination" of the state interests involved (*Zablocki v. Redhail,* 1978). *Zablocki* involved a challenge to a Wisconsin statute that required the consent of a judge to the marriage of a noncustodial parent who was subject to an order for child support. The statute conditioned the judge's consent on a finding that the person desiring to marry was in compliance with the support order and that extant children are not likely, by virtue of the marriage, to become "public charges." Marriage as a fundamental right had previously been upheld in *Loving v. Virginia* (1967) when the Court struck down Virginia's prohibition of interracial marriages. Even before that, in *Skinner v. Oklahoma* (1942) it had held that since marriage and procreation are fundamental to human survival, a state provision requiring sterilization of certain habitual criminal offenders would be subjected to strict scrutiny.

Predictably, Justice Rehnquist dissented alone in *Zablocki*. He would only have applied the rational basis test, under which the state's authority to refuse consent to marry would, as usual, have prevailed over the equal protection claim.

ILLEGITIMACY

Marriage itself having been protected as a fundamental right, the Supreme Court has also had to consider appropriate protection for the rights of children born out of marriage. The core case in point is *Levy v.*

Louisiana (1968). In *Levy,* Louisiana law did not allow illegitimate children to recover for the wrongful death of a parent. The law was predicated on the notion of "discouraging bringing children into the world out of wedlock." In *Levy,* Justice Douglas declared the law unconstitutional in typically short order. "Legitimacy or illegitimacy of birth," he wrote, "has no relation to the nature of the wrong allegedly inflicted on the mother." It was "invidious to discriminate against them" (*Levy v. Louisiana*: 1511).

Louisiana was twice again before the Supreme Court on questions involving illegitimacy. It won in 1971 in *Labine v. Vincent* when the Court upheld its intestacy law,[10] which excluded even an acknowledged illegitimate child from sharing equally with legitimate children in their father's estate. The Court was willing to continue its traditional deference to the states' powers over the laws respecting inheritance, one purpose of which was to ensure stability of land titles. Illegitimacy, it said in passing, "does not command extraordinary protection" (*Labine v. Vincent*: 2763). However, in *Weber v. Aetna Casualty & Surety Co.* (1972) Louisiana lost. This time its workmen's compensation statute denied to unacknowledged illegitimate children recovery equal to that provided legitimate children for the death of their natural father. The Court held that *Levy v. Louisiana* was controlling, and again only Rehnquist dissented.

In *Gomez v. Perez* (1973) the State of Texas was held to have discriminated against children born out of wedlock with regard to parental support. In a per curiam opinion the Court held that once a statute creates a judicially enforceable right of children for support, it may not deny the right of support to illegitimate children. In *New Jersey Welfare Rights Organization v. Cahill* (1973), eight members of the Court concurred in overturning a New Jersey provision that excluded from public assistance families containing illegitimate children. In none of these cases, however, did the Court consider at length the level of review that was appropriate.

Jimenez v. Weinberger (1974) was the first of the illegitimacy cases from the 1970s that questioned a federal statute. It reviewed a provision of the Social Security Act that conditioned disability benefits for certain illegitimate children on a showing that the child lived with the parent and that the parent contributed to the child's support. Illegitimate children who were so only because of "nonobvious defects in their parents' ceremonial marriage" or who had been legitimate under state law were allowed disability benefits with no requirement of actual dependency. The Court's majority found the distinction between the two classes of illegitimate children to bear no reasonable relationship to a valid governmental interest. However, in *Matthews v. Lucas* (1976) the Supreme Court reviewed yet another provision of the Social Security Act; this one made eligibility of illegitimate children for survivor's benefits conditional on a showing that the deceased parent was living with the child at time of death and was contributing to the child's support. A six-member majority endorsed Blackmun's opinion, which explicitly rejected the suggestion that illegitimacy was a suspect classification requiring strict scrutiny (*Matthews v. Lucas*: 2762). The majority found the classification permissible because it was reasonably related to the "likelihood of dependency at death." Stevens, Brennan, and Marshall argued in dissent that the classification was another consequence of the traditional thinking of the illegitimate as less deserving persons than legitimate.

Now things began to get confused. In *Trimble v. Gordon* (1977) a provision of the Illinois Probate Code that allowed illegitimate children to inherit by intestate succession from their mother, but not from the father, while allowing legitimate children to inherit from both parents, was struck down. Three justices joined Rehnquist in dissent. They found no distinction between this Illinois provision and the one in Louisiana that was held constitutional in *Labine v. Vincent*. Powell wrote for the majority in *Trimble* that, even though a suspect classification was not involved, the standard of review used by the Court was not toothless, and Powell thought that *Trimble* and *Labine* had been joined too easily. The Illinois statute reviewed in *Trimble* required that for the child to inherit there must be both the acknowledgment of the child by the father and the marriage of the parents. Powell found this to be an unacceptable burden. Without expressly overruling *Labine,* Powell's decision in *Trimble* appeared to have made it a dubious precedent, yet when he wrote again in *Lalli v. Lalli* (1978) he sustained a New York law that allowed an illegitimate child to inherit only when a court had determined its paternity. Powell found the paternity order in this instance to be a reasonable state requirement (*Lalli v. Lalli*: 528). The line between acceptable and unacceptable burdens was at best indistinct.

While the cases on illegitimacy have not adopted the suspect classification/strict scrutiny standard, they do reflect much the same sort of uncertain heightened scrutiny that we witnessed in the sex discrimination cases that followed *Craig v. Boren* in 1976. Heightened scrutiny is a level of review that is highly contextual and fact bound. Each case seems to turn on the balancing of specific facts and interests, with no presumptions in favor or against state legislation. Prediction in these cases is difficult at best, and it is not all that easy to make sense of them after the fact.

The last three cases on illegitimacy do at least offer the virtue of consistency. They all involved statutes of limitation. The first case, *Mills v. Habluetzel* (1982), reviewed a Texas statute that provided for a one-year limitation, running from the birth of a child, for a mother to file suit to establish paternity. In a unanimous opinion by Rehnquist, the Court held the one-year limit to restrict the rights of illegitimate children excessively. A two-year Tennessee statute was struck down unanimously in *Pickett v. Brown* (1983), and Pennsylvania's six-year statute was declared unconstitutional unanimously in *Clark v. Jeter* (1988).

THE TRADITIONAL FAMILY STRUCTURE

The Supreme Court, having been called upon to protect both marriage and illegitimate children through the Fourteenth Amendment, has also been impelled by circumstance to judge the size and structure of families under equal protection analysis. The first such case was *Dandridge v. Williams* (1970). It sustained a Maryland welfare grant that placed a limit on the monthly benefit any single family could receive against a challenge that such a policy discriminated against large families. The second case was *U.S.D.A. v. Moreno* (1973). *Moreno* challenged the federal Food Stamp Act's declaration that any household was ineligible for benefits if it contained a person unrelated to any other member of the household. Justice Brennan found this exclusion to be unconstitutional because it was not rationally related to a legitimate governmental interest. It was, in Brennan's view, enacted against "hippies" and "hippie communes" (*U.S.D.A. v. Moreno*: 2826). Its actual consequence was to refuse food stamps to a fifty-six-year-old diabetic who lived with another woman and her three children, to a married mother with three children (because she had offered refuge in her home to an emotionally disturbed twenty-year-old girl), and to a mother with a deaf daughter who required special education (because the mother agreed to share an apartment with another woman so that she and her daughter could afford to live near the school for the deaf). Rehnquist and Burger dissented because Congress's concern about unrelated people living together for the purpose of receiving food stamps was not "quite so irrational" as the majority made it appear. Traditional equal protection analysis did not require that every line be drawn with mathematical precision, they said. They were willing to defer to the Congress, even though it may have used a "blunt instrument" in attempting to achieves its ends.

U.S.D.A. v. Murry (1973) was a companion case to *Moreno.* Lula Mae Murry lived with her two sons and ten grandchildren. She became ineligible for food stamps when her former husband, who was not eligible for food stamps, claimed her two sons and one grandchild as tax dependents for the prior tax year. The exclusion as to tax dependency was contained in the Food Stamp Act of 1964. The Supreme Court's majority held, in an opinion by Justice Douglas, that the exclusion as to tax dependency bore no rational relationship to current need. This time there were four dissenters. The crux of their dissent was that the majority was too willing to second-guess Congress and too ready to require precision or "mathematical nicety."

With *Village of Belle Terre v. Boraas* (1974), the scene shifted again to the states' efforts to regulate families and households. The Village of Belle Terre, New York, had a zoning ordinance that generally limited the occupancy of single-family dwellings to traditional families or to groups with no more than two unrelated persons. This time Justice Douglas upheld the governmental interest, after what seemed to have been only the most limited scrutiny. He concluded that no fundamental right had been involved and there was no ascertainable group against which discrimination was directed. Justice Marshall, however, believed that the zoning ordinance violated both the freedom of association and the right of privacy, which here would have included the right to form a household of one's own choice.

In *Moore v. City of East Cleveland* (1977), a city went to even greater length to protect the traditional family through its zoning laws. It also limited single-family dwelling units to a traditional family, but it included as family, for most purposes, only the nuclear family. Grandparents, grandchildren, and cousins, for example, did not qualify as family. This provision was viewed as too restrictive and was held unconstitutional by all but Justices Rehnquist, Stewart, and White. They would have applied the same limited scrutiny used by Douglas in *Belle Terre.*

Once again, as the cases accumulate, confusion sets in. The majority in *Lyng v. Castillo* (1986) upheld recent amendments to the Food Stamp Act that had the effect of limiting the definition of a household to parents, children, or siblings who live together. The amendments treated all others, including relatives and unrelated persons who lived together, under a different standard. Despite the Court's prior holdings in *Moreno* and *Murry,* the majority sustained this under rational basis–minimum scrutiny review and found that Congress could rationally conclude that parents, children, or siblings who lived together would be more likely than others to purchase and prepare food together. Hence the relevancy of the classification to the food stamp program. Brennan, Marshall, and White found the legislative distinction to fail even the rational basis test, but the majority's deference to Congress was continued in the last case to be reviewed in this section.

Bowen v. Gilliard (1987) upheld (again by using the rational basis test) a 1984 amendment to the federal AFDC program that required families to include in the reported family unit any child receiving child support payments. Any support received in excess of 50 dollars per month was to be counted toward total family income for eligibility purposes. Brennan dissented at length. It was a dissent that cited even Plato and Tolstoy to weave a defense of the family against the modern state. He held the child's right to live with and receive the support of parents to be fundamental, so that the government's intrusion could not survive strict scrutiny.

POVERTY

Distinctions based on the ability to pay, on income, or on wealth have been applied by state and local governments or by the federal government across many policy areas and with varying purposes and consequences. The rhetoric of the Supreme Court has sometimes been strong and staunch against such distinctions, but the reality has just as often been inconsistent and confusing.

A majority of the court has been willing to apply strict scrutiny only against laws that raised state residency barriers against the influx of poor people, that raised property-based obstacles against the right to vote, or that placed indigent defendants at a serious disadvantage before the criminal courts. Each of these involved factors other than poverty. The right to vote and the right to travel from state to state have both been held to be fundamental rights, and the rights of the accused to equal justice are protected by the requirements both of fundamental fairness and under the incorporation of certain rights as fundamental within the meaning of the due process clause of the Fourteenth Amendment.

On several occasions certain members of the Warren Court wrote for majorities that proclaimed wealth-based distinctions to be suspect in much the same manner as those regarding race. As early as *Edwards v. California* (1941) the Court held that "mere property status" could not be used to qualify citizenship rights, as California's "Anti-Okie" law had clearly done.

The Supreme Court held in the 1950s that the charging of fees and of court costs in the criminal courts could not be an obstacle to equal justice for poor people. In *Griffin v. Illinois* (1956) the Court struck down Illinois's practice of charging defendants for a trial transcript, except in capital cases. In Illinois courts such a transcript was often essential to a full appellate review of a conviction. Justice Black's opinion in *Griffin* contained the aspirations for equal justice voiced in Magna Carta (1215) and repeated by the Supreme Court as early as in *Yick Wo v. Hopkins* (1886). The leading right to counsel cases contained the same aspirations, at least until *Ross v. Moffitt* (1974).[11]

Ross v. Moffitt represented the end (at least for the time) of the Supreme Court's liberality respecting the rights of indigents in the criminal justice system. Rehnquist wrote for a majority that was willing to deny an indigent the right to pursue further appeals at state expense once the first stage of appellate review had been concluded adversely. Absolute equality of resources before the bench was not a constitutional requirement, according to the majority view, from which only Brennan, Douglas, and Marshall dissented. That conclusion was sustained in 1989 even in cases involving the death penalty (see *Murry v. Giarratano,* 1989).

On the civil justice side, the first results were also liberal, but subsequent cases were more restrictive. In *Boddie v. Connecticut* (1971) a state law requiring the payment of court fees and costs incident to a divorce action, regardless of ability to pay, was held unconstitutional. The key to *Boddie* was that the state monopolized the divorce process so that an indigent divorce plaintiff had no alternative to suit. Following that line of reasoning, the Court held that indigents could be denied access to voluntary bankruptcy proceedings because other means of redress were open to debtors (*United States v. Kras,* 1973). Even more restrictive was the Court's ruling that a state welfare division could require a 25-dollar appellate filing fee for a petition to review a decision that had reduced welfare benefits (*Ortwein v. Schwab,* 1973). The per curiam opinion concluded that no fundamental right or interest was involved, but in dissent, Justice Douglas wrote that the majority had agreed to a scheme that made justice a "luxury for the wealthy" (*Ortwein v. Schwab*: 1175). Brennan and Marshall would have applied the precedent of *Boddie v. Connecticut* in all of these cases. The per curiam holding in *Ortwein* that no fundamental rights were implicated in the failure to provide for appellate review for indigents in welfare cases bears an interesting relation to the Court's 1970 decision in *Goldberg v. Kelly.*

Brennan's majority opinion in *Goldberg* held that procedural due process of law required a pre-termination evidentiary hearing before AFDC benefits could be terminated. The food, clothing, shelter, and medical care that would be purchased with such benefits were essential to the preservation of life, and only Justice Black (then in his later years) dissented in *Goldberg.* Procedural due process was also upheld in *Sniadach v. Family Finance Corp.* (1969), which struck down a state wage garnishment statute under which a debtor's wages could be seized without prior adversary hearing and in *Fuentes v. Shevin* (1972), which outlawed a procedure under which a debtor's property could be seized without prior notice or hearing. Why due process would require such evidentiary hearings but not a right of appeal (regardless of ability to pay) is not obvious. The majority in *Ortwein* simply concluded that due process does not mandate appellate review in civil cases, and it was also crucial that the poor were not seen as an ascertainable suspect class that might contain common victims of discrimination. That was at least consistent with the holding in *Dandridge v. Williams* (1970) that a state could impose an absolute maximum on welfare benefits, regardless of family size, thus denying "the most basis economic needs" to members of large indigent families and with *Lindsey v. Normet* (1972), which held that there was no constitutionally protected right to housing.

Other cases have followed the line that the poor do not constitute a discriminated class. For example, the denial of public funding for abortions for those who could not afford to pay for them was upheld in *Maher v. Roe* (1977), *Harris v. McRae* (1980), *Williams v. Zbaraz* (1980) and *Webster v. Reproductive Health Services* (1989).

We close this section with the interesting and important case of *San Antonio v. Rodriquez* (1973), which presented persistent and perplexing problems regarding the funding of public education. It involved adjacent school districts. The Edgewood Independent School District was an urban district in San Antonio. It had a relatively low per pupil property tax valuation ($4,686 per pupil). The adjacent district, Alamo Heights Independent School District, had a relatively high per pupil tax valuation (more than $49,000 per pupil). Edgewood actually spent $356 per pupil (from all combined sources) for the 1967–68 school year; Alamo Heights spent $594 per pupil for the same year. The suit began as a class action brought on behalf of the school children who lived in the poorer school district. They claimed that the Texas system of school financing discriminated on the basis of wealth in the provision of public education. The Supreme Court, however, held that public education was not a fundamental right that required strict scrutiny under the Fourteenth Amendment and that the funding distinctions between poor and affluent public school districts did not represent a form of invidious discrimination against an identifiable class of poor people.[12] Thus, strict scrutiny was not required, and the Court found that the state had met the burden of showing that its means of financing public education had a reasonable relationship to a legitimate state purpose. The principle of local control of public education was advanced by the use of independent school districts, even if one undesirable consequence of local control was disparity of resources.

San Antonio v. Rodriquez offers another excellent example of the inclusiveness or exclusiveness of our understanding of equality. If one believes that all public school students in the United States ought to be accorded equal educational opportunity, then it might be a logical necessity to ensure that the per pupil expenditures for education would be the same anywhere in the nation.[13] If, on the other hand, the state is the relevant domain for equality of education, it might only be necessary to ensure equal per pupil expenditures for all students within the state. If it is the local community that should be the proper domain for equal education, then it would be necessary only to provide equal funding for each student within the community. Finally, if education is thought to be the concern only of the family, then only the provision of equal educational support for each child of the family might be all that is required. It is simply a matter of how inclusive we think equality ought to be.

AGE

Both the young and the old are obvious subjects for discrimination. Age is like sex because there are certain physical differences between people that are associated with age and because age differences may contribute to social stereotypes. It has also been part of our tradition to relate to both the very young and the very old in a paternalistic manner, often even to try to protect them (just as with the "chivalrous" treatment of women).

The paternalistic treatment of youth in juvenile courts, which sometimes became harsh and insensitive rather than benevolent, was the subject of *In re Gault* (1967), in which the Supreme Court reviewed the case of Gerald Gault, age fifteen, who was sentenced to six years in a state reform school for making obscene phone calls (an offense for which an adult could have received a maximum sentence of two months in jail). Gerald's juvenile hearing was one for which his parents had received no notice of the charges against him, at which the complaining witness did not appear, and from which there was no right of appeal. Even recognizing that juvenile courts were specialized institutions whose purpose was to protect rather than punish, the Supreme Court held that Gerald had not been accorded due process of law.

Gault was followed two years later by *Tinker v. Des Moines Independent School District* (1969), in which the Court ruled that even school children had certain rights of political expression that were protected by the First Amendment. In 1975, the Court also included public school disciplinary proceedings under Fourteenth Amendment due process review (*Goss v. Lopez*), and in 1976 it ruled that a mandatory parental consent requirement for a minor female who sought an abortion was unconstitutional (*Planned Parenthood of Central Missouri v. Danforth*). "Constitutional rights," Justice Blackmun wrote, "do not mature and come into being magically only when one attains the state-defined age of majority" (*Planned Parenthood of Central Missouri*: 2843). *Belloti v. Baird* (1979) continued on much the same line. A person judged by a court to be a mature and fully competent minor ought to be able to seek an abortion even without parental notification or consent, the Court ruled in *Belloti*. We should note, however, that in recent cases the Supreme Court has upheld parental notification when a minor is involved, provided that some procedure for judicial nullification of the notification requirement is provided under applicable state law.

None of the cases reviewed in the paragraph above involved equal protection. They are indicative, however, of the Court's inclination to take the rights of young people more seriously than had been the case prior to *Gault* and *Tinker*. However, in both *Planned Parenthood v. Danforth* and in *Carey v. Population Services International* (1977) the Court did use language very much like that used in equal protection cases. *Carey* struck down a state law that prohibited the distribution of nonprescription contraceptives to those under sixteen years of age. Since the law invaded the fundamental right of privacy protected by the Court in *Griswold v. Connecticut* and *Roe v. Wade,* it could be justified, the Court ruled, only by a showing of a compelling state interest. The state argued that its legislation was permissible as a measure against "promiscuous sexual intercourse among the young" (*Carey v. Population Services International*: 2020). To prevail, however, that had to be more than a "bare assertion." Brennan found instead the "complete absence of supporting evidence" on the state's part.

Of course, these cases do not stand for the view that minors can never be the object of special legislation. Especially in instances involving the regulation of alcohol, sexually explicit material, or other matters broadly within the domain of public morality, protective legislation is likely to be sustained (*Ginsberg v. New York*, 1968). A recent example can be found in *City of Dallas v. Stanglin* (1989) in which the Court unanimously sustained a local ordinance prohibiting admission to dance halls of persons between fourteen and eighteen years of age, while using only the rational basis standard of review.

Cases involving older persons have generally held against the person objecting to age discrimination, and the Court purports to have applied the rational basis test. Thus, in *Massachusetts Board of Retirement v. Murgia* (1976) the Court upheld a state law that provided for mandatory retirement at age fifty for state police officers. It was evident even to the Court's majority that not all persons of fifty are equally ready for retirement. Indeed, fitness could have been determined by much more precise means, which the per curiam opinion acknowledged. Still, police officers over fifty were held not to be members of a victimized class, and the state's generalization about age was held to have a rational basis. Only Marshall dissented. He was willing to apply more exacting scrutiny and was persuaded by the fact that since Massachusetts was already routinely testing its officers' physical fitness, there was no reason that fitness could not be judged at age fifty and after.[14]

In 1979 in *Vance v. Bradley,* the Court was consistent with *Murgia* in sustaining a mandatory retirement age of sixty for foreign service officers. Again only Marshall dissented.

The Age Discrimination in Employment Act of 1967 covered issues such as those raised in *Murgia* and in *Vance,* but it was not until 1974 that the act was extended to cover state or local governmental employers. The result of the statute was to place the burden on the employer of showing that age was a "bona fide occupational qualification reasonably necessary to the normal operation of the particular business" (29 U.S.C., sec. 623(f)(1)). The act was sustained in its application to governmental employers in *EEOC v. Wyoming* (1983). However, in 1991 in *Gregory v. Ashcroft,* the Supreme Court held that Missouri state judges were appointees on a "policymaking level" and thus were covered by an exclusion in the federal Age Discrimination in Employment Act. Moreover, the court's majority in *Gregory* reiterated its previous rulings in

Murgia and in *Vance v. Bradley* that age is not a suspect classification, so that only the "rational basis" test is to be applied (*Gregory v. Ashcroft*: 2406). It is clear that but for congressional intervention, the Court sees no equal protection reason for overturning state mandatory retirement policies.

MENTAL RETARDATION

Only a single Supreme Court decision has considered mental retardation as the possible subject for discrimination, but it is a recent and important example of the Court's application of the Equal Protection Clause. The case involved a municipal zoning ordinance, which required a hearing for a special use permit for hospitals for the "insane or feeble-minded, or alcoholic or drug addicts, or penal or correctional institutions" (*City of Cleburne, Texas v. Cleburne Living Center,* 1985: 3252). Even while holding that mentally retarded persons did not constitute a suspect class for equal protection purposes, the Court struck down the city's ordinance. It did not have even a rational basis according to the Court, for the city did not require special use permits, for example, for boarding and lodging houses, fraternity or sorority houses, dormitories, hospitals, sanitariums, or nursing homes. The special use requirement for homes for mentally retarded persons was based on nothing more than "an irrational prejudice" (*City of Cleburne, Texas v. Cleburne Living Center:* 3260). Justice Marshall concurred with that result but was disturbed by the Court's rhetorical reluctance against heightened scrutiny review. Awareness of various forms of discrimination, Marshall argued, evolves across time. What once was acceptable without question may now be clearly suspect. By adopting heightened scrutiny for instances involving the mentally retarded or the handicapped, the Court would simply recognize the evolution of our understanding:

Courts, however, do not sit or act in a social vacuum. Moral philosophers may debate whether certain inequalities are absolute wrongs, but history makes clear that constitutional principles of equality, like constitutional principles of liberty, property, and due process, evolve over time; what once was a "natural" and "self evident" ordering later comes to be seen as an artificial and invidious constraint on human potential and freedom. (*City of Cleburne, Texas v. Cleburne Living Center:* 3268)

Justice Marshall's language in the *Cleburne* case offers a suitable conclusion to this chapter. We have reviewed cases involving aliens, voting and elections, residency, marriage, illegitimacy, traditional and nontraditional family structures, poverty, age, and mental retardation. Except for the early cases involving aliens and voting, the vast majority of the decisions date from the 1960s, but there was also a surge of decisions upholding equality in the 1970s. In a large sense all of the cases have involved a heightened awareness of the possible public usages of stereotypes and of unsubstantiated prejudices, even in the laws enacted by popularly elected legislators. Even when a majority of the Court recently has been unwilling to apply heightened scrutiny review to these laws, the fact that the issues are before the Court in itself represents the evolution of our understanding.

When the Court does apply heightened scrutiny—and especially when it applies strict scrutiny—it is in effect recognizing that certain prejudices and stereotypes have become highly visible and predominantly unacceptable. I am not sure that the differences between the justices of the Supreme Court as to the proper standard for equal protection review amount to anything more than their having different understandings regarding the propriety of particular distinctions among people. To be fair, the justices' disagreements on the degree of deference that ought to be accorded legislators may also represent a real division. A majority of the Court has been more deferential to legislators in recent decisions. But for whatever reason, even if the pace of the Court's recognition of human equality has slowed recently, the long-term trend over the past several decades has clearly favored inclusion. As that has happened the Supreme Court has broadened the circle of inclusionary equality in the United States.

12

EQUALITY FROM A MULTINATIONAL PERSPECTIVE

Today, the political theory which acknowledges the obligation of government . . . to provide jobs, medical care, old age pension, etc., extends to human rights and imposes an affirmative obligation to promote equality and liberty. The force of the idea of a state with obligation to help the weaker sections of its members seems to have increasing influence in constitutional law. The idea finds expression in a number of cases in America involving racial discrimination and also in the decisions requiring the state to offset the effects of poverty by providing counsel, transcript of appeal, expert witnesses, etc. Today, the sense that government has affirmative responsibility for the elimination of inequalities, social, economic, or otherwise, is one of the dominant forces in constitutional law.
—Justice Mathew of the Indian Supreme Court
in *State of Kerala v. Thomas*

In this chapter we will study equality provisions from the perspectives of the basic law of two other countries and under certain provisions of international law. My principal purpose is to show that understandings of equality outside the United States are more accepting of affirmative action and therefore more open to group- or bloc-regarding equality than often is the case in U.S. domestic law.

In the opinion of many observers, the United States is the quintessential land of individual-regarding equality. The deceptively simple idea that all human beings are equal and ought to be treated alike continues its appeal to many Americans, even if that is often only at a reflexive level of understanding. In the preceding chapters we have seen the doctrinal decline of justifications for racial and sexual distinctions and the conceptual victory of individual-regarding equality.

The appeal of individual-regarding equality is often so strong that programs that provide for some sort of affirmative action for members of traditionally disadvantaged groups may be rejected out of hand by those who espouse a continuing commitment to individualism. Indeed, from the cases reviewed in the previous several chapters, we can say that of the many issues raised in U.S. equal protection cases since the landmark *Brown* decision on racial discrimination in 1954, probably the most persistent and intractable conflict has involved policies that supporters call affirmative action and opponents call reverse discrimination. We saw those views posed in opposition to one another in a number of instances of racial discrimination in chapter 9 and of sexual discrimination in chapter 10. Moreover, in chapter 10 we learned that in 1987 the Supreme Court split 6 to 3 over the question of whether public employers may preferentially hire and promote women over white males (*Johnson v. Transportation Agency, Santa Clara County, California*).

The Court's majority in 1987, which occasionally still favored such preferences, was led by the then eighty-year-old Justice Brennan, since replaced by Justice Souter. That majority also included Justice Powell, who since has retired and been replaced by Justice Kennedy,[1] who as yet has been no friend of affirmative action. The completion of the 1990–91 term of the Court also brought the resignation of Justice Marshall, and his replacement, Clarence Thomas, has a record of having consistently opposed affirmative action.

The preferences of certain justices for individual-regarding equality and the difficulty encountered in achieving acceptance of affirmative action programs in the United States are not, however, necessarily typical of other countries and cultures. By examining the experiences of countries with somewhat different views on equality and affirmative action, India and Canada, we may gain a better perspective on the limitations of our own understanding of equality. We hope that the experiences of these two systems will shed some light on the conflict between individual-regarding and group- or bloc-regarding equality that we have witnessed in the United States.

Rae's conceptualization individual-regarding equality always involves a single class of individuals, all of whom are subject to the requirement that they should be treated alike. Group- or bloc-regarding equality always involves two or more groups, with the requirement that the groups as a whole receive equal treatment but not necessarily that individuals within groups be treated alike. Group-regarding equality commonly involves the measurement of success through the measurement of group outcomes; for example, does the ratio of "blacks to whites" in a particular work force match the ratio of those groups in the local community?

As we have seen, policies with implications for equality often involve choices between these two understandings. The most common Ameri-

can preference is for individual-regarding equality. Later, in the conclusion of this book, we will examine some of the underpinnings and consequences of American individualism that support this preference.

THE INDIAN EXPERIENCE

One obvious solution to the choice between individual-regarding and
group-regarding equality is to include an explicit choice in the constitution of a nation state. Several countries have done that, and India is one
of them. It might seem that such an initial choice would obviate the
necessity of judges frequently having to choose between competing
versions of equality. That has not been the case in India, for its courts
have labored as hard as any with the application of equality principles.

India's provisions regarding equality date from the constitutional
founding of the Indian nation in 1949 and are found in Articles 14, 15,
16, 29 (2) and 330 of the Indian Constitution. Article 15 (3) contains
explicit language on affirmative action affecting women and children
and what amounts to an even broader affirmative action clause was
added as Article 15 (4) in 1951.[2] Article 16 (4) included a broad affirmative action proviso from the beginning.[3] Article 330 reserves seats in
the Indian parliament for members of the scheduled castes and tribes,
but it establishes limits in time, even though its deadline has been
extended three times. Marc Galanter's massive study of Indian affirmative action programs provides the definitive background for the study of
these provisions. Obviously, we can only touch the surface of the subject in this chapter.

Galanter refers to India as a "compartmental" society in which many
groups maintain their diversity of statuses, life-styles, and religions.[4]
Caste, he notes, is one of the more "distinctive and pervasive features of
Indian society" (Galanter, 1984: 7). Caste contributes to a particular way
of viewing the society that involves graded hierarchies:

> The notion of graded inequality is explained and justified by the
> traditional Hindu notions of *dharma* and *karma*. Each caste group
> has its own *dharma*—the path which each of its members should
> follow in accordance with his nature and his station in life. The
> inequality of stations and the more onerous duties incumbent on
> some is explained and justified by the theory of *karma* and re-
> birth—that is, every human action has a positive or negative
> worth, and the moral balance of an individual's actions in previous

lives is manifested in the station into which he is reborn. Inequality
is thus explained and justified as the reflection of relative spiritual
merit accumulated in past existences. (Galanter, 1984: 11)

Galanter describes a traditional caste system that is at odds with
almost any contemporary understanding of human equality. In that tradition, at the bottom of the castes were the "Untouchables," but the
restrictions or disabilities that applied to Untouchables varied from
place to place in India. Discrimination against Untouchables and other
disadvantaged castes became an issue long before India's independence, but Gandhi's famous fast in 1932 against untouchability was
prominently associated with the movement to reform the caste system.
When independence finally came in 1947, events led to the inclusion of
Article 46 in the new constitution (Galanter, 1984: 28 et seq.).

As a "Directive of State Policy," Article 46 declared, "The State shall
promote with special care the educational and economic interests of the
weaker sections of the people" (Subbarao, 1985). Such directives are
not judicially enforceable, but the constitution still prescribes the duty
of the state to apply these principles (Galanter, 1984: 365).

Unlike Article 16 (4), which provided for affirmative action in public
employment from the beginning, the affirmative action proviso of Article 15 (4) was added by amendment in 1951 following a decision of the
Indian Supreme Court in *State of Madras v. Champakam Dorairajan*
(1951) (McKean, 1983: 253–53). That decision held that the state had
no power to reserve seats for backward communities in public educational institutions (as was explicitly provided, however, in the instance
of public employment under Article 16 [4]); hence paragraph (4) was
added by amendment to Article 15.

Coincidentally, the first key interpretation of Article 16 (4) was rendered on the same day in 1951 as the *Dorairajan* case. In *Venkataramana v. State of Madras* an official listing of public job openings indicated that of 83 positions, 19 would be reserved for *Harijans* (Untouchables), 5 for Muslims, 6 for Christians, 10 for backward Hindus, 32 for
non-Brahmin Hindus, and 11 for Brahmins. The petitioner was a Brah-
min, who under the listing would have been eligible for only 11 of the 83
positions, despite his qualifications. The Indian Supreme Court held
that *only* the reservation of jobs for *Harijans* and backward Hindus
could be sustained under 16 (4), for it was "impossible to say that
classes of people other than Harijans and Backward Hindus can be
called Backward Classes" (*Venkataramana v. State of Madras*: 230).

The determination of exactly who could be included as "backward classes" was an important issue, for it defined the difference between attempting to compensate for the social inequalities traditionally attributed to certain groups and the possible creation of entitlements even for more "advanced" groups (Galanter, 1984: 165 et seq.). The notion of entitlements has nonetheless proven to be a problem in India. Certain groups have "competed to be anointed with the `backward' label so as to become entitled to the benefits of compensatory discrimination" (Gadbois, 1986: 332).

The opinion of the Indian Supreme Court in *Venkataramana* was terse, and no criteria for determining the meaning of the words *backward classes* were offered. However, in 1963 in *Balaji v. State of Mysore* the Supreme Court reviewed a state order that had set aside positions for students from backward classes in public educational institutions. Mysore had appointed a Backward Classes Committee to advise the state government on criteria for determining who comprised "educationally and socially Backward Classes" (*Balaji v. State of Mysore*: 654).

The committee's report essentially equated socially "backward classes" with caste and community. At the risk of greatly oversimplifying a very complex Hindu social system, it can be noted briefly that traditionally there were four main divisions (*Varnas*) of Hindu society: *Brahmins* (priests), *Kshatriyas* (warriors), *Vaisyas* (merchants), and *Shudras* (servants). Each of the four *Varnas* is in turn divided into a larger number of caste groups (*jatis*). Untouchables (Gandhi called them "*Harijans*," which means children of God [Gadbois, 1986: 330]), were entirely outside the fourfold scheme and were traditionally referred to as outcastes (Kramer, 1982: 188–89). Today the term *scheduled castes* is roughly the same as the "Untouchables." They make up almost 15 percent (over 113 million) of India's population. The term *scheduled tribes* refers to India's aboriginal people, who make up about 7 percent (over 53 million) of the population and are physically concentrated in isolated parts of the country (Gadbois, 1986: 331).

The report of the Mysore committee in the *Balaji* case sought to divide the backward classes into those that were educationally "more backward" and only "backward," so it recommended that 28 percent of places in educational institutions be set aside for the "backward," 22 percent for the "more backward," 15 percent for scheduled castes and 3 percent for scheduled tribes—for a total reservation of 68 percent of the available places.[5]

The Indian Supreme Court found that the reservation of 68 percent of the places in educational institutions for backward classes was excessive and contrary to the purpose of Article 15 (4):

It is because the interest of society at large would be served by promoting the advancement of the weaker elements in the society that Article 15 (4) authorized special provisions to be made. But if a provision which is in the nature of an exception completely excluded the rest of society, that clearly is outside the scope of Art. 15 (4). It would be extremely unreasonable to assume that in enacting Art. 15 (4) the Constitution intended to provide that where the advancement of the Backward Classes or the Scheduled Castes and Tribes was concerned, the fundamental rights of the citizens constituting the rest of the society were to be completely and absolutely ignored. (*Balaji v. State of Mysore*: 662)

The Supreme Court suggested that the reservations should be less than 50 percent, and how much less than 50 percent they should be was contingent on the circumstances of each case.

It is worth noting that in the *Balaji* case the Indian Supreme Court cited with approval a program of another local government that called for the provision of financial assistance to students who sought higher education whose family incomes were below a certain prescribed minimum. That program, the Court said, "may afford relief to and assist the advancement of the Backward Classes in the State, because backwardness, social and educational, is ultimately and primarily due to poverty." The Indian Supreme Court also approved of that approach because it proceeded "on a rational, broad and scientific approach which is consistent with, and true to, the noble ideal of a secular welfare democratic State set up by the Constitution of this country" (*Balaji v. State of Mysore*: 664).

THE INDIAN EQUIVALENT OF THE *BAKKE* CASE

In 1976 in the case of *State of Kerala v. N. M. Thomas* the Indian Supreme Court rendered a decision on an ameliorative policy that was outside the affirmative provisions of Articles 15 (4) and 16 (4). The case involved the promotion of certain public employees, with provision for deferring the required passing of a certain examination for those promoted employees who were members of scheduled castes or scheduled tribes. Since Article 16 (4) calls only for the reservation of appointments for backward classes, promotions, especially ones with deferred examinations, are not covered.

The *Thomas* case has been called the "Indian equivalent of the *Bakke* decision" (McKean, 1983: 255). The Indian Constitution confers individual rights to equal treatment under law, however, the Indian government is also under the obligation to advance the disadvantaged segments of the population. This "compensatory discrimination involves tension between individuals or groups as objects of State policy" (Galanter, 1984: 381).

The complaint filed by Thomas concerned 51 vacancies that occurred for the position of "Upper Division Clerk" in 1972, 34 of which were filled by members of scheduled castes who had been exempted from the necessary qualifications for the position. Only 17 positions went to "qualified" persons. Nonetheless, the 34 individuals who had been promoted without the qualifications had accumulated the greatest seniority in the post of lower division clerk. The qualifications for the higher position included both seniority and a merit examination.

The temporary exemption from the passage of a merit examination was alleged by Thomas to be a violation of the general requirement of equal treatment under Article 16 (1), but the majority of the Indian Supreme Court held that this article prohibited only unreasonable distinctions and policies. Equal opportunity under Article 16 (1), the court said, required only that those who are "equally circumstanced" be treated equally. Here, according to the court, is how the exemption from the requirement of the merit examination can be reconciled with equal opportunity:

> The rule of classification is not a natural and logical corollary of the rule of equality, but the rule of differentiation is inherent in the concept of equality. Equality means parity of treatment under parity of conditions. Equality does not connote absolute equality. A classification in order to be constitutional must rest upon distinctions that are substantial and not merely illusory. The test is whether it has a reasonable basis free from artificiality and arbitrariness embracing all and omitting none naturally falling into that category. (*State of Kerala v. Thomas*: 499)

Under the *Thomas* standard the allowance of an extended period for the passage of a test for promotion accorded the members of scheduled castes and tribes was judged to be just and reasonable. Preference for the representation and promotion of the backward classes in public employment was a rational and permissible object of policy. Justice

Mathew's separate opinion in the *Thomas* case is consistent with that conclusion, but his justification offers a better explanation than others because it is more concrete:

> If we are all to be treated in the same manner, that must carry with it the important requirement that none of us should be better or worse in upbringing or education than anyone else which is an unattainable ideal for human beings of anything like the sort we now see. Some people maintain that equality of opportunity is an unsatisfactory concept. For, a complete formulation of it renders it incompatible with any form of human society. Take, for instance, the case of equality of opportunity for education. This equality cannot start in schools and hence requires uniform treatment in families which is an evident impossibility. To remedy this, all children might be brought up in state nurseries, but, to achieve the purpose, the nurseries would have to be run on vigorous uniform lines. (*State of Kerala v. Thomas*: 513–14)

Under Justice Mathew's reasoning, equality principles themselves suggest that government has an affirmative duty to eliminate inequalities and "to provide opportunities for the exercise of human rights and claims" (*State of Kerala v. Thomas*: 516).

According to Galanter, the outcome in *Thomas,* though somewhat uncertain, represents a significant doctrinal shift from previous decisions. He largely welcomed that shift, however, because it made judicial "reflection on compensatory equality unavoidable," and it provided the government "more ample means to pursue compensatory policies" (Galanter, 1984: 389–90).

The several separate opinions in *State of Kerala v. Thomas* offer excellent illustrations of different ways of thinking about equality. These indeed may help us to reconcile the apparently conflicting claims of individual-regarding and group- or bloc-regarding equality. The Indian reconciliation is somewhat different from the results in prominent affirmative action cases in the United States. For example, in *Swann v. Charlotte-Mecklenburg,* the affirmative obligation to achieve racial balance in public schools was based strictly on the premise that prior official wrongdoing of the school district (de jure discrimination) justified compensatory relief, such as busing and racial targets or quotas (see chapter 8). *Thomas,* to the contrary, sustains affirmative action even when the discrimination may have been entirely outside the domain of the current policy.[6]

The *Bakke* case, however, denied the explicit use of racial quotas and of compensatory equality (see chapter 9). The key vote cast by Justice Powell allowed the use of race as only one element in a policy that seeks to achieve a diverse student body. While Powell's solution still seemed to involve a racially conscious admissions program, race was moved off center stage by his solution and was replaced by the alternative goal of diversity. Indeed, it can reasonably be argued that Justice Powell's proposed solution to the issues in *Bakke* entirely obviates the use, even in certain limited circumstances, of racially conscious affirmative action policies.

If, for example, diversity in either a faculty or a student body is a legitimate educational objective, then it would seem to be appropriate to use race, ethnicity, religion, political orientation, or state of residence as factors (among others) that would contribute to diversity. However, it is somewhat difficult to imagine diversity as an end in itself. Presumably a justification for seeking diversity would be that it might be associated with different life values and perspectives, so that exchanges of views from diverse perspectives would enrich the educational environment. If that were the case, then the pursuit of diversity would have nothing to do either with compensation for the victims of traditional discrimination or with the amelioration of the currently disadvantaged. Affirmative action policies that recognize and seek to remediate the continuing consequences of traditional forms of discrimination or the reality of present disadvantaged would still require some independent justification against the claims of individual-regarding equality.

Firefighters Local No. 1784 v. Stotts, you may recall, represented a frontal conflict between the different justices' views on individual-regarding and group-regarding equality (see chapter 9). In a contest between seniority rules and affirmative action in *Stotts,* affirmative action lost 5 to 3. Affirmative action does not always lose in U.S. courts, but the acceptance of affirmative action remedies is at best reluctant for most.

The Indian cases represent not merely the presence of explicit affirmative action provisos in the Indian Constitution, though those provisions are an important contribution. Nor is it merely the case that the Indian decisions represent both the reality of a traditionally compartmentalized society and a contemporary preference among members of the Indian ruling elite for group-regarding equality because it may help to reduce historic disadvantages. The testament of *State of Kerala v. Thomas* is that equality of opportunity involves more than a formal, but perhaps simplistic, policy of individual-regarding equality. If people are indeed to have equality of opportunity, then the lesson of *Thomas* is that it is wrong to accept, but ignore, the handicaps that they bear, often from birth. In Justice Mathew words: "Formal equality of opportunity simply enables people with m[o]re education and intelligence to capture all the posts and to win over the less fortunate in education and talent even when the competition is fair. Equality of result is the test of equality of opportunity" (*State of Kerala v. Thomas*: 518).

One interesting aspect of Justice Mathew's opinion is that he drew, in part, on certain U.S. sources for authority. First, he relied on cases involving the rights of the accused in criminal courts, coupled with equal protection, to show that U.S. criminal justice came in the 1960s to require that an indigent criminal defendant not be disadvantaged by the inability to pay for counsel or for transcripts on appeal. Next, Mathew drew on the *Moynihan Report* (Moynihan, 1965) to show that the civil rights movement in the United States was transformed in the 1960s from one demanding liberty for individual black people to one calling for equality in group terms. This, Justice Mathew wrote, meant that the United States had begun to correct the discrepancy between its ideals and its practices. Mathew also saw affirmative action under the Indian Constitution not as an exception to equality but rather as "an emphatic way" of accomplishing equality of opportunity, even to the point of reserving coveted places for the "truly disadvantaged."[7]

Despite the language in *Thomas,* Galanter reports that compensatory equality has not fared all that well in the Indian courts. Between 1950 and 1977, he counted 113 reported suits that involved provision for compensatory equality. The Indian Supreme Court rendered decisions in 39; in less than half of them were the results in favor of affirmative policies. The outcomes in lower courts were even less favorable to compensatory equality (Galanter, 1984: 487).

We should also note that at about the same time that Galanter's book was being published in 1984, riots broke out in the Indian state of Gujarat over a promise of its government to increase reservations of positions in higher education and in public employment. The Gujarat riots were not isolated events. Indeed, Gadbois suggests that the "moral consensus" that supported compensatory programs at the birth of the Indian nation today has become an "angry debate" over the policy of reserving places for the disadvantaged (Gadbois, 1986: 341–42).

The angry debate has continued. In November 1990, Chandra Shekhar, newly named Janata Dal Socialist prime minister, vowed "to create a society of equals." Even so, Shekhar had come to office as a successor to V. P. Singh, whose efforts to reserve more government jobs for low-caste Indians through another affirmative action program had contributed to approximately 150 deaths by suicide or through political unrest in India in 1990 (Joshi, 1990). By March 1991, Shekhar was also forced out of office. Late in that month the continuing scourge of caste in India was sadly but profoundly illustrated by the hanging of three young Indians on a tree in the village of Mehrana near New Delhi. They died because one of them, a young woman of the Jat caste, had attempted to elope with a young man from the outcaste Harijan community. They were helped by a friend, another Harijan. The Jat-controlled village council sentenced the three of them to death for the outrage (Crossette, 1991). Clearly, we should not conclude that caste has been vanquished in India. But equally, we can by no means conclude that compensatory equality is universally popular amongst the Indian people.

We should note that Justice Mathew's version of equality of opportunity is not as simple and straightforward as it may seem at first glance (see chapter 13). James Fishkin, among others, has pointed out that requiring equality of results can indeed prove to be problematic in a variety of ways (Fishkin, 1983).

THE CANADIAN CHARTER OF
RIGHTS AND FREEDOMS

The Canadian Charter of Rights and Freedoms became part of the basic law of Canada through the Constitution Act of 1982. Prior to the charter, the Canadian Bill of Rights (1960) had declared the right to be free from "discrimination by reason of race, national origin, colour, religion or sex" and of "the right of the individual to equality before the law and equal protection of the law" (Canadian Bill of Rights, Section 1 [b]). That provision was, however, given a rather narrow meaning by Canadian courts.

The 1982 charter went considerably beyond earlier provisions and called in Section 15 (1) for equality *before* and *under* the law, as well as equal protection and equal benefit of the law. These forms of equality are to be provided "without discrimination," particularly without discrimination based on "race, national or ethnic origin, colour, religion, sex, age or mental or physical disability." Having covered those four forms of equality, Section 15 (2) goes on to provide explicitly for affirmative action. The proviso is that Section 15 (1) should not be read to preclude any policy or program whose purpose is the amelioration of disadvantaged individuals or groups, particularly those who are disadvantaged because of "race, national or ethnic origin, colour, religion, sex, age or mental or physical disability." The charter in effect calls for a three-stage inquiry. First comes the question of whether there has been a violation of one or more of the equality principles called for in 15 (1). Second, is the question of whether the discrimination (if any has been found) is nonetheless part of a genuine ameliorative policy for disadvantaged individuals or groups under Section 15 (2), Third, Section 1 of the charter provides that the rights and freedoms guaranteed by the charter are subject to "such reasonable limits prescribed by law as can be demonstrably justified in a free and democratic society," so Canadian courts must determine whether the discrimination (if any they have found) is justifiable under that standard. For example, in two cases in 1990 the Canadian Supreme Court held that the mandatory retirement age provisions of Canadian public university, while violative of Section 15 (1), were nonetheless sustainable as reasonable limitations on equality rights under Section 1 of the charter (*Harrison v. University of British Columbia* and *McKinney v. University of Guelph,* 1990).

The three stages of analysis and the plurality of equality in Section 15 (1) suggest that Canadian judges confront an interpretive task far more complex than that posed for U.S. judges by the Equal Protection Clause of the Fourteenth Amendment. What were the reasons for the plural equality provisions of Section 15 (1)? Equality before the law was in Section 1 (b) of the Canadian Bill of Rights, and it has a long history as well under the common law. It is a general statement that everyone is subject to the law—the same law—and that no one stands above the law. As a traditional requirement of consistency, some commentators have suggested that under the new charter it is as yet an open question whether equality before the law may go beyond that to evaluate the substance of policies (Eberts, 1985: 154). It seems that to do so would be redundant, for the principal Canadian commentators agree that the purpose of adding equality under the law to the new charter was to make it clear that some sort of substantive equality would also be required (Bayefsky and Eberts, 1985: 12; Gold, 1982: 124, Eberts, 1985: 155).

The requirement of equal protection of the law in the new charter seems an obvious effort to draw on case law from the United States, particularly on the various tests that have been developed by the Court (strict scrutiny, heightened scrutiny/rational basis, etc.) with which legislative enactments are measured (Bayefsky and Eberts, 1985: 13). Bayefsky argues that U.S. precedents seem to require equal protection as formal equality of opportunity, but she suggests that something approaching equality of results is also required in certain equal protection cases concerning "fundamental rights." Her example is *Shapiro v. Thompson* (1969), which, as we saw in chapter 11, struck down a discriminatory state residency requirement that kept a young woman who had recently arrived in Connecticut from receiving AFDC payments. Such outcomes, she noted, have not occurred in the United States "without corresponding displays of hand-wringing" (Bayefsky and Eberts, 1985: 19).

Finally, equal benefit of the law is said to have come from the 1979 decision in *Bliss v. Attorney General of Canada,* which involved the availability of unemployment benefits for a mother after the birth of a child. In *Bliss* the Canadian Supreme Court decided that the Canadian parliament could prescribe conditions for entitlement to unemployment benefits without violating Section 1 (b) of the extant Canadian Bill of Rights. The text of the federal report that accepted the addition of equal benefit of law language to Section 1 of the Charter of Rights and Freedoms, commented that the inclusion of those words would "extend the right to ensure that people enjoy equal benefits as well as protection of the law" (Bayefsky and Eberts, 1985: 23). While the equality of benefits provision implies some sort of equality of results with respect to the provision of money or other benefits by the government, the precise meaning of the words equality *before* and *under* the law and *equal protection* and *equal benefit* of the law is clearly open to judicial interpretation. However, in the Canadian cases that we review in this chapter we will see that Canadian courts have not, as yet, been much bothered by subtle distinctions among the four versions of equality set out in Section 1.

AFFIRMATIVE ACTION UNDER THE CANADIAN CHARTER OF RIGHTS AND FREEDOMS

Section 15 (2) of the charter explicitly avoids conflict between the general requirements of equality in 15 (1) and any "law, program or activity that has as its object the amelioration of conditions of disadvantaged groups or individuals." Conditions of disadvantage may include, but presumably are not limited to, "race, national or ethnic origin, colour, religion, sex, age or mental or physical disability." This list includes almost all the forms of discrimination that have been accumulated, case by case, in equal protection cases in the United States.

With respect to Section 15 (2) Bayefsky has cited the language of Gordon Fairweather, the chief commissioner of the Canadian Human Rights Commission, who testified in 1978 in support of the affirmative action proviso:

> Affirmative action programs should be allowed under the charter of rights and freedoms because sometimes just treating everybody equally does not eliminate the effects of discrimination. If some groups are already far behind and if the established way of doing things conspired to keep them behind, even unintentionally, then having a so-called equal chance with everyone else may not really give them a fair chance to catch up. Such a group may require a special program in order to bring them up to the point where they can take advantage of the same opportunities as everybody else. (Bayefsky and Eberts, 1985: 21)

One consequence of the proviso of 15 (2) is that, unlike U.S. affirmative action cases, amelioration is not contingent upon findings of prior de jure discrimination. Amelioration is supported by 15 (2) whatever may have the source or cause of the disadvantage. The relatively few cases that have been brought since 1985 under the charter sustain that conclusion. This is another example of compensatory equality in which a domain of allocation is used to compensate for inequality outside that domain. Nonetheless, the federal or provincial governments may have to meet a judicially determined standard for justifying such ameliorative programs. One example of that outcome appeared in the case of *Apsit, et al. v. Manitoba Human Rights Commission* (1985).

In the *Apsit* case Judge Jewers of the Manitoba Queen's Bench reviewed an affirmative action plan that had been approved by a provincial commission and that had granted to Indian groups and to certain individuals of native ancestry the first option to obtain licenses for the growing and harvesting of wild rice. Against that preference, an association of wild rice growers invoked Section 15 (1) of the charter. Judge Jewers acknowledged the discrimination under 15 (1) and found that 15 (2) applied, but he placed the burden on the Manitoba Human Rights Commission to show that its plan came within the "four corners" of 15 (2) and that the Indians and persons of native ancestry who were the objects of the affirmative plan were in fact "disadvantaged individuals" within the meaning of 15 (2). You may have noted that the issue raised in *Apsit* was much like the problem encountered in identifying backward classes under the Indian Constitution in *Balaji* case above.[8]

The next two Canadian cases involved conflicting judgments of provincial courts in British Columbia and Alberta. In *Regina v. LeGallant* (1985) the British Columbia Supreme Court considered whether a provision of its criminal code discriminates on the basis of age by restricting the defense of consent in cases involving youthful sexual offenders to persons three or fewer years older than the complainant, when the complainant was under fourteen years of age. The court held that it did discriminate, and it refused to apply Section 15 (2) by concluding (without much discussion) that the government's purpose of restricting the consent defense was not covered by the "amelioration of the disadvantaged" language of that section. The court then proceeded to determine whether this age discrimination could nevertheless be sustained by Section 1 because it was "demonstrably justified in a free and democratic society." The justification of the British Columbia government was that its provision would deter exploitation of young persons by older ones, but the British Columbia Supreme Court held, "exploitation by anyone—old or young—is equally abhorrent" (*Regina v. LeGallant*: 375). Thus the discrimination found under 15 (1) could not be justified either by Section 15 (2) or by Section 1.

The Alberta case was *Regina v. Bearhead* (1986). Alberta's criminal code provision on sexual consent was much the same as that of British Columbia. In *Regina v. Bearhead,* however, there was no reference at all to the proviso of Section 15 (2). The Alberta court found a violation of 15 (1) but sustained the consent provision on the grounds that it was designed to protect young females from becoming pregnant. As such it was held to be sustainable in a "free and democratic society" (*Regina v. Bearhead*: 217). This result was much like the decision of the U.S. Supreme Court in *Michael M. v. Superior Court of Sonoma County* (1981) (chapter 10) regarding a law under which only males could be held guilty of statutory rape.

Under the Fourteenth Amendment in the United States, equal protection judgments as to reasonableness of legislation must be made as an intrinsic part of equal protection inquiry. However, as both of these Canadian cases on sexual consent illustrate, under the Canadian charter legislation may be found to be discriminatory under 15 (1). However, that determination only moves the analysis on to the next steps, that is, of testing the law under the affirmative action proviso of 15 (2) and/or under the "free and democratic society" standard of Section 1.

In *Regina v. Oakes* (1986) the Canadian Supreme Court gave its first interpretation of Section 1.[9] The government's objective in justifying a limit on a right or freedom otherwise protected must "relate to con-

cerns which are pressing and substantial" before it can be held sufficiently important to override a right. Moreover, the government is required to show that the "means chosen are reasonable and demonstrably justified." This, the court said, involves a "proportionality" test.
Proportionality involves balancing the interests of society with those of
individuals and groups (*Regina v. Oakes*: 334 et seq.).[10]

We can offer only a few illustrations of the potential application of
Section 15 (2). In *Regina v. M.* (1985) the Manitoba Queen's Bench
faced the question of whether the exclusion of young offenders from
entitlement to earned remission of sentence violates a young person's
right to equality *before the law*. That court held the provision was a
violation of 15 (1) but that it was justified by the proviso of 15 (2). The
Young Offenders Act was viewed as a statute that discriminated in favor
of young offenders (*Regina v. M.*: 177).

Another case came from British Columbia. The intermediate appellate court there held that a provision for the commitment of a defendant
found not guilty by reason of insanity was an ameliorative measure
under 15 (2). The B.C. Court of Appeals, however, disagreed on the
application of 15 (2). The commitment procedure was not to protect the
criminally insane but to protect the public and thus could not be sustained under the proviso of 15 (2). However, the court did find the
measure to be sustainable under the "free and democratic society" standard of Section 1.

The first decision of the Supreme Court of Canada interpreting Section 15 of the charter was in April 1989 in *Andrews v. Law Society of
British Columbia*. The several opinions in *Andrews* consider the meaning of equality under Section 15 (1) at length, and the court concluded
that the exclusion of aliens from admission to the British Columbia bar
was a violation of 15 (1), even though alienage was not on the list of
discriminatory categories contained within the section. A majority of
the court found that the discrimination was not sustainable under Section 1, because the province's reasons for the exclusion of aliens were
not sufficiently substantial to override Section 15 equality rights. The
majority said that the burden on government to justify discrimination
must be onerous. Two justices dissented and would have applied only a
standard of reasonableness under Section 1. It is interesting that the
division on the Canadian Supreme Court was much like that on the U.S.
Supreme Court, that is, between those who would apply strict or heightened scrutiny and those who only would require the showing of a rational basis for legislation. The two Canadian Supreme Court decisions of
1990 sustaining mandatory age retirement under Section 1, *Harrison*

and *McKinney,* seemed to be quite deferential to provincial policy and did apply a reasonableness standard. Neither *Andrews* nor *Harrison* nor *McKinney* involved the affirmative action proviso of Section 15 (2), so as yet there has been no interpretation of that section by the Canadian Supreme Court.

AFFIRMATIVE ACTION IN INTERNATIONAL LAW

While we have neither the time nor the space to explore the nuances of the various provisions regarding equality under public international law, it is worth noting that several documents contain explicit affirmative action provisos. The International Convention on the Elimination of All Forms of Racial Discrimination (1965), the Convention on the Elimination of All Forms of Discrimination Against Women (1979), and the International Labour Organization's Convention Concerning Discrimination in Respect to Employment and Occupation (1958) all contain affirmative action provisos.

The International Covenant on Economic, Social and Cultural Rights (1966) provides in Articles 2 and 3 for the exercise of rights without discrimination. While that covenant has no affirmative action proviso, the debates that led to its current form indicated that the phrase "without discrimination" was seen as being different from "without distinction." Discrimination was "an unjustified differential treatment," while affirmative action based on race or sex, for example, was seen as "justified differential treatment." Thus an affirmative action proviso was thought to be unnecessary, even though other covenants do contain explicit language about it (McKean, 1983: 146 et seq.).[11]

In the instance of the Covenant on Civil and Political Rights (1966), the report of the relevant United Nations committee also stressed that ameliorative measures would not be deemed to be violations of that covenant, which also prohibited distinction based on such traits as race, color, or sex (McKean, 1983: 150).

The explicit affirmative action provisos in international agreements always are intended as temporary measures to be limited by the need for them. For example, the provisos of the convention against racial discrimination were based, in part, on the following:

The Canadian co-sponsor [of the provisos] said that until recently the need had been felt for a categorical proclamation of the right to non-discrimination and there had been a widespread suspicion of any special measures that might be regarded as relics of a discriminatory system, whereas the most urgent need now was to provide the facilities necessary to enable minorities to attain equality as rapidly as possible. The purpose of the clause . . . was to provide temporary "compensatory inequalities" in order to achieve true equality in fact for racial groups in inferior positions. (McKean, 1983: 153)

While the United States has ratified none of these international conventions, they have become, by ratification, part of the domestic law of a number of nations. Canada, for example, has ratified all those mentioned here. In addition, the conventions illustrate the broad recognition and support within the international community for affirmative action provisos within the general requirements of equal treatment. The United States, while not alone, is probably the most prominent member of the family of nations that continues to have a number of leaders, including several justices of the Supreme Court, who demand individual-regarding equality without conceding exceptions for affirmative action.

DECISIONS OF INTERNATIONAL TRIBUNALS

The most interesting example of a judicial opinion from an international tribunal on this subject comes from Judge Tanaka's assessment of apartheid in his dissenting opinion in the *South-West Africa Cases* (1966) before the International Court of Justice at the Hague. The issue in that case was whether the practice of apartheid in mandated territory was in violation of the obligations of the mandate. To resolve that issue it was necessary to consider a means for distinguishing between acceptable and unacceptable distinctions in public policy, which in the instance of apartheid was clearly a racial distinction. Judge Tanaka wrote that differences of treatment can be justified only by a "criterion of justice." The difference between just and unjust policies was between those that are positive and permissive and those that are negative and prohibitive. Apartheid was clearly the latter. Even so, Tanaka wrote that positive and permissive policies in Africa would be based not on race but on factors that may be associated in a particular time and place with race. "If there exists the necessity to treat one race differently from another, this necessity is not derived from physical characteristics or other racial qualification but other factors, namely religious, linguistic, educational, social, etc., which in themselves are not related to race or colour" (Brownlie, 1981: 461).

Hence, differences in religion, language, education, and custom sometimes may reasonably justify different treatment in public policy, while apartheid, being based predominantly or exclusively on race, cannot. The first sometimes can be supported by objective and reasonable justification, while the second cannot. That is not to suggest that all distinctions based on religion, language, education or custom are sustainable. Tanaka's opinion requires that all differences in treatment take into account the concrete circumstances of individual cases. "Equality being a principle and different treatment an exception, those who refer to the different treatment must prove its *raison d'être* and its reasonableness (Brownlie, 1981: 464)." The idea that there ought to be a presumption in favor of equality and that those who propose different treatments ought to carry the burden of proof is common in the literature on equality as mentioned in chapter 2 (Hochschild, 1981).

Judge Tanaka's opinion in the *South-West Africa Cases* is quite consistent with the provisos included within the various international conventions reviewed above, for they in each instance recognize the transitory nature of affirmative action—ameliorative programs are to be used only when necessary and only as long as necessary. Even when explicit provisos are not included, judicial opinions seem often to lead to the same outcome. For example, Article 14 of the European Convention for the Protection of Human Rights and Fundamental Freedoms (1950) establishes that the rights and freedoms provided for in the convention "shall be secured *without discrimination* on any ground such as sex, race, colour, language, religion, political or other opinion, national or social origin, association with a national minority, property, birth or other status." The French text of the convention provides that the rights and freedom are to be secured "*sans distinction aucune*" (without distinction of any sort), while the English version only forbids discrimination. The English text serves better to illustrate how distinctions in public policies inexorably confront the necessity for deciding between acceptable and unacceptable justifications, for only those that are unacceptable are held discriminatory. This distinction is made even more clear under the Canadian charter through the three-step process involving Sections 15 (1), 15 (2) and Section 1.

The European Convention on Human Rights contains its equality provision in Article 14. The landmark case on the interpretation of Article 14 is commonly cited as the *Belgian Linguistics Case* (1968). In that case, French-speaking parents who lived in Flanders, the predominantly Dutch-speaking areas of Belgium, brought suit claiming that the failure of Belgium to provide their children public education in their native tongue was a denial of the right to education and was also discriminatory on the grounds of language, one of the categories prohibited by Article 14. The decision makes it clear that while discrimination for reasons listed in Article 14 is forbidden, not all distinctions are discriminatory. Distinctions are discriminatory only if they have "no objective and reasonable justification." Whether a distinction in treatment is tenable also must be assessed with "regard being had to the principles which normally prevail in democratic societies" (this is like Section 1 of the Canadian charter). Finally, a distinction becomes discriminatory when there is no "reasonable relationship of proportionality between the means employed and the aim sought to be realized" (*Belgian Linguistics Case*: 34). The European Court of Human Rights went on to establish that the assessment of a particular distinction must be made contextually, taking into account the "legal and factual features which characterize the life of a society." Belgium accordingly was recognized as a "pluralingual State" comprised of several linguistic areas.

With minor exceptions, the court sustained Belgium's provision for unilingual regions as founded on "objective assessment of essentially different factual circumstances" "a fair balance between the protection of the interests of the community and respect for the rights and freedoms safeguarded by the Convention" (*Belgian Linguistics Case*: 44).

We now have seen examples from India, Canada, and various international conventions and tribunals that include and accept affirmative action as temporary policies of amelioration or remediation. However controversial they may be, their textual or decisional commitment to compensatory equality is more clear and firm than in the United States, where the Supreme Court's majority favoring affirmative action has at best been small and today is beleaguered if not defunct. In the most recent U.S. cases, affirmative action clear stands imperiled. Still, the differences between the United States and other jurisdictions may not be quite as great as they seem at first comparison.

None of the international conventions and none of the jurisdictions accept affirmative action as a permanent policy. All affirmative action programs are instead based either on remediation (which may imply compensation for past official discrimination) or amelioration for disadvantaged individuals or groups (whatever the source of the disadvantage). It may be true that policy makers in the United States have been more reluctant than elsewhere to approve affirmative action policies, but in those instances in which they have been approved, they have been essentially like the policies that we have found in other jurisdictions. Second, while the efficacy of an affirmative action program may best be measured by proportionate group results, none of the policies we have seen provide for group proportionality on a permanent basis, even though that might be quite acceptable under the concept of group-regarding equality. Indeed, the international conventions expressly repudiate permanent proportionality. It is clear, however, that India has had difficulty with demands for transformation of ameliorative policies into permanent entitlements.

Most analysts and policy-makers view individual-regarding equality as the only acceptable long-term solution. A compelling case can be made in the short-term, however, in favor of affirmative action and group-regarding equality. As discussed in chapter 9, Edwin Dorn has shown that for African-Americans in the United States now to achieve the same current success with respect to personal careers as whites will not decrease overall "black/white" differences, though it will keep those differences from becoming even larger. The only way to decrease the differences in success between "blacks and whites" "requires hiring blacks at a faster rate than whites during periods of rapid growth, and laying off blacks at a slower rate during periods of economic downturn" (Dorn, 1979: 122–23). Dorn's analysis leads inevitably to the conclusion that affirmative action is essential in the short run if de facto group-regarding equality is sought. It is in this sense that Justice Mathew was correct in *State of Kerala v. Thomas*.

It follows that group-regarding equality is an acceptable way of thinking about equality in the short run whenever a society continues to reflect group-based discrimination, whatever its sources, public or private, may have been. The affirmative action provisos from India, Canada, and from public international law affirm that and in so doing they provide important insights for equality in America.

Gadbois has argued that the biggest difference between India and the United States is the "pervasive system of graded inequality in India that begins at birth and follows the individual for the rest of his life." He argues, "It is much more difficult in India, by one's own efforts, to move up socially and economically" (Gadbois, 1986: 360). That offers a compelling justification for group-regarding equality in India. Whether upward mobility is any easier for the "truly disadvantaged" members of America's urban underclass is certainly open to question, but that, to be sure, can only be a question of degree. Steven Wasby's review of Galanter's book on compensatory equality in India concludes that India "comes down much harder than do we on the side of *equalizing*" (to remedy for historic disadvantages and to bring people to the point where equality of opportunity can operate) (Wasby, 1986: 383). That is certainly true in terms of Indian constitutional law and public policy. Whether Indian law and policy have as yet produced much meaningful social change is, however, another question.

Our own controversies over affirmative action continue. For example, late in 1990 the Bush administration was mired in still another conflict over affirmative action. It involved a question of equal educational opportunity. Apparently without first checking with the White House, the Civil Rights Division of the federal Department of Education ruled that colleges and universities that receive federal support were prohibited from offering scholarships exclusively designated for minority students (*New York Times*: December 18, 1990). That position probably was quite consistent with the private attitudes of key Republican leaders within the administration, but strongly negative reactions from educators around the country and the ensuing political fallout for the president made the position an impossible one to hold. The policy judgment was promptly reconsidered and, for all practical purposes, revoked.

13

CONCLUSION: EQUALITY FOR
FUTURE REFERENCE

It was indeed the nineteenth century to which I had awaked; there could be no doubt about that. . . . Now . . . the glaring disparities in the dress and condition of the men and women who brushed each other on the sidewalks shocked me at every step, and yet more the entire indifference which the prosperous showed to the plight of the unfortunate. Were these human beings, who could behold the wretchedness of their fellows without so much as a change of countenance?
—Edward Bellamy, *Looking Backward: 2000–1887,* 1888

Perhaps the key problem in fully appreciating human equality and in being appropriately skeptical about the legitimacy of the various pecking orders that exist in any society is that familiar things often seem both natural and inevitable. As Bellamy, author of the utopian novel *Looking Backward,* realized so well, hindsight sometimes reveals beliefs, values, and assumptions that, while once commonplace, unchallenged, and unwitting, in retrospect seem curious at best and pernicious at worst.

A society's outside observers also may have a special vantage point for clearly perceiving social reality. R. H. Tawney, the quintessential British egalitarian, suggested that anthropologists, social sciences's "professional outsiders," make excellent iconoclasts when they write about the "primitive people" of another society:

The centre of the[ir] system, they inform us, is the sanctity of class, which has a significance at once economic and religious and the conviction that prosperity will be blighted and morality undermined if that sanctity is impaired. And this system, it seems, is so venerable and all pervading, so hallowed by tradition and permeated with pious emotion, that not only does it seem inconceivable to its adherents that any other system should exist, but until attention is called to it by the irreverent curiosity of strangers, they are not even conscious of the fact of its existence. (Tawney, 1964: 35)

We also are sometimes unaware of the consequences of basic social facts of our own existence. Many of our society's former beliefs and practices were founded on perceptions of racial or sexual distinctions that, while once hallowed by many, are now more commonly seen as failed and foolish. These failed beliefs provide apt examples of prejudice that become clear only through the passage of time and through the perspectives offered by outsiders (Gunnar Myrdal's book on racism in America, *An American Dilemma* [1944], for example). Even so, other beliefs and understandings, though equally dubious, may be more enduring. They may avoid or withstand examination and persist because they operate closer to the core of our society's justificatory myths.

One of the best American examples of a continuing core belief is our understanding of individualism. It is not easy to say why individualism has been such an important and enduring American ideal, but reference to Tocqueville (who, it is often said, popularized the concept of individualism) and to surveys of contemporary American popular attitudes illustrate both the age and the current vitality of the concept—shall we say myth?—of American individualism. Closely allied with individualism is the ideal of merit, and the two together lead to an American fixation on a particular understanding of means-regarding equality of opportunity as our key manifestation of equality.

Our version of equality of opportunity is so American that it ranks with baseball, hotdogs, and apple pie. In confrontations between individualism and affirmative action programs, individualism is usually allied with "meritocracy," or the ideal of merit-based equality of opportunity. Yet affirmative action always involves an effort to ameliorate conditions of certain disadvantaged people through remedies that are group based and therefore are in ostensible conflict with both individualism and merit.

In this Conclusion I will show that confrontations between individualism and affirmative action largely result from the core position that individualism has occupied in American popular belief systems. I will argue that beliefs in individualism continue to be vital in America, despite the fact that individualism may no longer bear a close correspondence to important aspects of social reality. I will also argue that individualist ideology has made it much more difficult to devise and enforce affirmative action policies, which are aimed at the amelioration of group-based disadvantage. Finally, I will suggest a way in which it may be possible to resolve apparently intractable conflicts between individualism, on the one hand, and affirmative action policies, on the other, through what I call the distance-travelled concept.

EQUALITY OF OPPORTUNITY

At a relatively simple level of understanding, equality of opportunity seems to involve a principle of merit, so that those are rewarded who have some requisite talent or ability; often such merit is measured in some sort of competition. As we have seen, to implement that version of equality of opportunity it is necessary to make certain that an opportunity is publicly posted, that competition for it is open to all, and that the competition is procedurally fair. Actually such notions are much too simple, as we saw in chapter 2. To appreciate that you will only need to recall Rae's distinction between prospect-regarding and means-regarding equality of opportunity.[1]

The purpose of means-regarding equality of opportunity is not to create equal prospects of success, but rather to legitimate unequal results—to the winner goes the laurel wreath—or the job—or the place in medical school! That presupposes that winners possess particular talents or attributes that deserve recognition. It also follows that when there is no legitimate basis for differentiating people, that is, when, for all important and practical purposes they are equal, they deserve equal treatment. When a reward is indivisible and people are equally situated with respect to it, a simple lottery, as in prospect-regarding equality of opportunity, may be the most appropriate way to determine a winner.

It has often been suggested that simple procedural fairness, as in means-regarding equality of opportunity, may not be appropriate when certain potential competitors are handicapped by background or circumstances beyond their control. For example, in chapter 2 we mentioned Fishkin's "trilemma." Fishkin has suggested that the competing claims of means-regarding equality of opportunity, equality of life chances, and a preference in our society for the autonomy of the family create a trilemma. His point is that to have true means-regarding equality of opportunity would require that everyone have an equal starting point and no unfair handicaps or advantages. That was precisely Judge Tanaka's point in the *South-West Africa Case* that we reviewed in the preceding chapter. In a footrace, for example, fairness would require equal access to and time for appropriate nutrition and training, as well as racing shoes of comparable quality for all participants. In university or postgraduate admissions, fairness would require everyone to have had equal advantages and opportunities during childhood and youth. Yet the liberty that is an important part of our individualistic tradition includes the autonomy of the family and its liberty to enhance the life chances of its children, in so far as it can. Fishkin concludes that it is not possible to have all three elements of the "trilemma" at once (Fishkin, 1983: 4 et seq.). Given such a problem, individualism, in this instance mediated through the agency of the autonomous family, is usually preferred in the United States.

Most commonly the inequalities of life chances that contribute to Fishkin's trilemma are associated with socioeconomic status.[2] A child who is born with the ability to run fast over short distances is, subject to equal nutrition, training, and equipment, bound to succeed over less gifted runners. That is not usually the case with socially determined differences, such as a family's tendency to spend leisure time reading books rather than watching television. Differences that result from socioeconomic status, being socially determined, are in principle subject to compensatory or ameliorative measures, yet in our society merit-based means-regarding equality of opportunity usually attributes success not to socioeconomic background but to presumptive intrinsic individual merit. Only when we stop to think carefully (if we do) do our reflections reveal the possibility that individual achievements ought not to be viewed entirely apart from social settings or group affiliations. When we don't reflect on that possibility (and most often we don't), we tend instead to see ourselves and others as autonomous individuals—as self-made men or women—and our successes as being due entirely to our own merits.

INDIVIDUALISM IN AMERICAN IDEOLOGY

Alexis de Tocqueville, writing in the 1830s, first gave wide currency to the concept of individualism. He himself noted only that *individualism* was "a word recently coined to express a new idea."[3]

The prior term was *egoism,* which he defined as "a passionate love of self which leads a man to think of all things in terms of himself and to prefer himself to all" (Tocqueville, 1969: 506). He saw individualism quite differently. Unlike egoism, it had its structural as well as its psychological side. Individualism in Tocqueville's view involves the breaking of traditional ties that linked people in feudal or aristocratic societies and the retreat to a smaller circle of family and friends in a democratic society. In a sense, the larger society thus becomes more remote, both because of the absence of social ties and because of attitudes that sustain a preference for family and intimate friends; but in another sense individualism allows for involvement with the cause of humanity, or with a people as a whole, even though that may seem to be an esoteric abstraction. In aristocratic societies, Tocqueville wrote, men were more often immediately involved with others outside themselves, because of extensive social ties, but they were less likely to conceive of human fellowship as a whole (Tocqueville, 1969: 507).

When the idea of human equality is added to individualism, Tocqueville noted, the emergence of individual advancement, or, as he put it, of "indefinite perfectibility" is the result. His conclusion is simple but compelling. When people are bound by ties of birth or social rank, there is little reason to fight against what most will see as an inevitable fate. But when "castes disappear and classes are brought together," no avenues for advancement are foreclosed and all things are possible. Thus the seeds of merit-based, means-regarding equality of opportunity are sown (Tocqueville, 1969: 452).

Happily, self-advancement was constrained in the America Tocqueville observed by "self-interest properly understood." As he wrote, "Every American has the sense to sacrifice some of his private interests to save the rest" (Tocqueville, 1969: 527). In other words, it is in each person's interest to be hospitable, charitable, moderate, and temperate, for those are amenable traits when reciprocated by others. Self-interest that is mean-spirited is likely to be counterproductive in the long run. While this is perhaps not a very lofty perch for human brotherhood or sisterhood, Tocqueville thought that "self-interest properly understood" would probably raise actual human standards.

In certain ways Tocqueville had a happy vision of America. To be sure, he was concerned about pressures toward conformity with the preferences of a popular majority and also about the possibility of tyranny—whether that of a majority or of the newly emerging captains of industry, but many of the social changes he saw as inevitable, he also saw as being positive or benign. Perhaps it was the nearness of the frontier in 1833 and the ready prospects for personal advancement, at least for white settlers, that allowed self-interest to be properly understood and constrained. However, other voices from the seventeenth, eighteenth, and early nineteenth centuries spoke also of the pursuit of worldly self-interest, though not always so complacently. Thomas Hobbes, John Locke, Adam Smith, Thomas Malthus, and eventually Charles Darwin, Herbert Spencer, and William Graham Sumner also contributed to the ideology of individualism, even if, with nature, the pursuit of individual self-interest was sometimes seen as blood "red in tooth and claw."

NATURAL SELECTION AND THE SURVIVAL OF THE FITTEST

Darwin's interpretation of Malthus came in 1838. In Malthus he "found a quantitative deterministic formulation of the superfecundity principle." In short, the idea that population progresses geometrically, while food supply increases only arithmetically, exerts continuous pressure and contributes to the struggle for survival. The origin and extinction of species and individuals were thus linked to the struggle for existence. As Schweber put it, Darwin now understood the "creative power of death" (Schweber, 1977: 295–99).

Michael Ghiselin has suggested that Darwin's debt to nineteenth-century economic and political thought is profound. This was a time when the old aristocratic order (which Tocqueville had contrasted with America) was breaking up. The organization of society based upon "God's will," the divine right of kings and aristocratic privilege had made state and society primary and most individuals secondary, at best. Ghiselin's key point is this:

A reconsideration of the nature of society, by stressing the importance of the individual, did far more than demolish the philosophical arguments for despotism. Treating social entities not as manifestations of abstract forms, but as the consequence of interactions among individuals, brought about the scientific investigation of society. Human associations, like biological species, are populations and conceiving of them as such was fundamental to the kind of thinking Darwin owed to his reading of Malthus. (Ghiselin, 1969: 60)

Ghiselin's point is made even more forcefully by Karl Polanyi. He argues that the emerging market economy required the availability of labor as a commodity, and that in turn required the fungibility of human beings as units of labor.[4] To produce such units, it was necessary to transform society, to destroy the vestiges of feudalism—the manor, the parish, the village, the community—that linked people and protected them from hunger. Polanyi argues that the acceptance of poverty by the mass of citizens was the price to be paid for the highest stage of prosperity under market capitalism. "The improvidence of the poor was a law of nature, for servile, sordid and ignoble work would otherwise not be done" (Polanyi, 1957: 118).

Darwin's adoption of natural selection indirectly undergirded others in their efforts to provide rationalizations for market capitalism. Herbert Spencer was the most notable example, and his American disciple was William Graham Sumner, a social scientist at Yale.

Spencer simply took Darwin's work and unabashedly applied it to human beings in society. As Montagu has said, "Darwin and Spencer gave the industrialists of the nineteenth century a cosmic sanction for free competition" (Montagu, 1952: 33). That this involved a stark view of society was revealed in an 1879 lecture of Sumner, the American protagonist of laissez-faire capitalism:

> Many economists seem to be terrified that distress and misery still remain on earth and promise to remain as long as the vices of human nature remain. Many of them are frightened at liberty, especially under the form of competition, which they elevate into a bugbear. They think it bears harshly on the weak. They do not perceive that here "the strong" and "the weak" are terms which admit no definition unless they are made equivalent to the industrious and the idle, the frugal and the extravagant. They do not perceive, furthermore, that if we do not like the survival of the fittest, we have only one possible alternative, and that is the survival of the unfittest. The former is the law of civilization; the latter is the law of anti-civilization. (Sumner, 1914: 68)

Viewing people chiefly as units of labor, some industrious, some indolent, is, according to C. B. Macpherson, a direct outgrowth of the particular kind of individualism that emerged to serve the needs of a capitalist market economy. Macpherson called this "possessive individualism" and argued, "Its possessive quality is found in its conception of the individual as essentially the proprietor of his own person and capacities, owing nothing to society for them" (Macpherson, 1962: 3). This view Macpherson found especially in the writing of Hobbes, thus, "The *Value,* or Worth of a man, is as of all other things, his Price." It is important here to note that the atomistic, market-oriented individualism of the emergent capitalist-industrial economy remains a pervasive element of the world view of many Americans even today. J. R. Pole sees within this sort of individualism what he calls a principle of *interchangeability,* which, as we shall see, is much the same as fungibility. This principle involves the understanding that, with appropriate training and experience, people could readily trade places:

> The individualist principle disassociates people from the context of family, religion, class, or race and when linked with the idea of

equality in the most affirmative sense—a sense widely accepted
throughout a large part of American history—it assumes the co-
ordinate principle of interchangeability. (Pole, 1978: 293)

The idea of interchangeability is seductive. Note, for example, the
appeal of the recent popular movie, *Trading Places,* in which a vagrant
was successfully transformed overnight into a high-powered invest-
ment analyst (while the analyst became a vagrant). Earlier, Mark
Twain's *The Prince and the Pauper* had much the same plot. The most
affirming power of equality in our society has involved high aspirations
for upward mobility of the lowly. Yet, interchangeability has another
side. The myth of individual freedom and parity of contract between
employers and employees that became part of substantive economic
due process in the last quarter of the nineteenth century and that held
on until 1937, is an excellent example of individualism run amok. The
last gasps of substantive economic due process are now gone in both
word and deed,[5] but individualism in America lives on in other forms
and places—not all of them happy or appropriate.

CONTEMPORARY INDIVIDUALISM

James Kluegel and Eliot Smith's recent study of Americans' beliefs
about inequality illustrates the persistence of these ideas. Along with
other scholars, they call these ideas the "dominant ideology" about
economic inequality. The ideology they describe has the following elements:

The major premise of the ideology is that opportunity for economic
advancement based on hard work is plentiful. From this premise,
the following propositions are derived:

a. Individuals are responsible for their own economic fate.
b. Where one ends up depends upon the effort one puts into acquiring and applying the necessary skills and attitudes and on
one's own native talent.
c. Individual outcomes are proportionate to individual inputs (talent and effort).
d. The resulting unequal distribution of economic rewards is equitable and fair. (Kluegel and Smith, 1986: 5)

In Rae's terms, here we encounter again a perfect example of indi-
vidually oriented means-regarding equality of opportunity. This per-

spective would indicate that we live in a world in which we compete with equal rules and no unfair advantages or handicaps so that we can demonstrate our superior talents and efforts.

Kluegel and Smith's 1980 sample of more than 2,200 Americans shows that a clear majority of Americans holds such beliefs. It may be true these days that Americans have come to have some doubts about education as the invariant route to upward mobility, and that they probably understand that children from wealthy families have an advantage in life over children from poor ones. But while some of us also understand that minorities and women continue to experience certain serious disadvantages in our society, others believe that minorities and women have better than average opportunities. Nonetheless, when asked to analyze their own life prospects, most Americans are fervent believers in the dominant ideology. Reference to previous studies suggests that there may have been a modest decline in this ideology over the past three decades, but even so, it has not yet been seriously impaired (Kluegel and Smith, 1986: 52).

It should not be surprising that the most willing believers in the dominant ideology are those who, compared to others, have already succeeded. White males with high status are most apt to be the true believers of individualism. To the extent that there is dissent, it is among African-Americans. At each level of socioeconomic status, about half of the African-American respondents deny that opportunities are readily available to themselves, and many report that they have personally experienced barriers to success. Such respondents have had the opportunity to do some reality testing of the dominant ideology on their own (Kluegel and Smith, 1986: 68 et seq.).

Kluegel and Smith also asked about individual and structural causes of achieving wealth or of experiencing poverty. Structural explanations, of course, suggest that wealth or poverty results from causes that are to some extent beyond the control of the rich or poor. Such explanations are found most often among women, young adults, nonwhites, and those with relatively low incomes and relatively little education. Conversely, the true believer in the dominant ideology of individual responsibility, they found to "resemble Ronald Reagan: an older, white, male, Westerner with a relatively high income" (Kluegel and Smith, 1986: 91).

In another recent study, Paul Sniderman focused on questions about race and inequality. It was based on two opinion surveys, one national and one from the San Francisco–Oakland Bay area (both conducted in 1972). It is intriguing to see how the analyses from two independent studies—Kluegel and Smith's and Sniderman's—converge. Sniderman takes the individualist theme of self-reliance[6] and adds to it another American theme, which he calls *moralism* and defines as the "readiness of Americans to scrutinize, to criticize, to reproach, not just others, but themselves as well—indeed, perhaps particularly themselves and their institutions (Sniderman, 1985: 34). Using the combinations of these two ideas, he develops four orientations. The individualist (the person who is high on self-reliance and low on moralism) holds that African-Americans are responsible for their own fate and rejects the idea that powerful whites keep them down. The progressive (the person who is high on moralism and low on self-reliance) sees African-Americans as victims and sees rich and powerful whites as being responsible for that condition. The fundamentalist (the person who is high on both moralism and self-reliance) relies on a biblical explanation of racial inequality but tends also to believe in individual responsibility. Finally, the historicist (the person who is low on both moralism and self-reliance) sees racial inequality as the consequence of past discrimination rather than a matter of current personal or social responsibility (Sniderman, 1985: 36 et seq.).

Given those four orientations, Sniderman finds that individualists make up 57 percent of the national sample, but only 35 percent of Bay Area respondents. The smaller number of individualists in the Bay Area is matched by a greater number of progressives.

Sniderman uses his four categories effectively to analyze differences with respect to pro-equality policies. The two policy questions he employed involved quite modest commitments, and neither of them necessarily involved group-based affirmative action.[7] A separate set of questions concerned support for racial equality as an abstract principle rather than public policies.[8]

Most respondents favored racial equality as an abstract principle, but only progressives and historicists tended to favor equality as public policy. That left individualists and fundamentalists in opposition to equality as public policy, and they were also relatively low in support for equality as an abstract principle. Since both fundamentalists and individualists were relatively low in formal education, Sniderman examined the impact of education on attitudes. At all education levels, however, individualists were low on support for equality both as an abstract principle and in public policy. This result was highlighted by focusing on specific questions about equality for minorities, women, and the poor. Individualists score high on indices of equality for all three categories. According to individualists, African-Americans, women, and the poor

have only themselves to blame if they do not succeed in America. Here
is Sniderman's apt conclusion:

> Individualism, then, is an ethic: It is a bedrock belief in an ethic
> of self-reliance. Individuals must take care of themselves. They
> must not pretend to be victims of circumstance, or ask for special
> favors, in an effort to get others to do for them what they should do
> for themselves. It is up to them to do what it takes to get ahead.
> (Sniderman, 1985: 97)

There is no reason to press this point further. The continuities between current attitudes and the individualism of the eighteenth and
nineteenth centuries are evident.

Nonetheless, Jennifer Hochschild suggests a possible distinction in
contrasting attitudes about equality in social, political, and economic
domains of life. Her point is that it is chiefly in the economic realm that
we commonly use principles of differentiation, that is, we believe that
there are significant differences between people in most economic contexts, so we are able to legitimate economic success or failure. In social
and political realms, we are more likely to use principles of equality,
that is, an assumption that all people have a legitimate prima facie claim
to equal resources (Hochschild, 1981: 46 et seq.).

Hochschild's research was, however, based on a small number of in-
depth interviews. Sniderman's results suggest that a strong individualist orientation may spill over into political and social domains, though
admittedly the orientation is most evident in the economic realm.

Just as Hochschild suggested a possibly important distinction between principles of equality and differentiation, *Habits of the Heart*, by
Bellah and others, suggests that we need to distinguish two other sorts
of individualism. The sort we have been examining in this chapter
Bellah calls *utilitarian individualism.* It is marked by the pursuit of
material self-interest, albeit often by sober, frugal, and industrious
means. Franklin's "Poor Richard" suggests the prototype. The second
kind of individualism Bellah calls *expressive individualism.* It involves
the present enjoyment of life through whatever means one chooses—
classical music, books, art, and foreign travel for some; bowling, baseball, beer, and honky-tonks for others (Bellah et al., 1986). Expressive
individualism seems to have much in common with *self-actualization,* as
described in Maslow's hierarchy of needs (Maslow, 1962).[9]

In Bellah's terms we have been concerned with the consequences utilitarian individualism has had for disadvantaged groups in American society. The expressive individualism that Bellah describes may sometimes be lonely, relativistic, and even solipsistic, but it does not seem to have the obvious negative consequences for others that utilitarian individualism clearly has had, during the "halcyon" days of Social Darwinism, or even today.

RECONCILING CONFLICTS BETWEEN INDIVIDUAL AND GROUP CLAIMS

Even under more sympathetic circumstances, such as those outlined in the previous chapter, group-regarding claims for affirmative action are rarely, if ever, offered as permanent solutions, and they may become more difficult to sustain over extended periods of time (note the recent riots in India over reservation of jobs or places in universities for Untouchables, as well as the rhetoric against "quotas" that the Bush administration currently employs). At best, affirmative action policies are accepted as temporary exceptions to the claims of individual-regarding equality. And our review of other countries and of international agreements suggests that affirmative action claims may be even more problematic in the United States than elsewhere.

A key difficulty with adhering to individual-regarding equality in preference to group-based affirmative action claims is that the notion of the autonomous self-reliant individual is part of a myth whose best days are past, if indeed it was ever necessary or appropriate. Each of us these days is likely to be a product of a complex set of interrelated factors. The many groups of which we are part, the larger social, political, and economic forces and institutions that determine, direct, or constrain many of our choices; the natural resources as well as the environmental and technological factors that contribute both to the means of production and to what is produced—the aggregate market forces that are little influenced by our own tiny contributions—all these things, and probably others we have not yet imagined, may have made the idea of the autonomous self-reliant individual an anachronism.

Throughout this book we have seen that group-regarding equality represents an alternative view that stresses groups and group outcomes (Sindler, 1978: 4). Surely discrimination by race, national origin, sex, or other categories has always been directed at groups, even if it is individuals within those groups who necessarily experience the reality of being the convenient targets. It makes sense today to think of groups rather than individuals as appropriate units of analysis in a variety of social settings, yet that perception runs counter to the powerful ideology of individualism that we have described. The answer to the contest between individual-regarding and group-regarding understandings of equality may lie in developing a way of thinking that will help us better to differentiate between the beneficiaries and the victims of larger forces in society.

As we have seen, group claims to compensatory remedies are usually founded on an ascertained history of group-based disadvantage or discrimination. When a group has such a history, a current individual's mere inclusion in a group is often taken as sufficient evidence of a socially determined disadvantage. Of course, that may or may not be true for any particular individual, but whether a particular individual is disadvantaged or not is rarely considered. If we measure equality by a group-regarding standard and we establish an individual's membership in a group, that individual's condition would not even be relevant. Such categorizations can become problems for exceptional individuals within a group, especially for a "gifted" member or an otherwise disadvantaged group, who may be unable to escape the presumption that he or she has been the individual beneficiary of a compensatory program, rather than being quite capable of succeeding on his or her own (Carter, 1991).

If, however, we were to make the effort to measure specific individual disadvantages—for example, poverty, illiteracy, or residence in a decaying inner-city neighborhood—we would be able to compare individuals fairly in the context of means-regarding equality of opportunity. The advantage would be that it would allow us to retain individuals as our unit of analysis, while evaluating individual *means* in the context of disadvantages that individuals have actually experienced. This would help bridge the models of individual justice and group justice proposed by Fallon and Weiler and discussed in Chapter 9.

THE DISTANCE-TRAVELLED CONCEPT

The *distance-travelled concept* may help to develop an understanding of the means by which affirmative action can be achieved while countering arguments that reject group-regarding equality and continue to insist on individual-regarding equality. All the justices who wrote opinions in the *Bakke* case seemed to share certain assumptions about the benchmark scores of medical school candidates. They assumed that the scores of candidates could be compared by using strict numerical equivalencies, that is, one score of 560 is equal to any other score of 560, and a 560 is better than a 520. They also assumed that such scores were demonstrably related in some way or another to success in medical school or medical practice. Higher scorers were therefore more "meritorious" as medical school applicants than lower scorers.

Such assumptions *may* be sensible, but they also may be quite problematic. Such assumptions also support many compensatory programs, that is, such programs compensate for the lower scores of disadvantaged candidates.

The following two examples illustrate the notion of distance travelled.

> Individual *A*: child of a single-parent family with six siblings. The single at-home parent is a recipient of AFDC payments. The home is in government-subsidized housing in inner-city Detroit. The child, a graduate of an inner-city public school system with low district average SAT scores, attends Wayne State University at night while working full time as a paralegal in a law office. At the conclusion of *A*'s undergraduate education, *A* receives a social work degree with a 3.1 cumulative grade point average. *A* takes the Law School Admissions Test (LSAT) and achieves a score of 31 (about the 50th percentile).

> Individual *B*: child of an intact nuclear family, with a younger brother. Father is CEO of a large bank holding company in New York City; the mother is a published novelist. The family lives in suburban Connecticut. *B* attends and graduates from a private prep school, one that reputedly is one of the top college prep schools in the country. Upon graduation, *B* attends Dartmouth College. At the conclusion of *B*'s undergraduate education, *B* receives a degree in economics with a 3.1 cumulative grade point average. *B* takes the LSAT and achieves a score of 31 (about the 50th percentile)

Assume now that a law school has one place left in its entering class and must choose between these two candidates. Which one is more meritorious? The distance-travelled concept suggests that, given their relative backgrounds, *A*'s performance may represent a more substantial achievement and more substantial merit than does *B*'s. That certainly makes intuitive sense. Candidate *A* has made it *against* all odds, while B has accomplished less given the advantages that have been available. Note that neither race nor gender has been mentioned in either instance, but some readers may have inferred that *A* might be an African-American female and that *B* might be a white male. Should that be reversed, however, it would make no difference under the distance-travelled concept.

Distance travelled is both race and gender neutral and allows for fair comparison between two individuals without regard to group identity, yet it takes into account most (but probably not all) of the real consequences of social advantage and disadvantage. A distance-travelled idea was suggested by Justice Douglas's dissent in *DeFunis v. Odegaard* (1974). It is also consistent with Amy Gutmann's concerns about group-regarding equality that we noted in Chapter 9 above (Gutmann, 1987: 211). Still, the idea of taking distance travelled into account will itself no doubt prove to be somewhat controversial, for it would transform race-conscious affirmative action into a remedy for all of those who are seriously disadvantaged by socioeconomic conditions (Holmes, 1991).

This means of evaluating performance might also alert us to the deceptive quality of the numbers that otherwise we may tend to take too seriously. Keep in mind that the benchmark scores in *Bakke* consisted of interviewer's summaries, overall GPA, science GPA, MCAT scores, letters of recommendation, and extracurricular activities. Five committee members rated the candidates in 1973, giving each candidate a score from 0 to 100; in 1974, there were six committee members, so the total possible score was 600. In both years a minimum GPA of 2.5 was required (*Regents of the University of California v. Bakke, 1978: 2739*). These scores were treated as reliable measures in the medical school admission process, yet simple inspection of the criteria used and of the method of scoring suggests that the scores were uncertain at best. Some of the items included in the index were necessarily subjective; it was not clear how each item considered might be related to success in medical school; and there was no demonstration that differences in the individual items, or in the overall index score, were statistically significant. The University of California and the Justices of the U.S. Supreme Court nonetheless treated the differences in benchmark scores as significant ones, while we have attempted to demonstrate that in the instance of *A* and *B* above even identical scores may have disparate meanings.

Most admissions decisions and many employment decisions also assume that it is best to take higher scores on employment tests or other indices because they represent greater merit. Thus, using the examples of our hypothetical *A* and *B* applicants above, while we might choose *A,* with an LSAT of 31 over *B,* with the same LSAT score of 31, we certainly would take *B* if he had an LSAT of 42 (about the 95th percentile) over *A,* if she had an LSAT of 36 (about the 76th percentile), assuming that their backgrounds and qualifications otherwise remained exactly as described in the hypothetical situations described above. That might represent a serious error, however.

Once certain minimum acceptable qualifications for law school, for medical school, or for employment are established and met by certain applicants, it might be reasonable to select from qualified applicants by lot; that would be consistent with prospect-regarding equality of opportunity. The idea of random selection, once acceptable qualifications are met, may appear startling, yet it has by no means always been demonstrated that we are correct in choosing for jobs or for higher education, those students with the highest standardized test scores or GPA's. What if scores above a certain level represent "surplus talent," which may be quite unrelated to adequate job or academic performance, or even to superlative performance? Consider, for example, the routine daily tasks performed by a dentist, a physician in family practice, or by an attorney in general practice, and ask whether extraordinary intellectual ability is required in their daily work, or whether most of the work is routine. Of course, there is no easy way to prove this point, but it does make intuitive sense. Even on those occasions when high intellectual ability may be requisite, certain differences between otherwise qualified individuals may be simply a matter of the time it takes different individuals to complete a task. Standardized tests reward the ability to work quickly, a situation less frequent in real life.

We may have devised admissions and selections systems through which we award the opportunity to make relatively large incomes to those who are able to win a particular kind of academic or intellectual race, possibly a race that often is irrelevant to actual performance in school or on the job. The apparent virtues of an individual-regarding competitive meritocracy that is based on means-regarding equality of opportunity one day may prove (in many instances) to be as much of an illusion as perceived racial or sexual differences eventually have already proven to be.

The best expositor of unease about the victory of means-regarding equality is Michael Young, whose dystopia was described in *The Rise of the Meritocracy* (1959). Writing about a twenty-first century society in which the measurement of IQ has been perfected, Young describes a hierarchical society in which equality has been dismissed as an absurdity, for science has disclosed, rigorously and systematically, the "real" differences between people. Rewards in that society are apportioned strictly according to those differences.

Young portrays a society in which merit has run amok—even with the "perfect" measure of intelligence. It clearly would be absurd to devise a social system in which people are ranked hierarchically solely according to IQ, assigned jobs, and rewarded according to that single criterion, however well it might be measured. It seems likely that most of the positions in society which are occupied by most of the people most of the time require only a level of intelligence and ability with some broad "normal" range. Even if we accept, as probably we should, that some positions (the theoretical physicist or concert pianist, for example) require a particular kind of intelligence or talent that most people may not have, there is no particular reason why those special kinds or levels of intelligence or talent ought to be made universal standards, just as there is no particular reason that they should be disproportionately rewarded by society. The most troublesome aspect suggested by Young's book is that we already do distribute many rewards based almost entirely on success in school or on standardized tests. We accept those outcomes as commonplace and appropriate, and most of us do not realize that they may be problematic.

The distance-travelled concept serves to remind us that the numbers people accrue in their lives are not necessarily equivalent or valid measures of individual talent. We need to know a good deal more about a person than a raw score if we are to put his or her abilities and motivations in proper perspective. That especially is the case if we are to take into account the consequences of historic or present disadvantage or discrimination.

We also may need a broader understanding of motivation than that traditionally suggested by economic incentives. For example, C. B. Macpherson called for the abandonment of possessive individualism and of unlimited material acquisition as the best measures of people and for a broader understanding of human purpose (Macpherson, 1962, 1977). Amy Gutmann has written about disentangling human equality from the "web of individualism" (Gutmann, 1987). That would not be easy, and it would require us to see ourselves and others in new and different ways. Yet we have seen how the Equal Protection Clause of the Fourteenth Amendment has helped to transform our understanding of the similarities and differences between people. Most of the important transformations of understanding have occurred in this century.

Policy distinctions based on race, sex, ethnicity, alienage, residence, age, handicap, and wealth or poverty have often been challenged. Sometimes they have been rejected by the U.S. Supreme Court—and by courts in other jurisdictions.

Most often, when the U.S. Supreme Court has rejected distinctions on the ground that they deny the equal protection of the law, it has been because of judges' understanding and support for individual-regarding equality. We have also sometimes seen the Supreme Court enforce, however reluctantly, group- or bloc-regarding equality to sustain certain remedial policies, when some showing of de jure discrimination has been made. In the preceding chapter we saw that such group-based remedial or ameliorative policies have more often been employed in India, Canada, and under certain international agreements, than in the United States. It may prove useful to recognize that we are not alone in having confronted these problems. It may be even more useful to learn that ours is neither the only nor necessarily the best resolution. However, in all jurisdictions the claims of individual-regarding equality are still supposed to prevail in the long run. Group-regarding remedies clearly are transitory.

You may recall that in chapter 9 we considered Fallon and Weiler's suggestion that affirmative action remedies ought to be confined to those situations in which "group-based subordination" was "aided and abetted by government and by law." They accepted affirmative action when historic discrimination "had an enduring impact, measurable now in economic and social disparities between racial groups" and where historical discrimination had produced a group identity. Whenever such factors converge, they held that a "Model of Social Justice" warrants "affirmative discrimination" (Fallon and Weiler, 1985: 35 et seq.). In his recent book, Michel Rosenfeld proposes a somewhat more complicated six-pronged constitutional justification that is generally consistent with Fallon and Weiler's.[10] Surely both models are appropriate when such factors have converged, as they suggest, to produce almost invariable group-based disadvantages, but it is precisely such a convergence of complex factors that ought to be transitory, as affirmative action policies eventually produce measurable results.

So long as the convergence of historic discrimination, economic and social disadvantage, and group identification persist, affirmative action programs are perfectly reasonable—and even essential—if a disadvantaged group is to have any prospect of effective and prompt amelioration. If that is true, then President Bush's rhetorical opposition to "quotas" may prove to be good politics but bad social policy. Yet it takes both insight and candor to transcend political rhetoric against "quotas." For example, a recent column in *Time* magazine argued that quotas are not really the issue. Acknowledging the propriety of taking race into account in order to get beyond race, the *Time* columnist suggested that even the implementation of affirmative action programs "does not guarantee the ability to get beyond race." The real question, he suggested, is how we choose to deal with the inevitable and real problem of racism in America (Cose, 1991).

All the while, those provoked to anger and discontent by affirmative action programs argue what is sometimes demonstrably absurd, if only they would take a look at the real world around them—especially at life in America's older inner cities. Professor Lino Graglia, for example, answers his own question about the consequences of affirmative action by arguing, "In a word, it means that if you are white, you are a member of a legally dispreferred race and, therefore, in an extremely vulnerable position in competition with persons who are members of other races" (Graglia, 1991). Professor Graglia himself presently lives in Texas and holds an endowed professorship at the University of Texas Law School. Somehow he seems so far to have survived his own racial vulnerability.

Others in fact have examined the "problem of the innocent white male" and are more cautious than Graglia in assessing the disadvantages that whites may suffer. Michel Rosenfeld suggests that affirmative action is an acceptable compromise between the perpetuation of white male advantage, on the one hand, and "radical and immediate" compensation to the seriously disadvantaged, on the other (Rosenfeld, 1991: 324).

Given such controversy, it should be easy to see the potential appeal of a distance-travelled concept. It would avoid race by taking into account socioeconomic disadvantages, yet we know that such disadvantages have been strongly correlated with race in America for a very long time. Another benefit of considering the distance-travelled by disadvantaged Americans is that we would not be limited to temporary remedial policies. Under distance travelled any individual, of whatever age, race, sex, or religion, could be recognized and evaluated for the particular constellation of advantages and disadvantages that has been his or hers. By assessing the real circumstances of individuals we would indeed be raising means-regarding equality of opportunity to a higher level of understanding.

In this conclusion we have highlighted American individualism as the foundation of our preferences for individual-regarding equality in general and for "merit-based means-regarding equality of opportunity" in particular. We have introduced the distance-travelled concept in an effort to transcend distinctions between groups and individuals, and to reveal our all too often unexamined adherence to "merit" and to "meritocracy" as they are applied in our administration of equality of opportunity. My principal purpose has been to argue that we can take historic and contemporary social disadvantages properly into account by carefully assessing what specific achievements may represent for each individual and by being sure not to attribute more importance to such measures than they actually warrant. If we take distance travelled into account, we will be able to achieve the purposes of affirmative action programs, but without the costs of categorization by race, sex, or other concepts. The goal of encouraging diversity, as championed by Justice Powell in *Bakke,* might yet be continued, for its own reasons, on independent grounds.

We close by returning to where we began. If this book can be summed up in a single sentence, it is that assumptions of human equality are always appropriate and that the burden of proof should always be on those who want to justify treating people differently—for whatever reasons. Our historical difficulty has not been with the principle of equality but with the inferior reasons we have accepted for deviating from that principle.

NOTES

CHAPTER 1. INTRODUCTION

1. Rae's book is the product of his collaboration with Douglas Yates, Jennifer Hochschild, James Marone, and Carol Fessler, through a series of seminars at Yale University.

2. What are in fact "better" or "lesser" qualifications (in terms of the abilities essential for successful performance in medical school, or indeed in medical practice) is by no means a simple matter.

3. See, for example, McGlen and O'Connor, 1983.

CHAPTER 2. UNDERSTANDING KEY CONCEPTS OF EQUALITY

1. Title VII is that part of the 1964 Civil Rights Act that prohibits discrimination in employment. When employment tests operate so as to exclude applicants who share a particular attribute (gender, for example) at a rate higher than for other applicants, employers may be required to show that a valid job requirement is identified by the tests. The application of this rule was curtailed by the Supreme Court in 1989, as we shall see in chapter 9.

2. I should acknowledge that in many instances we may have to be satisfied with qualitative judgments that involve a high degree of subjectivity. Yet, if we are aware of the extremely problematic character of our evaluations of others, at a minimum we ought to be more careful and cautious in our judgments. Nonetheless, our subjective and qualitative judgments will have to suffice so long as they are the best available, and therefore at the time are inevitable.

3. According to Rae, "A grammar of equality is an account of the ways in which such judgments (how to apply equality in actual human communities) form coherent patterns of similarity and difference, consistency and contradiction" (Rae, 1981: 16). The structural problems referred to are various structural aspects of real societies, such as the division of labor.

CHAPTER 3. RECONSTRUCTION AND EQUAL PROTECTION

1. The Fourteenth Amendment, Section 1, provides: "No State shall make or enforce any law which shall abridge the privileges or immunities of citizens of the United States; nor shall any State deprive any person of life, liberty or

property, without due process of law; not deny to any person within its jurisdiction the equal protection of the laws."

2. See especially Baer, 1983; Berger, 1977; Curtis, 1986; James, 1956; and ten Broek, 1965.

3. Hereafter cited as the *Globe.*

4. Even seemingly impassioned pleas for human brotherhood often failed to grasp the possibility of a *broad domain,* of social equality between the races on American soil. For example, Sen. Ben Wade, a Radical leader from Massachusetts, proposed to his colleagues in 1860: "I know it is said that the African is an inferior race, incapable of defending his own rights. My ethics teach me, if it be so, that this fact, so far from giving me a right to enslave him, requires that I be more scrupulous of his rights; but I know that, whether he be equal to me or not, he is still a human being; Negroes are still men. Senators will bear me witness that there are thousands now in bondage who are much more white than black—yea tens of thousands of such; but, whether white or black, I say again, they are still human; they are animated by the same hopes, they are afflicted with the same sorrows, they are actuated by the same motives that we are. Like us, they may be deprived of every right, they may be treated like brutes; their souls may be ignored; you may whip, scourge and trample them in the dust, if you will; but they, being human, will arise from the utmost degradation; and still stand forth in the image of God, the conscious candidate of immortal life" (Hyman, 1967: 12).

5. The Thirteenth Amendment, which was approved by the Congress on January 13, 1865, and upon ratification by the states became part of the Constitution on December 13, 1865, confirmed the Emancipation Proclamation and, in theory, abolished the distinction between slave and freeman. The Fifteenth Amendment, approved by Congress in February 1869, and ratified on February 13, 1870, protects the right to vote against discrimination because of race, color, or previous condition of servitude.

6. See especially Charles Fairman, 1949, and William Crosskey, 1984.

7. See especially Alexander Bickel, 1955; Frank and Munro, 1950; ten Broek, 1965; and Berger, 1977.

8. This particular senator's analysis was clouded by his starkly racist views: "It is impossible that two distinct races should exist harmoniously in the same country, on the same footing of equality before the law. The results must be a disgusting and deteriorating admixture of races such as is presented in the Spanish States of America by the crossing of the Castillian with the Aztec and Negro. The prejudice of color is one of those facts implanted by Providence for wise purposes. Among others it is doubtless for the purpose of preserving a race homogeneous, which is the source of its true strength and permanent improvement. Physiologists instruct us that a race may be improved by the union of valuable qualities among the same race or others of similar characteristics, but not by the indiscriminate amalgamation of superior with greater inferior races" (*Globe,* January 31, 1866: 542).

9. In Section 2 the amendment provides for a reduction in representation in proportion to the number of male citizens denied the franchise.

10. The *McCulloch* decision in 1819 held that Congress had the power to create a national bank, despite the absences of a specific grant of power in Article I, Section 8. By examining the powers that *were* specifically granted in Section 8, in the context of the grant of the power to "make all laws which shall be necessary and proper for carrying into execution the foregoing powers,"

Chief Justice John Marshall established the doctrinal foundation for implied powers that endures today.

11. The Fifteenth Amendment, guaranteeing the right to vote, was ratified four years later.

12. Domains of allocation, it is important to remember, may be broad or narrow. Relative to all classes of things that might be allocated, the rather short list of civil rights originally covered by the Fourteenth Amendment seems a rather narrow domain of allocation. Stevens's words suggest a much broader *domain* (Rae, 1981: 46).

CHAPTER 4. EARLY INTERPRETATIONS OF EQUAL PROTECTION

1. Eric Foner has aptly summed up the results of the disputed election: "Among other things 1877 marked a decisive retreat from the idea, born during the Civil War, of a powerful national state protecting the fundamental rights of American citizens. Yet the federal government was not rendered impotent in all matters—only those concerning blacks" (Foner, 1988: 582–83).

2. The police powers of the states are the general powers of sovereign governments to legislate to protect public health, safety, education, and welfare.

3. A reason that was expressly repudiated by the Supreme Court 84 years later in *Loving v. Virginia* (1967).

4. Foner notes that blacks delegated to the 1868 Georgia Constitutional Convention, "expressed little interest in marrying white women, but some felt constrained to point out that the "purity of blood" lauded by their opponents had 'already been somewhat interfered with' by planters assaulting or cohabiting with female slaves" (Foner, 1988: 321).

CHAPTER 5. LAISSEZ-FAIRE AND ECONOMIC EQUAL PROTECTION

1. *Laissez-faire capitalism* involves the view that the economic system functions best when there is no interference by the government. *Substantive due process* involves the federal courts in judging whether state legislation results in a denial of liberty or property without due process of law. Due process in this context is substantive because it inevitably involves the federal courts in judging the substance of state legislation as to its "reasonableness" (see *Lochner v. New York* [1905]).

2. Stone's words were suggestive rather than conclusive: "Nor need we enquire . . . whether prejudice against discrete and insular minorities [in this instance religious, national, or racial minorities] may be a special condition which tends seriously to curtail the operation of those political processes ordinarily to be relied on to protect minorities, and which may call for a correspondingly more searching judicial inquiry" (*Carolene Products Case*: 784).

CHAPTER 6. THE PATH TO *BROWN V. BOARD OF EDUCATION*

1. In *Corrigan v. Buckley* (1926), however, the Supreme Court sustained racially restrictive covenants that accomplished between "private parties" what

the Louisville ordinance could not. The *Corrigan* case was a major defeat and disappointment for the NAACP (Vose, 1955).

2. A grandfather clause confers an exemption from voter qualifications that can readily be applied by a voting registrar to enfranchise whites, while excluding African-Americans. The example in *Guinn* was the exemption from literacy requirements of voters, or the descendants of voters, who had been qualified voters on January 1, 1866, or any time prior to that—a date that effectively excluded African-American voters.

3. In *Smith v. Allright* (1944) the Supreme Court overruled *Grovey v. Townsend,* holding that the nomination by the Democratic party in Texas was tantamount to election, making the party primary, in effect, an act of the state.

4. It should be noted that the NAACP, through the efforts of Charles Houston, Thurgood Marshall, and others, had successfully challenged the exclusion of African-Americans from the University of Maryland Law School in *Murray v. Pearson* (1936), a suit brought and won in state courts.

5. *Cumming* is the 1899 case in which it was held that a local school board could choose to support secondary education for white students, while providing none for African-Americans.

6. The *Morgan* decision was consistent with an 1878 holding of the Supreme Court in *Hall v. DeCuir,* although there the court held a Louisiana antisegregation statute unconstitutional as an invasion of congressional power to regulate interstate commerce.

7. In accordance with the practice then in effect, two end tables nearest the kitchen were conditionally reserved for Negroes. At each end those tables were to be reserved initially for Negroes and, when occupied by Negroes, curtains were to be drawn between them and the rest of the car. If the other tables were occupied before any Negro passengers presented themselves at the diner, then those two tables also were to be available for white passengers and Negroes were not to be seated at them while in use by white passengers (*Henderson v. United States*: 844).

8. This was the beginning of the Montgomery bus boycott, which led to the creation of the Montgomery Improvement Association and to the rise to leadership of Martin Luther King, Jr. (Garrow, 1988: chapter 1; Branch, 1988, chapter 5).

9. It should be noted in passing that *Shelley v. Kraemer* (1948) held that "in granting judicial enforcement of restrictive agreements . . . , the State has denied petitioner the equal protection of the law" (*Shelley*: 845). In finding state action the Supreme Court was willing to mute the impact of the *Civil Rights Cases of 1883.*

10. The first set of rules required "Negro" students to "sit apart at a designated desk in an anteroom adjoining the classroom; to sit at a designated desk on the mezzanine floor of the library, but not to use the desks in the regular reading room; and to sit at a designated table and to eat at a different time from the other students in the school cafeteria" (*McLaurin v. Oklahoma State Regents*: 853).

11. *De facto segregation* refers to segregation that exists in fact but that cannot be shown to be related, directly or indirectly, to governmental action. *De jure desegregation* refers to segregation that is the direct or indirect consequence of some governmental action or policy. Once explicit forms of discrimination are overturned, the question of whether segregation is de facto or de jure is often a problem of proof in court, so that the standard of proof required and the

evidence deemed admissible often become as important as the conceptual distinction.

CHAPTER 7. SEGREGATION AND DESEGREGATION—
THE CONSEQUENCES OF *BROWN*

1. See Berger, 1977; and ten Broek, 1965.

2. As noted before, de jure (by law) discrimination is that which results from or involves, directly or indirectly, the actions of a government. De facto (in fact) discrimination exists in fact, but is not officially prescribed, encouraged, or condoned.

3. *Brown I* refers to the set of cases decided on May 17, 1954, which declared segregated public schools to be unconstitutional. Further hearings were held on the enforcement of that decision, and on May 31, 1955, the Supreme Court in *Brown II,* remanded the cases to lower federal courts for enforcement "with all deliberate speed."

4. Since the District of Columbia is not a state, it is not covered by the Fourteenth Amendment. The Supreme Court has used the Due Process Clause of the Fifth Amendment, which applies to the federal government, to achieve much the same purpose as the Equal Protection Clause of the Fourteenth.

5. "Stair-step" plans usually integrated the first grade of classes during the first year of the plan, the first and second grades during the second year of the plan, and so on. Thus it would take twelve years from the beginning of such a plan to achieve integration from the first through twelfth grades.

6. The federal Department of Health, Education and Welfare (HEW) was then responsible for federally supported educational programs.

7. The Civil Rights Act of 1964, by far the strongest federal civil rights legislation since Reconstruction, resulted from a combination of factors that included the rise and influence of the "civil rights movement" led by Martin Luther King, Jr., and others, the assassination of President Kennedy, and the unusual presidential leadership and support of President Lyndon Johnson.

8. Federal Courts of Appeals, commonly called circuit courts, are multiple-member courts. Ordinarily circuit judges hear cases sitting in panels of three. An en banc rehearing consists of a hearing before all the appellate judges within the circuit, who review the previous decision of a panel.

9. Freedom of choice plans allowed any student to attend any school of choice, while voluntary transfer plans allowed free transfer to a school of choice.

10. Judge Johnson, an Eisenhower appointee, was one of the rare liberals on a U.S. District bench in the South. As a Republican, President Eisenhower did not have to clear his federal judicial appointments with Southern Democratic senators.

CHAPTER 8. INTEGRATION, BUSING, AND GROUP-
REGARDING EQUALITY

1. By 1965, when the *Swann* suit was filed, only 2 percent (490 students) of the African-American students in Charlotte were in schools with whites. Moreover, more than 80 percent of the 490 African-American students attended one school in which there were only seven white students (Schwartz, 1986: 8).

Remember, this was ten years after the "all deliberate speed" enforcement decision in *Brown II*. With a few exceptions, federal district judges in the South were deliberate indeed.

2. The system included 550 square miles—22 miles east-west and 36 miles north-south. In the 1968 school year there were 84,000 students in 107 schools, 71 percent white and 29 percent African-American (*Swann v. Charlotte-Mecklenberg Board of Education*: 1271).

3. Burger's holdout and his eventual concession are described at length in Schwartz, 1986: 111. Traditionally the chief justice, if he is in the majority, assigns the writing of the opinion of the court to himself or to another justice. If the chief justice is not in the majority, the senior justice in the majority assigns the opinion.

4. Literally "at first sight." In law it involves facts presumed to be true unless disproved by evidence to the contrary.

5. Powell wrote: "This plan requiring transportation of from 18,600 to 25,000 students, consisting of from 32% to 42% of the entire school population, was ordered despite the District Court's conclusion that such a plan would involve a 'risk' to health and probably to impingement of education for students younger than the sixth grade" (*Austin Independent School District v. United States*, 518–19). Austin had some time before annexed much of the surrounding vacant land, thus avoiding the encirclement by suburban districts that proved to be problematic for metropolitan desegregation in Detroit.

6. According to Justice Rehnquist, the district court's finding that the presence of racially imbalanced schools, the use of optional attendance zones and other recent actions of the local school board cumulatively were in violation of the Equal Protection Clause was not sustained by sufficient findings of fact. The case was remanded for further hearings with the specific admonition that, "where mandatory racial segregation has long since ceased," it must be determined "if the school board intended to and did in fact discriminate." "Only if systemwide discrimination is shown may there be a systemwide remedy" (*Dayton I*: 2769). We will see that in *Dayton II,* affirmed by the Supreme Court in 1979, the facts were eventually found sufficient to sustain a systemwide remedy.

CHAPTER 9. AFFIRMATIVE ACTION PROGRAMS IN HIGHER EDUCATION AND EMPLOYMENT

1. DeFunis had been admitted to the University of Washington Law School by order of a state trial judge in 1971. By the time his case was before the U.S. Supreme Court for review in February 1974, he was about to enter his last semester of law school. On the day after argument of the case, counsel for the law school acknowledged by letter to the court that DeFunis had registered for his final semester. Counsel also advised that he would be allowed to graduate no matter what the Supreme Court might rule. Five members of the court held that the court's ruling would be moot (of no practical significance) and declined to rule on the merits. Four members, including Justice William O. Douglas, wanted to decide the case. Justice Brennan noted that the issue in DeFunis was inescapable and would eventually be before the court in another case. Maverick as he often was, Douglas alone filed his opinion on the merits of the case. At conference Douglas had said that he was "suspicious of tests and maybe we ought to say that all at the bottom of the class must be taken in" (Schwartz, 1988: 33).

2. The index score was calculated chiefly from each applicant's Law School Admissions Test (LSAT) score and from the applicant's grade point average for the junior and senior years. Those with index scores of 77 or higher were usually admitted. Those with 74.5 or less were usually rejected. Those with index score between those numbers were reviewed by the admissions committee. DeFunis's score of 76.23 placed him in the middle group. His application was rejected after admissions committee review. Two groups were excepted from the automatic rejection point of 74.5. Returning military veterans who had previously been admitted were routinely readmitted. Minority applicants with scores of 74.5 or below were separately reviewed (Sindler, 1978: 34 et seq.).

3. Douglas noted that the Equal Protection Clause did not mandate the LSAT. He argued: "A black applicant who pulled himself out of the ghetto into a junior college may thereby demonstrate a level of motivation, perseverance, and ability that would lead a fairminded admissions committee to conclude that he shows more promise for law study than the son of a rich alumnus who achieved better grades at Harvard" (*DeFunis v. Odegaard*: 1713). The difference was that decisions could be based on individual attributes, rather than on race. The LSAT was likely, in Douglas's view, to lead to the selection of the "organization man" and to exclude minorities. Since the LSAT was unlikely to unearth the special attributes of minority students, he thought it would be appropriate to review minority applicants separately so as "to probe their capacities and potentials" and to be sure that "racial factors do not militate against an applicant or on his behalf" (*DeFunis v. Odegaard*: 1715).

4. Justice Powell's opinion presented the following data in a footnote (*Regents of the University of California v. Bakke*: 2741):

	SGPA	OGPA	Verbal	MCAT (in percentiles)		
				Quanti-tative	Science	General Information
Class entering in 1973						
Bakke	3.44	3.46	96	94	97	72
Average of regular admittees	3.51	3.49	81	76	83	69
Average of special admittees	2.62	2.88	46	24	35	33
Class entering in 1974						
Bakke	3.44	3.46	96	94	97	72
Average of regular admittees	3.36	3.29	69	67	82	72
Average of special admittees	2.42	2.62	34	30	37	18

SGPA = Science Undergraduate Point Average
OGPA = Overall Undergraduate Point Average

5. As we have seen before, according to Justice Black's 1944 opinion in *Korematsu v. United States,* certain classifications, most notably racial ones, have been held to be suspect and must survive the "most exacting judicial scrutiny" if they are to be upheld. Routine classifications are subjected only to the rational basis or rational purpose test, that is, does there appear to be an intelligible and acceptable reason for the classification? Great deference, ap-

proaching a presumption of rationality, is accorded legislative enactments under the rational purpose test. A category somewhere between suspect classifications and those presumed to be rational has eventually evolved. Today it is most commonly applied to instances of alleged sexual discrimination. Sexual classifications are subjected to "heightened scrutiny." To pass this level of review, the classification must serve important governmental objectives and must be substantially related to the achievement of those objectives (*Craig v. Boren,* 1976).

6. This is the "heightened scrutiny" standard of review accorded sex-based discrimination in *Craig v. Boren*. See note 5 this chapter.

7. As we saw in chapter 5, a corporation, obviously an artificial entity, has long been held to have the status of a person for most purposes of legal and constitutional protection.

8. Title VII provides: "It shall be an unlawful employment practice for an employer . . . to fail or refuse to hire or to discharge any individual, or otherwise to discriminate against any individual with respect to his compensation, terms, conditions, or privileges of employment because of such individual's race, color, religion, sex or national origin" (42 U.S.C.A., section 2000e–2[a]).

9. The standards for statistical significance of the American Psychological Association were adopted (Jackson, 1976: 70).

10. Since the Equal Protection Clause of the Fourteenth Amendment applies only to the states, equal protection has been held to apply to the federal government only through the Due Process Clause of the Fifth Amendment (*Bolling v. Sharpe*).

11. A class action is one brought on behalf of all those who are similarly situated with respect to a right or cause of legal action. Stotts sought relief for all the "black firemen" who were being let go.

12. Disparate impact analysis in Watson requires that the plaintiff identify a particular practice; next, the plaintiff may offer statistical evidence to show that the practice in question has the effect of disproportionately excluding members of a group. Such a showing shifts the burden of going forward to the employer, who must show that it has legitimate business reasons for the practice. If that is done, the burden shifts back to the plaintiff who must show that other devices, with the disparate effect, would also serve the employer's legitimate business purposes.

13. This discussion deliberately omits consideration of minority business enterprise set-aside programs, such as the one rejected by the Court in *City of Richmond v. Croson* in 1989. While important issues certainly were raised in that case, the conflict between individual-regarding and bloc-regarding equality is adequately presented in the other cases we have reviewed.

14. A collateral attack would allow review of the consent decrees only to show that they were issued by a court that had no jurisdiction or to show that they were procured by fraud. Nonparties who would bring a collateral attack on a judgment would not be allowed to relitigate the merits of the case.

CHAPTER 10. EQUAL PROTECTION AND SEX DISCRIMINATION

1. The completion of legal education by itself was no small achievement for the time. In 1872, Dr. Edward H. Clark, at one time a professor at Harvard Medical School, renounced his support for the entry of women into medical

education and announced his conclusion that higher education was detrimental to the health of young women. The following excerpt represents his observations on the impact of academic work on a young woman. It comes from his 1873 book, published the same year that the *Bradwell* case was decided:

The stream of vital and constructive force evolved within her was turned steadily to the brain, and away from the ovaries and their accessories. The result of this sort of education was, that these last-mentioned organs, deprived of sufficient opportunity and nutriment, first began to perform their functions with pain, a warning of error that was unheeded; then, to cease to grow; next to set up once a month a grumbling torture that made life miserable; and, lastly, the brain and the whole nervous system, disturbed, in obedience to the law, that, if one member suffers, all the members suffer, became neuralgic and hysterical. (Clark, *Sex in Education,* 1873, quoted in Dorenkamp et al., 1985: 44–45)

2. Here are the perceptions of a male physician who was the author of a book about "woman's nature" that was widely read in the 1850s: "The attribute of modesty certainly lends the most powerful aid to the other charms of woman. It is one of the qualities given to her in order to be a strong fence for her children, for it binds her to the domestic altar—her children could not but endure damage and loss, should she leave home to plunge into the torrent of public affairs, or mingle freely with the distracting world! Her modesty, gentleness, and timidity, assimilate her to the characters of children, whose best playfellow, nurse and instructress she is. Come out from the world, and be separate from it, is peculiarly a command for her" (from Charles D. Meigs, *Woman: Her Diseases and Remedies,* as quoted in Dorenkamp et al., 1985: 8–9).

3. If women suffered such disability as jurors, then should they not also be excluded from serving as judges? So went the argument by a Texas state senator against the appointment of Sarah T. Hughes as the first female to sit as a trial judge of a Texas district court in 1935: "In the first place she is a married woman and she should be home washing dishes. . . . There is another reason why I do not believe Mrs. Hughes is eligible to hold the office. Under our Constitution only men may serve on juries and in cases where juries are waived with a woman on the bench we would be confronted with the specticle [sic] of a woman not eligible to decide the facts as a member of a jury deciding them from the bench. . . . It is generally recognized that probably 80 per cent of a trial judge's acts are discretionary and the average woman is so constituted that she responds to intuition rather than knowledge or aptness in deciding matters needing instant action" (Riddlesperger, 1980: 18–19).

4. The National Woman's party grew out of the Congressional Union, which was founded in 1913.

5. Certain federal statutes call for three-judge courts, composed usually of two circuit judges and one district judge. One of the instances is when the constitutionality of a federal statute is challenged. When a three-judge federal court is used, the route of appeal is directly to the U.S. Supreme Court.

6. This would have produced a net tax reduction of about $15 (Baer, 1983: 144).

7. In *Califano v. Goldfarb* (1977) the Supreme Court again held the provision

of survivor's benefits on a more liberal basis to widows than to widowers to rest on "archaic and overbroad generalizations."

8. This was due, to some degree, to the strong Mormon influence in Utah.

9. *Lehr v. Robertson* (1983) involved a similar point. There the Supreme Court upheld a New York law that guaranteed the mother the right to veto an adoption but accorded the same right only to fathers who had affirmatively sought to establish a relationship with an illegitimate child. White, Marshall, and Blackmun dissented on the grounds that the provision of notice of pending proceedings is a fundamental requirement of due process. No state interest was served, they wrote, by denying the father notice when his identity and location were well known. Due process, rather then equal protection, decided the matter for them.

10. We should note in passing another "easy" case from the year before. In *Wengler v. Druggists Mutual Insurance Co.* (1980) the Supreme Court struck down a provision of the Missouri workman's compensation law that limited a husband's entitlement to a death benefit for his wife's death unless he was physically or mentally incapacitated or could prove actual dependence.

11. Even then it was favored by 52.5 percent of the American public (McGlen and O'Connor, 1983: 380).

12. We have noted before that since the Fourteenth Amendment applies only to the states, equal protection as to the federal government must rest on the due process clause of the Fifth Amendment.

13. A state provision that provided for single sex colleges had been upheld as recently as 1971 in *Williams v. McNair.*

14. In academic year 1966–67, women represented about 4 percent of law school students. During the 1970s law schools instituted affirmative action programs for female applicants. For a while, women could gain admission with somewhat lower numbers (undergraduate grade point average and LSAT score) than male applicants. It soon became obvious that it would not be necessary to admit women with lower numbers, because the number of well-qualified female applicants offered an ample applicant pool. In academic year 1988–89 women represented about 41 percent of total law school J.D. enrollments. It is not unusual these days for entering law school classes to have more women than men (Law School Admissions Services, 1991: 35).

15. Male-only state military academies in Virginia (VMI) and South Carolina (The Citadel) were challenged but upheld at the trial court level in 1991. The first appeals of the these cases were not yet decided as of the completion of this book.

CHAPTER 11. BREAKING NEW GROUND
FOR CATEGORICAL DISCRIMINATION

1. As we saw in chapter 3, the debates in the Thirty-ninth Congress on what was to become the Fourteenth Amendment included references to the natural rights of "Jews, Gypsies, Chinese, Negroes, [and] all men of every color and condition" (*Globe,* December 13, 1865: 40–41).

2. *Yick Wo* is commonly cited as an example of a facially neutral statute that may have been applied in a discriminatory manner. Tribe reports that Yick Wo indeed may not have been the object of discrimination. San Francisco officials insisted on a version of the facts that was quite different from that related by Justice Matthews in his opinion (Tribe, 1988: 1483, n. 3).

3. Even these rulings had their limits. In 1947 in *Oyama v. California* the Supreme Court upheld the right of a minor American citizen of Japanese ancestry to own land that had been purchased in his name but paid for by his father, a Japanese alien ineligible for naturalization. The California Alien Land Law called for the land to be confiscated by the state because the purchase in the son's name was viewed as a mere subterfuge. The Supreme Court, however, took the son's right as a U.S. citizen as the primary question. His right to own land was held to be protected both by the Fourteenth Amendment and by federal legislation enacted under the authority of that amendment.

4. Tribe notes that several scholars have suggested that the alienage cases are better classified under the Supremacy Clause than under the Fourteenth Amendment (Tribe, 1988: 1550, n. 57).

5. *Baker v. Carr* and *Reynolds v. Sims* initiated the complex subject of legislative reapportionment, the so-called one man-one vote rule. Reapportionment has been the subject of such extensive treatment in a variety of books that we will not review reapportionment cases here. See, for example, the bibliography collected by Henry J. Abraham (1980: 412).

6. Even apart from reapportionment, the cases on election and voting rights are legion. Only a few of the prominent examples are reviewed in this section.

7. As we have seen before, the "rational basis" test presumes the validity of a state law and requires only that a rational basis or purpose for the law be shown for it to pass equal protection review. A year after Rosario a majority of the Court again sustained a law designed to protect political parties. This time a California statute prohibited access to the ballot as an independent candidate if the prospective candidate had been registered as a member of a party within one year prior to the preceding primary election. Justice White wrote that this served the reasonable objective of preventing the excessive splintering of political parties and interests. However, the case was remanded because the majority of the Court found that another provision, which required a certain number of signatures by voters who had not voted in a previous party primary, might be "unduly onerous" in restricting access to the ballot (*Storer v. Brown*, 1974). Also in *American Party of Texas v. White* (1974), Justice White upheld all but one of the provisions of Texas law that prescribed the means by which political parties could have their candidates for office placed on the general election ballot. The single exception was the practice of including only the candidates of the two major parties on absentee ballots.

8. More recently than "the beginning of the Republic," *Edwards v. California* (1941) invoked the right to travel during the "Great Depression" against California's "Anti-Okie" law.

9. We reviewed *Stanley v. Illinois* (1972) in chapter 10. It struck down an irrebuttable state presumption that all unmarried fathers are unqualified to raise their children.

10. Intestacy occurs when an individual dies without leaving a will.

11. See *Powell v. Alabama* ("special circumstances rule" in capital cases, 1932), *Betts v. Brady* (generalized "special circumstances" rule, 1942), *Gideon v. Wainwright* (right to counsel in all serious cases, 1963), *Douglas v. California* (right to counsel on appeal, 1963), *Argersinger v. Hamlin* (right to counsel in certain misdemeanors, 1972), and *Scott v. Illinois* (right to counsel on prospect of incarceration, 1979).

12. It is important to remember that the absolute exclusion from free public education of the children of illegal aliens was held unconstitutional in *Plyler v.*

Doe (1982). State funding formulas that contribute to the unequal funding of public school districts have, however, been held unconstitutional recently in several state cases brought under provisions of state constitutions.

13. Equal funding in terms of absolute dollars (*lot-regarding equality*) is only one possibility. *Lot-regarding equality* involves the equal distribution of resources regardless of individual desire, purpose, or need. *Person-regarding equality* involves the distribution to individuals or groups according to their needs. Since needs can differ, so could the allocation of resources. Special education of children with learning disabilities, for example, might be more costly on a per pupil basis that would the education of the average student (Rae, 1981: chapter 5).

14. In two cases decided late in 1990, the Supreme Court of Canada held that while the equality provisions (Section 15) of the Canadian Charter of Rights and Freedoms were violated by mandatory age retirement policies in Canadian public universities, the policies were nonetheless reasonable limitations under Section 1 of the Charter, and thus were upheld (*McKinney v. University of Guelph* and *Harrison v. University of British Columbia,* 1990).

CHAPTER 12. EQUALITY FROM A
MULTINATIONAL PERSPECTIVE

1. As chapters 9 and 10 above revealed, Kennedy has been involved in two affirmative action cases, *Martin v. Wilks* (1989) on racial affirmative action and *Price Waterhouse v. Hopkins* (1989) on affirmative action for women. His two votes were against affirmative action. Admittedly, we should be careful about generalizing from only a few cases.

2. Article 14 provides for: "Equality before the law:—The State shall not deny to any person equality before the law or the equal protection of the laws within the territory of India." Article 29 (2) prohibits discrimination in state-aided educational institutions. Article 15 prohibits discrimination on grounds of religion, race, caste, sex, or place of birth, but paragraph (4) adds: "Nothing in this article . . . shall prevent the State from making any special provision for the advancement of any socially or educationally backward classes of citizens or for the Scheduled Castes and the Scheduled Tribes" (Subbarao, 1985).

3. Article 16 provides for equality of opportunity in public employment, but paragraph (4) provides: "Nothing in this article shall prevent the State from making any provision for the reservation of appointments or posts in favor of any backward class of citizens which, in the opinion of the State is not adequately represented in the services under the State (Subbarao, 1985).

4. Rajeev Dhavan, a leading Indian scholar, disputes Galanter's conclusion and suggests that he, along with other American scholars, tends to ignore the impact of India's capitalist economy (Dhavan, 1986: 367).

5. Provision is made for listing "scheduled castes" and "scheduled tribes" under Articles 340 and 341 of the Indian Constitution.

6. As we saw in chapter 2 Rae himself calls this *compensatory inequality.* You may recall that compensatory inequality in this sense occurs when a domain of allocation (the things that a present agency controls for the purpose of distribution) is unequally distributed to compensate for unequal distributions in a larger domain of account (a domain of account consists of the class of things over which a particular group or class seeks equal distribution). Compensatory

inequality in the sense suggested by Rae occurs only when domains of account and domains of allocation do not coincide. Thus, unlike *Swann,* the University of California attempted to pursue a policy of compensatory equality, which led to the *Bakke* case.

7. Some readers will recognize the phrase the "truly disadvantaged" as the title of a book by William Julius Wilson (1987). Wilson's point is that "true" disadvantaged persons in the United States are part of an urban underclass that happens to be predominantly black. This underclass, however, is not strictly a racial phenomenon, for Wilson shows that many members of the black middle class profited from the civil rights movement of the 1950s and 1960s and fled from the ghetto into "Middle America." The underclass was left behind.

8. The opinion of the Court of the Queen's Bench was overturned, but only on technical grounds of mootness (*Apsit et al. v. Manitoba Human Rights Commission,* 1988).

9. The court said that any Section 1 inquiry must begin with the premise that the "impugned limit violates constitutional rights and freedoms." Thus the burden of proving that a limit is "reasonable and demonstrably justified" falls to those who would justify it. The standard of proof is by a preponderance of the evidence.

10. The court added that there were three components to the proportionality test: (1) "the measures must be carefully designed to achieve the objective in question," which is to say that they must be "rationally connected to the objective" rather than being arbitrary, irrational or unfair; (2) the means chosen should "impair as little as possible" the right in question; and (3) there must be proportionality in the effects of the limits and importance of the governmental objective (*Regina v. Oakes*: 337). Prior to the decision in *Regina v. Oakes,* a provincial court had suggested in *Black v. Law Society of Alberta* (1986) that four questions were involved in the application of Section 1: (1) the discriminatory policy must be clear and made by recognized authority; (2) it must bear a rational relationship to a valid governmental objective; (3) the limitation must maintain and enhance a free and democratic society more than would the affirmation of an equality right; and (4) no less intrusive means would equally serve the same purpose (*Black v. Law Society of Alberta*: 153). Either the *Oakes* or the *Black* tests seem very much like the heightened scrutiny standard in the United States first enunciated in *Craig v. Boren* (1976).

11. For example, Article 1, paragraph 4 of the International Convention on the Elimination of All Forms of Racial Discrimination (1965) provides: "Special measures taken for the sole purpose of securing adequate ·advancement of certain racial or ethnic groups of individuals requiring such protection as may be necessary in order to ensure such groups or individuals equal enjoyment or exercise of human rights and fundamental freedoms shall not be deemed racial discrimination, provided, however, that such measures do not, as a consequence, lead to the maintenance of separate rights for different racial groups and that they shall not be continued after the objectives for which they were taken have been achieved."

In similar manner, Article 2, paragraph 2, provides: "State Parties shall, when the circumstances so warrant, take, in the social, economic, cultural and other fields, special and concrete measures to ensure the adequate development and protection of certain racial groups or individuals belonging to them, for the purpose of guaranteeing them the full and equal enjoyment of human rights and fundamental freedoms. These measures shall in no case entail as a consequence the maintenance of unequal or separate rights for different racial groups after the objectives for which they were taken have been achieved."

The provisions of the other conventions mentioned in the text above are much the same as those quoted in this note.

CHAPTER 13. CONCLUSION: EQUALITY
FOR FUTURE REFERENCE

1. In prospect-regarding equal opportunity: two persons, J and K, have equal opportunities for X, if each has the same probability of attaining X. In *means-regarding* equal opportunity: two persons, J and K, have equal opportunities of X, if each has the same instruments for attaining X (Rae, 1981: 65-66, and see chapter 2 above). Briefly, in prospect-regarding settings in which equality of opportunity is ideally achieved, everyone would have the same probability of success, as in a nonskill game, such as a lottery with one ticket per contestant. In means-regarding settings in which perfect equality of opportunity is achieved, the player would have equal rules through which they can demonstrate their possibly unequal talents, as in a fairly run footrace.

2. Dahrendorf's category d, as explained in chapter 2 (Dahrendorf, 1969).

3. In fact, a certain conception of individualism in connection with the rights of property figured prominently in the works of Hobbes, Locke, and Harrington (Macpherson, 1962).

4. Fungibility simply refers to the ready substitution of one thing for another. For example, bushels of wheat of the same quality are entirely interchangeable.

5. See the discussion of economic equal protection and laissez-faire in chapter 5. The most commonly cited case on substantive economic due process is *Lochner v. New York* (1905). *Lochner* held that it was a violation of the liberty guaranteed to employers and employees by the due process clause of the Fourteenth Amendment for a state to regulate the working hours of bakery employees. Laissez-faire economics was the ruling ideology of the day.

6. The notion of self-reliance may remind us of Ralph Waldo Emerson's 1841 essay on "Self-Reliance." Emerson's self-reliance was, however, of somewhat different nature than economic individualism. He wrote chiefly of the man "who has ventured to trust himself" and his own moral sense, rather than to be ruled entirely by the opinions of others.

7. The two questions were: (1) Should the government in Washington see to it that blacks get fair treatment in jobs or leave this to state and local communities; and (2) Do you think the government in Washington should see to it that white and black children go to the same schools?

8. These involved: (1) attitudes toward neighborhoods—whether whites have a right to keep blacks out and whether blacks have a right to live where they want; and (2) attitudes toward desegregation versus strict segregation.

9. The six factors, summarized:

(1) that there exists a class who have been the object of discrimination which has produced deprivation, to which the state has contributed, and the basis of the discrimination was a "morally irrelevant characteristic" shared by members of the class;

(2) present adverse effects can be traced to past deprivation;

(3) the class as a whole is substantially disadvantaged in the competition for some scarce good;

(4) affirmative action offers a reasonable prospect of compensating for the disadvantage;

(5) there is no other better alternative; and

(6) the burden on the innocent member of a "nonpreferred group" suffers no greater competitive disadvantage than he or she might have experienced had the group favored by affirmative action not suffered substantial disadvantage. (Rosenfeld, 1991: 332)

10. We should note that Bellah et al., suggest other forms of individualism, specifically "biblical individualism" and "civic individualism." Both of these involve a basis for important relationships with others, rather than intrinsically different individualistic orientations.

BIBLIOGRAPHY

BOOKS AND ARTICLES

Abraham, H. J. (1980). *The Judicial Process: An Introductory Analysis of the Courts of the United States, England and France.* 4th ed. New York: Oxford University Press.

Armor, D. J. (1989). "After Busing: Education and Choice," *Public Interest* (Spring 1989): 24.

Aristotle (1962). *Nicomachean Ethics,* translated by M. Ostwald. New York: Bobbs-Merrill.

Baer, J. A. (1983). *Equality under the Constitution: Reclaiming the Fourteenth Amendment.* Ithaca, N.Y.: Cornell University Press.

Bayefsky, A. F., and M. Eberts (eds.) (1985). *Equality Rights and the Canadian Charter of Rights and Freedoms.* Toronto: Carswell.

Beale, H. K. (1930, 1958). *The Critical Year: A Study of Andrew Johnson and Reconstruction.* New York: Frederick Ungar.

Beard, C. A. (1918). *Contemporary American History, 1877–1913.* New York: Macmillan.

Beard, C. A., and M. Beard (1965). *An Economic Interpretation of the Constitution of the United States.* New York: The Free Press (originally published 1915).

Bellah, R. N., et al. (1986). *Habits of the Heart: Individualism and Commitment in American Life.* New York: Harper & Row.

Bellamy, E. (1888). *Looking Backward: 2000–1887.* Chicago: Packard and Co.

Berger, R. (1977). *Government by Judiciary: The Transformation of the Fourteenth Amendment.* Cambridge, Mass.: Harvard University Press.

Berle, A. A., and Means, G. C. (1932). *The Modern Corporation and Private Property.* New York: Macmillan.

Berlin, I. (1956). "Equality," *Proceedings of the Aristotelian Society,* New Series, 56.

——— (1961). "Equality as an Ideal," in F. Olafson (ed.), *Justice and Social Policy: a Collection of Essays.* Englewood Cliffs, N.J.: Prentice-Hall.

Bickel, A. M. (1955). "The Original Understanding and the Segregation Decision," *Harvard Law Review* 69 (Nov. 1955): 1.

——— (1978). *The Supreme Court and the Idea of Progress.* New Haven, Conn.: Yale University Press.

Blaustein, A. B., and R. L. Zangrando (1968). *Civil Rights and the American Negro: A Documentary History.* New York: Trident Press.

Branch, T. (1988). *Parting the Waters: America in the King Years, 1954–63.* New York: Simon and Schuster.

Brownlie, I. (ed.) (1981). *Basic Documents on Human Rights*. Oxford: Clarendon Press.

Carter, S. L. (1991). *Reflections of an Affirmative Action Baby*. New York: Basic Books.

Congressional Quarterly Service (1968). *Revolution in Civil Rights*. 4th ed. Washington, D.C.: Congressional Quarterly Inc.

Congressional Quarterly Weekly Report (June 29, 1991). "Another Round of Quotas," p. 1760.

Congressional Quarterly Weekly Report (August 3, 1991). "Civil Rights: No Deal," p. 2170.

Cose, E. (1991). "Are Quotas Really the Problem?" *Time* (June 24, 1991).

Crossette, B. (1991). "India's Descent," *New York Times Magazine* (May 19, 1991).

Crosskey, W. W. (1954). "Charles Fairman, 'Legislative History,' and the Constitutional Limitations on State Authority," *University of Chicago Law Review* 22 (Autumn, 1954): 1.

Curtis, M. K. (1986). *No State Shall Abridge: The Fourteenth Amendment and the Bill of Rights*. Durham, N.C.: Duke University Press.

Dahrendorf, R. (1969). "On the Origin of Inequality Among Men," in A. Beteille (ed.), *Social Inequality*. Harmondsworth, England: Penguin Books.

Dhavan, R. (1986). "Marc Galanter's Competing Equalities," *Law and Policy* 8, no. 3: 365.

Donald, D. (1960). *Charles Sumner and the Coming of the Civil War*. New York: Alfred A. Knopf.

Dorenkamp, A. G., J. F. McClymer, M. M. Moynihan, and A. C. Vadum (1985). *Images of Women in American Popular Culture*. Orlando, Fla.: Harcourt Brace Jovanovich.

Dorn, E. (1979). *Rules and Racial Equality*. New Haven, Conn.: Yale University Press.

Du Bois, W.E.B. (1935). *Black Reconstruction: An Essay Toward a History of the Part Which Black Folk Played in the Attempt to Reconstruct Democracy in America*. New York: S. A. Russell Co.

Dworkin, R. M. (1977). *Taking Rights Seriously*. Cambridge, Mass.: Harvard University Press.

Eberts, M. (1985). "The Equality Provisions of the Canadian Charter of Rights and Freedoms and Government Institutions," in Claire Becton and A. Wayne Mackay (eds.), *The Courts and the Charter*. Toronto: University of Toronto Press.

Emerson, R. W. (1954). *Basic Selections from Emerson*. New York: New American Library.

Fairman, C. (1949). "Does the Fourteenth Amendment Incorporate the Bill of Rights? The Original Understanding," *Stanford Law Review* 2 (December 1949): 5.

Fallon, R. H., Jr., and P. C. Weiler (1985). "Firefighters v. Stotts: Conflicting Models of Racial Justice," *Supreme Court Review* (1984): 1.

Fishkin, J. S. (1983). *Justice, Equal Opportunity and the Family*. New Haven, Conn.: Yale University Press.

Fiss, O. M. (1976). "Groups and the Equal Protection Clause," *Philosophy and Public Affairs* 5: 107.

Foner, E. (1988). *Reconstruction: America's Unfinished Revolution, 1863–1877*. New York: Harper and Row.

Frank, J. P., and R. F. Munro (1950). "The Original Understanding of 'Equal Protection of the Laws.' " *Columbia Law Review* 50 (February 1950): 131.

Friedman, L. (ed.) (1969). *Argument: The Oral Argument before the Supreme Court in Brown v. Board of Education of Topeka, 1952–55.* New York: Chelsea House Publishers.

Gadbois, G. H., Jr. (1986). "Affirmative Action in India: The Judiciary and Social Change," *Law and Policy* 8, no. 3: 329.

Gaillard, F. (1988). "On and Off the Bus in Charlotte," *Progressive* (April 1988): 21–23.

Galanter, M. (1984). *Competing Equalities: Law and the Backward Classes in India.* Berkeley: University of California Press.

Garrow, D. J. (1988). *Bearing the Cross: Martin Luther King, Jr., and the Southern Christian Leadership Conference.* New York: Vintage Book Edition.

Ghiselin, M. (1969). *The Triumph of the Darwinian Method.* Berkeley: University of California Press.

Gold, M. (1982). "A Principled Approach to Equality Rights: A Preliminary Inquiry," in E. P. Belobaba and E. Gertner (eds.), *The New Constitution and the Charter of Rights: Fundamental Issues and Strategies* (Special Symposium Edition of the *Supreme Court Law Review*) (1982): 130–61.

Goldstein, L.F. (1988). *The Constitutional Rights of Women: Cases in Law and Social Change.* Madison: University of Wisconsin Press.

Gould, S. J. (1980). *The Panda's Thumb: More Reflections in Natural History.* New York: W. W. Norton & Co.

Graglia, L. (1991). " 'Affirmative Action,' the Constitution, and the 1964 Civil Rights Act." *Measure* no. 92 (February 1991): 1.

Graham, H. J. (1950). "The Early Antislavery Backgrounds of the Fourteenth Amendment." *Wisconsin Law Review* 3 (April 1950): 479 and 4 (May 1950): 610.

——— (1968). *Everyman's Constitution.* New York: W. W. Norton & Co.

Griffin, J. H., and T. Freedman (1956). *Mansfield, Texas: A Report of the Crisis Situation Resulting from Efforts to Desegregate the School System.* New York: Anti-Defamation League of B'nai B'rith (Field Reports on Desegregation in the South).

Gutmann, A. (1987). *Democratic Education.* Princeton, N.J.: Princeton University Press.

——— (1980). *Liberal Equality.* Cambridge, England: Cambridge University Press.

Hayek, F. A. (1944). *The Road to Serfdom.* London: Routledge & Kegan Paul.

Hochschild, J. (1981). *What's Fair: American Beliefs about Distributive Justice.* Cambridge, Mass.: Harvard University Press.

Huber, J., and W. H. Form (1973). *Income and Ideology.* New York: Free Press.

Hyman, H. M. (1967). *The Radical Republicans and Reconstruction: 1861–1870.* New York: Bobbs-Merrill.

Jackson, D. W. (1976). "A New Vision of Equality: Testing the Effects of Gatekeeping Criteria," in S. Wasby (ed.), *Civil Liberties: Policy and Policy Making.* Lexington, Mass.: Lexington Books.

James, J. B. (1956). *The Framing of the Fourteenth Amendment.* Urbana: University of Illinois Press.

Kelly, A. H. (1956). "The Fourteenth Amendment Reconsidered: The Segregation Question." *Michigan Law Review* 59 (June 1956): 1049.

Kendrick, B. (1914). *The Journal of the Joint Committee of Fifteen on Reconstruction*. New York: Columbia University.

Kirp, D. L., M. G. Yudof, and M. S. Franks. (1986). *Gender Justice*. Chicago: University of Chicago Press.

Kluegel, J. R., and E. R. Smith (1986). *Beliefs about Inequality: American's Views of What Is and What Ought to Be*. New York: Aldine de Gruyter.

Kluger, R. (1975). *Simple Justice: The History of Brown v. Board of Education and Black America's Struggle for Equality*. New York: Alfred A. Knopf.

Korngold, R. (1955). *Thaddeus Stevens: A Being Darkly Wise and Rudely Great*. Westport, Conn.: Greenwood Press.

Kousser, J. M. (1980). "Separate but *not* Equal: The Supreme Court's First Decision on Racial Discrimination in Schools," *Journal of Southern History* 46: 36.

——— (1986). *Dead End: The Development of Nineteenth-Century Litigation on Racial Discrimination in Schools*. New York: Oxford University Press.

Kramer, D. C. (1982). *Comparative Civil Rights and Liberties*. Washington, D.C.: University Press of America.

Law School Admissions Services, Inc. (1991). *Law Services: The Official Guide to U.S. Law Schools*. Newtown, Penn.: Law School Admissions Services, Inc.

Lofgren, C. A. (1987). *The Plessy Case: A Legal-Historical Interpretation*. New York: Oxford University Press.

Lurie, J. (1984). "The Fourteenth Amendment: Use and Application in Selected State Court Civil Liberties Cases, 1870–1890—A Preliminary Assessment," *Journal of Legal History* 28: 297.

McGlen, N. E., and K. O'Connor (1983). *Women's Rights: The Struggle for Equality in the 19th and 20th Centuries*. New York: Praeger.

McKean, W. (1983). *Equality and Discrimination Under International Law*. Oxford: Clarendon Press.

Macpherson, C. B. (1962). *The Political Theory of Possessive Individualism*. Oxford: The Clarendon Press.

——— (1977). *The Life and Times of Liberal Democracy*. Oxford: Oxford University Press.

Maslow, A. H. (1962). *Toward a Psychology of Being*. New York: Van Nostrand.

Metcalf, G. R. (1983). *From Little Rock to Boston: The History of School Desegregation*. Westport, Conn.: Greenwood Press.

Montagu, A. (1952). *Darwin: Competition and Cooperation*. New York: Henry Schuman.

——— (1957). *The Natural Superiority of Women*. New York: Macmillan.

Moynihan, D. P. (1965). *The Negro Family: The Case for National Action*. Washington, D.C.: Office of Policy Planning and Research, U.S. Department of Labor.

Murphy, W. F. (1962). *Congress and the Court*. Chicago: University of Chicago Press.

Myrdal, G. (1944). *An American Dilemma*. New York: Harper and Bros.

O'Neill, T. (1987). *Man of the House: The Life and Political Memoirs of Speaker Tip O'Neill*. New York: Random House.

O'Neill, T. J. (1981). "The Language of Equality in a Constitutional Order," *American Political Science Review* 75: 626.

Orwell, G. (1946). *Animal Farm*. New York: Harcourt Brace.

Peltason, J. W. (1961). *Fifty-Eight Lonely Men: Southern Federal Judges and School Desegregation*. New York: Harcourt, Brace and World.

Polanyi, K. (1957). *The Great Transformation*. Boston: Beacon Hill Press.

Pole, J. R. (1978). *The Pursuit of Equality in American History.* Berkeley: University of California Press.

Prichett, C. H. (1948). *The Roosevelt Court.* New York: Macmillan.

—— (1961). *Congress versus the Supreme Court.* Minneapolis: University of Minnesota Press.

Rae, D., et al. (1981). *Equalities.* Cambridge, Mass.: Harvard University Press.

Riddleberger, P. W. (1979). *1866: The Critical Year Revisited.* Carbondale: Southern Illinois University Press.

Riddlesperger, J. W., Jr. (1980). "Sarah T. Hughes: Biography of a Federal District Judge." Master's thesis, North Texas State University.

Rosenfeld, M. (1991). *Affirmative Action & Justice: A Philosophical and Constitutional Inquiry.* New Haven, Conn.: Yale University Press.

Rousseau, J. J. (1967). *The Social Contract and the Discourse on the Origin of Inequality,* translated by L. G. Crocker. New York: Pocket Books.

Ruffins, P. (1988). "Activists Fight Desegregation Rollback," *Black Enterprise* (September 1988): 25.

Schwartz, B. (1988). *Behind Bakke: Affirmative Action and the Supreme Court.* New York: New York University Press.

—— (1986). *Swann's Way: The School Busing Case & the Supreme Court.* New York: Oxford University Press.

Schweber, S. S. (1977). "The Origin of the *Origin* Revisited." *Journal of the History of Biology,* 10: 229.

Sindler, A. P. (1978). *Bakke, DeFunis and Minority Admissions: The Quest for Equal Opportunity.* New York: Longman.

Smith, A. (1776). *An Inquiry into the Nature and Causes of the Wealth of Nations.* New York: Modern Library Edition, 1937.

Sniderman, P. M. (1985). *Race and Inequality: A Study in American Values.* Chatham, N.J.: Chatham House.

Spencer, H. (1850). *Social Statics.* New York: D. Appleton Edition, 1892.

—— (1972). *On Social Evolution* (edited by J.D.Y. Peel). Chicago: University of Chicago Press.

Subbarao, G.C.V. (1985). *Computerised Constitution of India.* Hyderabad: Law Academy Private Ltd.

Sumner, W. G. (1914). *The Challenge of the Facts and Other Essays.* New Haven, Conn.: Yale University Press.

—— (1940). *Folkways.* Boston: Ginn & Co.

—— (1963). *Social Darwinism: Selected Essays.* Englewood Cliffs, N.J.: Prentice-Hall.

Tawney, R. H. (1964). *Equality.* London: Allen and Unwin.

ten Broek, J. (1965). *Equal under Law.* New York: Collier Books.

Tocqueville, A. de. (1969). *Democracy in America.* Garden City, New York: Anchor Books.

Trefousse, H. L. (1968). *The Radical Republicans: Lincoln's Vanguard for Racial Justice.* Baton Rouge: Louisiana State University Press.

Tribe, L. (1988). *American Constitutional Law.* Mineola, N.Y.: Foundation Press.

Vose, C. (1955). "NAACP Strategy in the Covenant Cases," *Western Reserve Law Review* 6: 101.

Wasby, S. L. (1986). "Indian 'Compensatory Discrimination' and American 'Affirmative Action': Some Parallels—A Review of Galanter's *Competing Equalities,*" *Law and Policy* 8, no.3: 379.

Wasserstrom, R. (1980). "Preferential Treatment," in *Philosophy and Society*

Issues: Five Studies. Notre Dame, Ind.: University of Notre Dame Press.

Westen, P. (1982). "The Empty Idea of Equality," *Harvard Law Review* 95: 537–96.

———— (1990). *Speaking of Equality: An Analysis of the Rhetorical Force of 'Equality' in Moral and Legal Discourse.* Princeton, N.J.: Princeton University Press.

Wilkinson, J. H., III (1979). *From Brown to Bakke: The Supreme Court and School Integration: 1954–78.* New York: Oxford University Press.

Wilson, W. J. (1987). *The Truly Disadvantaged: The Inner City, The Underclass and Public Policy.* Chicago: University of Chicago Press.

Wolgast, E. H. (1987). *The Grammar of Justice.* Ithaca, N.Y.: Cornell University Press.

Woodward, C. V. (1955). *The Strange Career of Jim Crow.* New York: Oxford University Press.

Young, M. (1959). *The Rise of the Meritocracy.* Harmondsworth, England: Penguin Books.

CASES

Canadian Cases

Andrews v. Law Society of British Columbia, 27 D.L.R.[1] (4th) 600 (1986), 10 C.R.R.[1] D/5719 (1989).

Apsit, et al. v. Manitoba Human Rights Commission, 22 C.R.R.[1] 225 (1985).

Black v. Law Society of Alberta, 20 C.R.R. 153 (1986).

Bliss v. Attorney General of Canada, (1979) 1 S.C.R.[1] 183.

Harrison v. University of British Columbia, 13 C.H.R.R.[1] D/317 (1990).

McKinney v. University of Guelph, 13 C.H.R.R. D/171 (1990).

Regina v. Bearhead, 18 C.R.R. 362 (1985).

Regina v. LeGallant, 18 C.R.R. 362 (1985).

Regina v. M., 19 C.R.R. 145 (1986).

Regina v. Oakes, 19 C.R.R. 308 (1986).

Indian Cases

Balaji v. State of Mysore, AIR[2] 1963 SC 649.

State of Kerala v. N. M. Thomas, AIR 1976 SC 490.

State of Madras v. Champakam Dorairajan, AIR 1951 S.C. 226.

Venkataramana v. State of Madras, AIR 1951 S.C. 229.

International Cases

Belgian Linguistics Case (Case Relating to Certain Aspects of the Laws on the Use of Languages in Education in Belgium), Judgment of 23rd July, 1968, European Court of Human Rights, E.C.R.A., Series A, vol. 6.

1. D.L.R. refers to the Dominion Law Reports. C.R.R. refers to the Canadian Rights Reporter. S.C.R. refers to the Supreme Court Reports. C.H.R.R. refers to the Canadian Human Rights Reporter.
2. All India Reports.

South-West Africa Cases (Second Phase), International Court of Justice, ICJ Rep. 1966.

United States Cases[3]

Albemarle Paper Co. v. Moody, 422 U.S. 405, 95 S.Ct. 2362 (1975).
Alexander v. Holmes County Board of Education, 396 U.S. 19, 90 S.Ct. 29 (1969).
Alexander v. Louisiana, 405 U.S. 625, 92 S.Ct. 1221 (1972).
Ambach v. Norwick, 441 U.S. 68, 99 S.Ct. 1589 (1979).
American Party of Texas v. White, 415 U.S. 767, 94 S.Ct. 1296 (1974).
American Sugar Refining Co. v. Louisiana, 179 U.S. 89, 21 S.Ct. 43 (1900).
Argersinger v. Hamlin, 407 U.S. 25, 92 S.Ct. 2006 (1972).
Arizona Governing Committee, etc. v. Norris, 463 U.S. 1073, 103 S.Ct. 3492 (1983).
Atchison, Topeka & Santa Fe Railway v. Vosburg, 238 U.S. 56, 35 S.Ct. 675 (1915).
Attorney General of New York v. Soto-Lopez, 476 U.S. 898, 106 S.Ct. 2317 (1986).
Austin Independent School District v. United States, 429 U.S. 990, 97 S.Ct. 517 (1976).
Bachtel v. Wilson, 204 U.S. 36, 27 S.Ct. 243 (1907).
Baker v. Carr, 369 U.S. 186, 82 S.Ct. 691 (1962).
Bakke (See *Regents of the University of California v. Bakke*)
Ball v. James, 451 U.S. 355, 101 S.Ct. 1811 (1981).
Barbier v. Connally, 113 U.S. 27, 5 S.Ct. 357 (1884).
Barksdale v. Springfield School Committee, 237 F.Supp. 543 (D.Mass, 1965).
Bates v. City of Little Rock, 361 U.S. 516, 80 S.Ct. 412 (1960).
Bell v. School City of Gary, Indiana, 213 F.Supp. 819 (N.D. Indiana, 1963), 324 F2d 209 (7th Cir., 1963).
Belloti v. Baird, 443 U.S. 622, 99 S.Ct. 3035 (1979).
Betts v. Brady, 316 U.S. 455, 62 S.Ct. 1252 (1942).
Board of Education of Oklahoma City v. Dowell, ___ U.S. ___ , 111 S.Ct. 630 (1991).
Boddie v. Connecticut, 401 U.S. 371, 91 S.Ct. 780 (1971).
Bolling v. Sharpe, 347 U.S. 497, 74 S.Ct. 693 (1954).
Bowen v. Gilliard, 483 U.S. 587, 107 S.Ct. 3008 (1987).
Bradley v. School Board of City of Richmond (*Richmond I*), 382 U.S. 103, 86 S.Ct. 224 (1965).
Bradley v. School Board of City of Richmond (*Richmond II*), 416 U.S. 696. 94 S.Ct. 2006 (1974).
Bradwell v. Illinois, 83 (16 Wallace) U.S. 130, 21 L.Ed. 442 (1873).
Branche v. Board of Education of Town of Hempstead, 204 F.Supp. 150 (E.D.N.Y., 1962).
Brennan, Corning Glass Works v. (See Corning Glass Works v. Brennan)
Briggs v. Elliot, 132 F.Supp. 776 (E.D.S.C., 1955).
Brown v. Board of Education of Topeka (*Brown I*), 347 U.S. 483, 74 S.Ct. 686 (1954).

3. Citations to pages of cases in the text are to the second series citation (L.Ed or S.Ct), rather than to the *U.S. Reports.*

Brown v. Board of Education of Topeka (Brown II), 349 U.S. 294, 75 S.Ct. 753 (1955).
Buchanan v. Warley, 245 U.S. 60, 38 S.Ct. 16 (1917).
Bullock v. Carter, 405 U.S. 134, 92 S.Ct. 849 (1972).
Burdine, Texas Department of Community Affairs v. (See *Texas Department of Community Affairs v. Burdine*)
Bush v. Kentucky, 107 U.S. 110, 1 S.Ct. 625 (1883).
Caban v. Mohammed, 441 U.S. 380 99 S.Ct. 1760 (1979).
Cabell v. Chavez-Salido, 454 U.S. 432, 102 S.Ct 735 (1982).
Califano v. Goldfarb, 430 U.S. 199, 97 S.Ct. 1021 (1977).
Califano v. Jobst, 434 U.S. 47, 98 S.Ct. 95 (1977).
Califano v. Webster, 430 U.S. 313, 97 S.Ct. 1192 (1977).
Califano v. Westcott, 443 U.S. 76, 99 S.Ct. 2655 (1979).
California Federal Savings and Loan Association v. Guerra, 479 U.S. 272, 107 S.Ct. 683 (1987).
Carey v. Population Services International, 431 U.S. 678, 97 S.Ct. 2010 (1977).
Carolene Products Case (See *United States v. Carolene Products*)
Carrington v. Rash, 380 U.S. 89, 85 S.Ct. 775 (1965).
Chappelle v. Greater Baton Rouge Airport District, 431 U.S. 159, 97 S.Ct. 2162 (1977).
Cipriano v. City of Houma, 395 U.S. 701, 89 S.Ct. 1897 (1969).
City of Cleburne, Texas v. Cleburne Living Center, 473 U.S. 432, 105 S.Ct. 3249 (1985).
City of Dallas v. Stanglin, 490 U.S. 19, 109 S.Ct. 1591 (1989).
City of Los Angeles v. Manhart, 435 U.S. 702, 98 S.Ct. 1370 (1978).
City of Phoenix v. Kolodziejski, 399 U.S. 204, 90 S.Ct. 1990 (1970).
City of Richmond v. Croson Co., 488 U.S. 469 109 S.Ct. 706 (1989).
The Civil Rights Cases, 109 U.S. 3, 3 S.Ct. 18 (1883).
Clark v. Jeter, 486 U.S. 456, 108 S.Ct. 1910 (1988).
Clements v. Fashing, 457 U.S. 957, 102 S.Ct. 2836 (1982).
Cleveland Board of Education v. LaFleur, 414 U.S. 632, 94 S.Ct. 791 (1974).
Columbus Board of Education v. Penick, 443 U.S. 449, 99 S.Ct. 2941 (1979).
Connolly v. Union Sewer Pipe Co., 184 U.S. 540, 22 S.Ct. 431 (1902).
Cooper v. Aaron, 358 U.S. 1, 78 S.Ct. 1401 (1958).
Corning Glass Works v. Brennan, 417 U.S. 188, 94 S.Ct. 2223 (1974).
Corrigan v. Buckley, 271 U.S. 323, 46 S.Ct. 521 (1926).
Cotting v. Godard, 183 U.S. 79, 22 S.Ct. 30 (1901).
County of San Mateo v. Southern Pacific Railroad, 116 U.S. 138, 6 S.Ct. 317 (1885).
County of Washington v. Gunther, 452 U.S. 161, 101 S.Ct. 2242 (1981).
Craig v. Boren, 429 U.S. 190, 97 S.Ct. 451 (1976).
Crane v. New York, 239 U.S. 195, 36 S.Ct. 85 (1915).
Crawford v. Board of Education of the City of Los Angeles, 458 U.S. 527, 102 S.Ct. 3211 (1982).
Crescent Cotton Oil Co. v. Mississippi, 257 U.S. 129, 42 S.Ct. 42 (1921).
Cumming v. County Board of Education of Richmond County, Georgia, 175 U.S. 528, 20 S.Ct. 197 (1899).
Dandridge v. Williams, 397 U.S. 471, 90 S.Ct. 1153 (1970).
Davis v. Bandemer, 478 U.S. 109, 106 S.Ct. 2797 (1986).
Davis v. Board of School Commissioners of Mobile County, 402 U.S. 33, 91 S.Ct. 1289 (1971).

Dayton Board of Education v. Brinkman (Dayton I), 433 U.S. 406, 97 S.Ct. 2766 (1977).
Dayton Board of Education v. Brinkman (Dayton II), 443 U.S. 526, 99 S.Ct. 2971 (1979).
DeFunis v. Odegaard, 416 U.S. 312, 94 S.Ct. 1704 (1974).
Dominion Hotel v. Arizona, 249 U.S. 265, 39 S.Ct. 273 (1919).
Dothard v. Rawlinson, 433 U.S. 321, 97 S.Ct. 2720 (1977).
Douglas v. California, 372 U.S. 353, 83 S.Ct. 814 (1963).
Dred Scott v. Sanford, 60 U.S. (19 Howard) 393, 15 L.Ed. 691 (1857).
Dunn v. Blumstein, 405 U.S. 330, 92 S.Ct. 995 (1972).
Edwards v. California, 314 U.S. 160, 62 S.Ct. 164 (1941).
EEOC v. Wyoming, 460 U.S. 226, 103 S.Ct. 1054 (1983).
Examining Board v. Otero, 426 U.S. 572, 96 S.Ct. 2264 (1976).
Evans v. Buchanan, 393 F.Supp 428 (D.C.Del., 1975).
Ex parte Virginia, 100 U.S. 339, 25 L.Ed. 676 (1880).
Fay v. New York, 332 U.S. 261, 67 S.Ct. 1613 (1947).
Feeney, Personnel Administrator of Massachusetts v. (See *Personnel Administrator of Massachusetts v. Feeney*)
Firefighters Case (See *Local No. 93, International Association of Firefighters v. City of Cleveland*)
Firefighters Local Union No. 1784 v. Stotts, 467 U.S. 561, 104 S.Ct. 2576 (1984).
Foley v. Connelie, 435 U.S. 291, 98 S.Ct. 1067 (1978).
Fong Yue Ting v. U.S., 149 U.S. 698, 13 S.Ct. 1016 (1893).
Forbush v. Wallace, 405 U.S. 970, 92 S.Ct. 1197 (1972).
Frontiero v. Richardson, 411 U.S. 677, 93 S.Ct. 1764 (1973).
Fuentes v. Shevin, 407 U.S. 67, 92 S.Ct. 1983 (1972).
Fullilove v. Klutznick, 443 U.S. 448, 100 S.Ct. 2758 (1980).
Gaines (See *Missouri ex rel Gaines v. Canada*)
Gault (See *In re Gault*)
Geduldig v. Aiello, 417 U.S. 484, 94 S.Ct. 2485 (1974).
General Electric v. Gilbert, 429 U.S. 125, 97 S.Ct. 401 (1976).
Gideon v. Wainwright, 372 U.S. 335, 83 S.Ct. 792 (1963).
Ginsberg v. New York, 390 U.S. 629, 88 S.Ct. 1274 (1968).
Goesaert v. Cleary, 335 U.S. 464, 69 S.Ct. 198 (1948).
Goldberg v. Kelly, 397 U.S. 254, 90 S.Ct. 1011 (1970).
Goldfarb, Califano v. (See *Califano v. Goldfarb*)
Gomez v. Perez, 409 U.S. 535, 93 S.Ct. 872 (1973).
Gong Lum v. Rice, 275 U.S. 78, 48 S.Ct. 91 (1927).
Goss v. Board of Education of the City of Knoxville, 373 U.S. 683, 83 S.Ct. 1405 (1963).
Goss v. Lopez, 419 U.S. 565, 95 S.Ct. 729 (1975).
Graham v. Richardson, 403 U.S. 365, 91 S.Ct. 1848 (1971).
Green v. County School Board of New Kent County, Virginia, 391 U.S. 430, 88 S.Ct. 1689 (1968).
Gregory v. Ashcroft, ___ U.S. ___, 111 S.Ct. 2395 (1991).
Griffin v. County School Board of Prince Edward County, Virginia, 377 U.S. 218, 84 S.Ct. 1226 (1964).
Griffin v. Illinois, 351 U.S. 12, 76 S.Ct. 585 (1956).
Griffiths (See *In re Griffiths*)
Griggs v. Duke Power Co., 401 U.S. 424, 91 S.Ct. 849 (1971).
Griswold v. Connecticut, 381 U.S. 479, 85 S.Ct. 1678 (1965).

Guerra, California Federal Savings and Loan Association v. (See *California Federal Savings and Loan v. Guerra*)

Grovey v. Townsend, 295 U.S. 45, 55 S.Ct. 622 (1935).

Guinn v. United States, 238 U.S. 347, 35 S.Ct. 926 (1915).

Gulf, Colorado & and Santa Fe Railway Co. v. Ellis, 165 U.S. 150, 17 S.Ct. 255 (1897).

Gunther, County of Washington v. (See *County of Washington v. Gunther*)

Hall v. De Cuir, 95 U.S. 485, 24 L.Ed. 547 (1878).

Hampton v. Mow Sun Wong, 426 U.S. 88, 96 S.Ct. 1895 (1976).

Harper v. Virginia State Board of Elections, 383 U.S. 663, 86 S.Ct. 1079 (1966).

Harris v. McRae, 448 U.S. 297, 100 S.Ct. 2671 (1980).

Hartford Steam Boiler Inspection and Insurance Co. v. Harrison, 301 U.S. 459, 57 S.Ct. 838 (1937).

Hayes v. Missouri, 120 U.S. 68, 7 S.Ct. 350 (1887).

Heim v. McCall, 239 U.S. 175, 36 S.Ct 78 (1915).

Henderson v. United States, 339 U.S. 816, 70 S.Ct. 843 (1950).

Hill v. Stone, 421 U.S. 289, 95 S.Ct. 1637 (1975).

Hirabayashi v. United States, 320 U.S. 81, 63 S.Ct. 1375 (1943).

Hishon v. King & Spaulding, 467 U.S. 69, 104 S.Ct. 2229 (1984).

Hogan, Mississippi University for Women v. (See *Mississippi University for Women v. Hogan*)

Hooper v. Bernalillo County Assessor, 472 U.S. 612, 105 S.Ct. 2862 (1985).

Hoyt v. Florida, 368 U.S. 57, 82 S.Ct. 159 (1961).

Illinois State Board of Elections v. Socialist Workers Party, 440 U.S. 173, 99 S.Ct. 983 (1979).

In re Gault, 387 U.S. 1, 87 S.Ct. 1428 (1967).

In re Griffiths, 413 U.S. 717, 93 S.Ct. 2851 (1973).

International Union, UAW v. Johnson Controls, ___ U.S. ___, 111 S.Ct. 1196 (1991).

Jefferson County Board of Education (See *United States v. Jefferson County Board of Education*)

Jimenez v. Weinberger, 417 U.S. 628, 94 S.Ct. 2496 (1974).

Johnson v. Transportation Agency, Santa Clara County, California, 480 U.S.616, 107 S.Ct. 1442 (1987).

Kahn v. Shevin, 416 U.S. 351, 94 S.Ct. 1734 (1974).

Keyes v. School District No. 1, Denver, 413 U.S. 189, 93 S.Ct. 2686 (1973).

Kirchberg v. Feenstra, 450 U.S. 455, 101 S.Ct. 1195 (1981).

Korematsu v. U.S., 323 U.S. 214, 65 S.Ct. 193 (1944).

LaFleur, Cleveland Board of Education v. (See *Cleveland Board of Education v. LaFleur*)

Kramer v. Union Free School District, 395 U.S. 621, 89 S.Ct. 1886 (1969).

Kras (See *United States v. Kras*)

Labine v. Vincent, 401 U.S. 532, 91 S.Ct. 1017 (1971).

Lalli v. Lalli, 439 U.S. 259, 99 S.Ct. 519 (1978).

Lehr v. Robertson, 463 U.S. 248, 103 S.Ct. 2985 (1983).

Levy v. Louisiana, 391 U.S. 68, 88 S.Ct. 1509 (1968).

Lindsey v. Normet, 405 U.S. 56, 92 S.Ct. 862 (1972).

Local No. 28, Sheet Metal Workers' v. EEOC, 478 U.S. 421, 106 S.Ct. 3019 (1986).

Local No. 93, International Association of Firefighters v. City of Cleveland, 478 U.S. 501, 106 S.Ct. 3063 (1986).

Lochner v. New York, 198 U.S. 45, 25 S.Ct. 539 (1905).
Louisville, New Orleans and Texas Railway Co. v. Mississippi, 133 U.S. 587, 10 S.Ct. 348 (1890).
Loving v. Virginia, 338 U.S. 1, 87 S.Ct. 1817 (1967).
Lyng v. Castillo, 477 U.S. 635, 106 S.Ct. 2727 (1986).
McCabe v. Atchison, Topeka & Santa Fe Railway Co., 235 U.S. 151, 35 S.Ct. 69 (1914).
McCready v. Virginia, 94 U.S. 391, 24 L.Ed. 248 (1877).
McCulloch v. Maryland, 17 U.S. (4 Wheat.) 316, 4 L.Ed. 579 (1819).
McDonald v. Board of Election Commissioners of Chicago, 394 U.S. 802, 89 S.Ct. 1404 (1969).
McLaurin v. Oklahoma State Regents, 339 U.S. 637, 70 S.Ct. 851 (1950).
McNeese v. Board of Education, 373 U.S. 668, 83 S.Ct. 1433 (1963).
Magoun v. Illinois Trust & Savings Bank, 170 U.S. 283, 18 S.Ct. 594 (1898).
Maher v. Roe, 432 U.S. 464, 97 S.Ct. 2376 (1977).
Manhart, City of Los Angeles v. (See *City of Los Angeles v. Manhart*)
Marston v. Lewis, 410 U.S. 679, 93 S.Ct. 1211 (1973).
Martin v. Wilks, 490 U.S. 755, 109 S.Ct. 2180 (1989).
Martinez v. Bynum, 461 U.S. 321, 103 S.Ct. 1838 (1983).
Massachusetts Board of Retirement v. Murgia, 427 U.S. 307, 96 S.Ct. 2562 (1976).
Matthews v. Lucas, 427 U.S. 495, 96 S.Ct. 2755 (1976).
Memorial Hospital v. Maricopa County, 415 U.S. 250, 94 S.Ct. 1076 (1974).
Metropolitan County Board of Education of Nashville and Davidson County, Tennessee v. Kelly, 511 F.Supp. 1363, 687 F.2d 814, Cert. denied, 103 S.Ct. 834 (1983).
Metropolitan Life Ins. Co. v. Ward, 470 U.S. 869, 105 S.Ct. 1676 (1985).
Michael M. v. Superior Court of Sonoma County, 450 U.S. 464, 101 S.Ct. 1200 (1981).
Milliken v. Bradley (Milliken I), 418 U.S. 717, 94 S.Ct. 3112 (1974).
Milliken v. Bradley (Milliken II), 433 U.S. 267, 97 S.Ct. 2749 (1977).
Mills v. Habluetzel, 456 U.S. 91, 102 S.Ct. 1549 (1982).
Minnesota Rate Case (Chicago, Milwaukee and St. Paul Railway Co. v. Minnesota), 134 U.S. 418, 10 S.Ct. 462 (1890).
Minor v. Happersett, 88 (21 Wallace) U.S. 162, 22 L.Ed. 627 (1875).
Mississippi University for Women v. Hogan, 458 U.S. 718, 102 S.Ct. 3331 (1982).
Missouri ex rel Gaines v. Canada, 305 U.S. 337, 59 S.Ct. 232 (1938).
Monroe v. Board of Commissioners of the City of Jackson, Tennessee, 391 U.S. 450, 88 S.Ct. 1700 (1968).
Montgomery County Board of Education (See *United States v. Montgomery County Board of Education*)
Moore v. City of East Cleveland, 431 U.S. 494, 97 S.Ct. 1932 (1977).
Moreno (See *U.S.D.A. v. Moreno*)
Morgan v. Kerrigan, 388 F.Supp. 581 (D. Mass.,1974), 509 F.2d 580 (1974), Cert. denied, 421 U.S. 963, 95 S.Ct. 1950 (1975).
Morgan v. Virginia, 328 U.S. 373, 66 S.Ct. 1050 (1946).
Muller v. Oregon, 208 U.S. 412, 28 S.Ct. 324 (1908).
Munn v. Illinois, 94 US. 133, 24 L.Ed. 77 (1877).
Murgia (See *Massachusetts Board of Retirement v. Murgia*)
Murray v. Giarratano, 492 U.S. 1, 109 S.Ct. 2765 (1989).
Murray v. Pearson, 182 A. 590 (1936).
Murry (See *U.S.D.A. v. Murry*)

Nashville Gas Co. v. Satty, 434 U.S. 136, 98 S.Ct. 347 (1977).
Neal v. Delaware, 103 U.S. 370, 26 L.Ed. 567 (1881).
New Jersey Welfare Rights Organization v. Cahill, 411 U.S. 619, 93 S.Ct. 1700 (1973).
Newport News Shipbuilding & Dry Dock Co. v. EEOC, 462 U.S. 669, 103 S.Ct. 2622 (1983).
Nixon v. Condon, 286 U.S. 73, 52 S.Ct. 484 (1932).
Nixon v. Herndon, 273 U.S. 536, 47 S.Ct. 446 (1927).
Norris, Arizona Governing Committee v. (See *Arizona Governing Committee v. Norris*)
Nyquist v. Mauclet, 432 U.S. 1, 97 S.Ct. 2120 (1977).
O'Brien v. Skinner, 414 U.S. 524, 94 S.Ct. 740 (1974).
Oklahoma City (See *Board of Education of Oklahoma City v. Dowell*)
Orient Insurance Co. v. Daggs, 172 U.S. 557, 19 S.Ct. 281 (1899).
Orr v. Orr, 440 U.S. 268, 99 S.Ct. 1102 (1979).
Ortwein v. Schwab, 410 U.S. 656, 93 S.Ct. 1172 (1973).
Oyama v. California, 332 U.S. 633, 68 S.Ct. 269 (1948).
Pace v. Alabama, 106 U.S. 583, 1 S.Ct. 637 (1883).
Palko v. Connecticut, 302 U.S. 319, 58 S.Ct. 149 (1937).
Parham v. Hughes, 441 U.S. 347, 99 S.Ct. 1742 (1979).
Pasadena City Board of Education v. Spangler, 427 U.S.424, 96 S.Ct. 2697 (1976).
Patsone v. Pennsylvania, 232 U.S. 138, 34 S.Ct. 281 (1914).
Personnel Administrator of Massachusetts v. Feeney, 442 U.S. 256, 99 S.Ct. 2282 (1979).
Phillips v. Martin-Marietta Corp., 400 U.S. 542, 91 S.Ct. 496 (1971).
Pickett v. Brown, 462 U.S. 1, 103 S.Ct. 2199 (1983).
Planned Parenthood of Central Missouri v. Danforth, 428 U.S. 52, 96 S.Ct. 2831 (1976).
Plessy v. Ferguson, 163 U.S. 537, 16 S.Ct. 1138 (1896).
Plyler v. Doe, 457 U.S. 202, 102 S.Ct. 2382 (1982).
Porterfield v. Webb, 263 U.S. 225, 44 S.Ct. 21 (1923).
Powell v. Alabama, 287 U.S. 45, 53 S.Ct. 55 (1932).
Price Waterhouse v. Hopkins, 490 U.S. 228, 109 S.Ct. 1775 (1989).
Quaker City Cab Co. v. Pennsylvania, 277 U.S. 389, 48 S.Ct. 553 1928).
Quarles v. Oxford Municipal Separate School District, 868 F.2d 750 (5th Cir., 1989).
Quilloin v. Walcott, 434 U.S. 246, 98 S.Ct. 549 (1978).
Quinn v. Millsap, 491 U.S. 95, 109 S.Ct. 2324 (1989).
Quong Wing v. Kirkendall, 223 U.S. 59, 32 S.Ct. 192 (1912).
Reagan v. Farmers Loan and Trust Co., 154 U.S. 362, 14 S.Ct. 1047 (1894).
Reed v. Reed, 404 U.S. 71, 92 S.Ct. 251 (1971).
Regents of the University of California v. Bakke, 438 U.S. 265, 98 S.Ct. 2733 (1978).
Reynolds v. Sims, 377 U.S. 533, 84 S.Ct. 1362 (1964).
Richmond I and II (See *Bradley v. School Board of City of Richmond*)
Roe v. Wade, 410 U.S. 113, 93 S.Ct. 705 (1973).
Rogers v. Paul, 382 U.S. 198, 86 S.Ct. 358 (1965).
Rosario v. Rockefeller, 410 U.S. 752, 93 S.Ct. 1245 (1973).
Ross v. Moffitt, 417 U.S. 600, 94 S.Ct. 2437 (1974).

Rostker v. Goldberg, 453 U.S. 57, 101 S.Ct. 2646 (1981).

Salyer Land Co. v. Tulare Lake Basin Water Storage District, 410 U.S. 719, 93 S.Ct. 1224 (1973).

San Antonio v. Rodriquez, 411 U.S. 1, 93 S.Ct. 1278 (1973).

Schlesinger v. Ballard, 419 U.S. 498, 95 S.Ct. 572 (1975).

Schweiker v. Wilson, 450 U.S. 221, 101 S.Ct. 1074 (1981).

Scott v. Illinois, 440 U.S. 367, 99 S.Ct. 1158 (1979).

Seattle School District (See *Washington v. Seattle School District*)

Shapiro v. Thompson, 394 U.S. 618, 89 S.Ct. 1322 (1969).

Sheet Metal Workers Case (See *Local No. 28, Sheet Metal Workers v. EEOC*)

Shelley v. Kraemer, 334 U.S. 1, 68 S.Ct. 836 (1948).

Singleton v. Jackson Municipal Separate School District, 348 F2d 729 (5th Cir., 1965); 355 F2d 865 (5th Cir., 1966).

Sipuel v. Board of Regents, 332 U.S. 631, 68 S.Ct. 299 (1948).

Skinner v. Oklahoma, 316 U.S. 535, 62 S.Ct. 1110 (1942).

Slaughter-House Cases, 83 U.S. (16 Wallace) 36, 21 L.Ed. 394 (1873).

Smith v. Allright, 321 U.S. 649, 64 S.Ct. 757 (1944).

Smyth v. Ames, 169 U.S. 466, 18 S.Ct. 418 (1898).

Sniadach v. Family Finance Corp., 395 U.S. 337, 89 S.Ct. 1820 (1969).

Sosna v. Iowa, 419 U.S. 393, 95 S.Ct. 553 (1975).

Soto-Lopez (See *Attorney General of New York v. Soto-Lopez*)

Stanley v. Illinois, 405 U.S. 645, 92 S.Ct. 1208 (1972).

Stanton v. Stanton, 421 U.S. 7, 95 S.Ct. 1373 (1975).

State of Ohio v. Deckebach, 274 U.S. 392, 47 S.Ct. 630 (1927).

Steele v. Louisville & Nashville Railroad Co., 323 U.S. 192, 65 S.Ct. 226 (1944).

Storer v. Brown, 415 U.S. 724, 94 S.Ct. 1274 (1974).

Stotts (See *Firefighters Local Union No. 1784 v. Stotts*)

Strauder v. West Virginia, 100 U.S. 303, 25 L.Ed. 664 (1880).

Sugarman v. Dougall, 413 U.S. 634, 93 S.Ct. 2842 (1973).

Swann v. Charlotte-Mecklenburg Board of Education, 300 F. Supp. 1358 (W.D. N.C., 1969); 431 F.2d 138 (4th Cir., 1970); 402 U.S. 1, 91 S.Ct. 1267 (1971).

Sweatt v. Painter, 339 U.S. 629, 70 S.Ct. 848 (1950).

Takahashi v. Fish and Game Commission, 334 U.S. 410, 68 S.Ct. 1138 (1948).

Taylor v. Louisiana, 419 U.S. 522, 95 S.Ct. 692 (1975).

Terrace v. Thompson, 263 U.S. 197, 44 S.Ct. 15 (1923).

Texas Department of Community Affairs v. Burdine, 450 U.S. 248, 101 S.Ct. 1089 (1981).

Tigner v. Texas, 310 U.S. 141, 60 S.Ct. 879 (1940).

Tinker v. Des Moines Independent School District, 393 U.S. 503, 89 S.Ct. 733 (1969).

Toll v. Moreno, 458 U.S. 1, 102 S.Ct. 2977 (1982).

Trimble v. Gordon, 430 U.S. 762, 97 S.Ct. 1459 (1977).

Truax v. Corrigan, 257 U.S. 312, 42 S.Ct. 124 (1921).

Truax v. Raich, 239 U.S. 33, 36 S.Ct. 7 (1915).

Turner v. Department of Employment Security, 423 U.S. 44, 96 S.Ct. 249 (1975).

Turner v. Fouche, 396 U.S. 346, 90 S.Ct. 532 (1970).

United States v. Carolene Products Co., 304 U.S. 144, 58 S.Ct. 778 (1938).

United States v. Cruikshank, 92 U.S. 542, 23 L.Ed. 588 (1876).

United States v. Harris, 106 U.S. 629, 1 S.Ct. 601 (1883).

United States v. Jefferson County Board of Education, 372 F.2d 837 (5th Cir., 1966).

United States v. Kras, 409 U.S. 434, 93 S.Ct. 631 (1973).
United States v. Montgomery County Board of Education, 395 U.S. 225, 89 S.Ct. 1670 (1969).
United States v. Paradise, 480 U.S. 149, 107 S.Ct. 1053 (1987).
United States v. Wong Kim Ark, 169 U.S. 649, 18 S.Ct. 456 (1898).
United Steelworkers v. Weber, 443 U.S. 193, 99 S.Ct. 2721 (1979).
U.S.D.A. v. Moreno, 413 U.S. 528, 93 S.Ct. 2821 (1973).
U.S.D.A. v. Murry, 413 U.S. 508, 93 S.Ct. 2832 (1973).
Vance v. Bradley, 440 U.S. 90, 99 S.Ct. 2230 (1979).
Village of Belle Terre v. Boraas, 416 U.S. 1, 945 S. Ct. 1536 (1974).
Virginia v. Rives, 100 U.S. 313, 25 L.Ed. 667 (1880).
Vlandis v. Kline, 412 U.S. 441, 93 S.Ct. 2230 (1973).
Vorchheimer v. School Board of Philadelphia, 430 U.S. 703,97 S.Ct. 1671 (1977).
Wards Cove Packing Co., Inc., v. Antonio, 490 U.S. 642, 109 S.Ct.2115 (1989).
Washington v. Davis, 426 U.S. 229, 96 S.Ct. 2040 (1976).
Washington v. Seattle School District No. 1, 458 U.S. 457, 102 S.Ct. 3187 (1982).
Washington, Alexandria & Georgetown Railroad Co. v. Brown, 84 U.S (17 Wallace) 445, 21 L.Ed. 675 (1873).
Watson v. Fort Worth Bank and Trust, 487 U.S. 977, 108 S.Ct. 2777 (1988).
Weber (See *United Steelworkers v. Weber*)
Weber v. Aetna Casualty & Surety Co., 406 U.S. 164, 92 S.Ct. 1400 (1972).
Webster, Califano v. (See *Califano v. Webster*)
Webster v. Reproductive Health Services, 492 U.S. 490, 109 S.Ct. 3040 (1989).
Weinburger v. Wiesenfeld, 420 U.S. 636, 95 S.Ct. 1225 (1975).
Wengler v. Druggists Mutual Insurance Co., 446 U.S. 142, 100 S.Ct. 1540 (1980).
West Chester and Philadelphia Railroad Co. v. Miles, 55 Pa. 209 (1867).
Westcott, Califano v. (See *Califano v. Westcott*)
Williams v. McNair, 401 U.S. 951, 91 S.Ct. 976 (1971).
Williams v. Mississippi, 170 U.S. 213, 18 S.Ct. 583 (1898).
Williams v. Zbaraz, 448 U.S. 358, 100 S.Ct. 2694 (1980).
Williamson v. Lee Optical Co., 348 U.S. 483, 75 S.Ct. 461 (1955).
Wimberly v. Labor and Industrial Relations Commission of Missouri, 479 U.S. 511, 107 S.Ct. 821 (1987).
Winston-Salem/Forsyth County Board of Education v. Scott, 404 U.S. 1221, 92 S.Ct. 1236 (1971).
Wong Kim Ark (See *United States v. Wong Kim Ark*)
Wong Wing v. United States, 163 U.S. 228, 16 S.Ct. 977 (1896).
Wygant v. Jackson Board of Education, 476 U.S. 267, 106 S.Ct.1842 (1986).
Yick Wo v. Hopkins, 118 U.S. 356, 6 S.Ct. 1064 (1886).
Zablocki v. Redhail, 434 U.S. 374, 98 S. Ct. 673 (1978).
Zobel v. Williams, 457 U.S. 55, 102 S.Ct. 2309 (1982).

DOCUMENT

Congressional Globe, 39th Congress, 1st Session, December 4, 1865 through June 13, 1866.

NEWSPAPERS

Austin Statesman, June 6 and 7, 1950.
Holmes, S. (1991). "Mulling the Idea of Affirmative Action for Poor Whites." *New York Times* (August 18, 1991).

Joshi, V. (1990). "India's New Chief Vows 'a Society of Equals,'" *Fort Worth Star Telegram* (November 10, 1990).

CONVENTIONS OR TREATIES[4]

Canadian Charter of Rights and Freedoms (1982).
Constitution of India (1949).
Convention on the Elimination of All Forms of Discrimination against Women (1979).
European Convention for the Protection of Human Rights and Fundamental Freedoms (1950).
International Covenant on Civil and Political Rights (1966).
International Covenant on Economic, Social and Cultural Rights (1966).
International Convention on the Elimination of All Forms of Racial Discrimination (1965).
International Labour Organization. Convention Concerning Discrimination in Respect to Employment and Occupation (1958).
International Labour Organization. Convention Concerning Equal Remuneration (1951).

STATUTES

Age Discrimination in Employment Act, 29 U.S.C., sec. 621 et seq.
Article 3107, Texas Revised Civil Statutes, 1923.
Education of the Handicapped Act, 20 U.S.C., sec. 1401 et seq.
Equal Pay Act of 1963, 29 U.S.C.A. section 206(d).
Federal Unemployment Tax Act, 26 U.S.C.A., section 3304 (a)(12).
Food Stamp Act of 1964, 7 U.S.C., sec. 2011 et seq.
Magna Carta (1215). In *Sources of Our Liberties,* translated and reprinted Richard L. Perry (1972). New York: New York University Press.
Pregnancy Discrimination Act of 1978, 42 U.S.C.A. sections 2000e(k), 2000e(l).
Title IX, of the 1972 Education Amendments, 20 U.S.C.A., sections 1681(a) and 1682.
U.S. Civil Rights Act of 1964, Title VI (sections 601 et seq.) and Title VII (sections 701 et seq.) as amended, sections 2000d and 2000e et seq.
U.S. Civil Rights Act of 1964, sections 701(k), 703 (e)(1), 42 U.S.C.A., as amended by the Pregnancy Discrimination Act (see below).
8 U.S.C., sec. 41 (for current version see 42 U.S.C.A. sec. 1981).

4. The texts of most of these international agreements can be found in Brownlie, Ian (ed.). 1981. *Basic Documents on Human Rights.* Oxford: Clarendon Press.

INDEX

Abortions, 146; parental consent for, 191; public funding for, 189
Accommodations. *See* Public accommodations
Admission criteria, issues about, 116–24
AFDC. *See* Aid to Families with Dependent Children
Affirmative action, 23, 84, 140, 141, 226, 234, 248n1; accepting, 195, 203; in Canada, 196, 207–8, 215; controversies over, 216; de facto segregation and, 110; dissent on, 133; diversity and, 203; group-regarding equality and, 215, 228–29; in India, 196, 197–205, 215; individual-regarding equality and, 212; individualism and, 218; international law and, 211–15; purposes of, 236; race-conscious, 135, 146, 231, 235; remediation by, 58; transitoriness of, 213–15; UN and, 211; women and, 162, 165
Affirmative Action and Justice (Rosenfeld), x
Affirmative duty, 106, 114, 195, 202
Age discrimination, 190–93; in Canada, 206, 210–11
Age Discrimination in Employment Act of 1967, 192
Aid to Families with Dependent Children (AFDC), 155, 179, 187, 189, 207
Alabama Department of Public Safety, set-asides by, 131
Albemarle Paper Co. v. Moody (1975), 17, 119, 125–26, 135
Alexander v. Holmes County Board of Education (1969), 101
Alexander v. Louisiana (1972), 146
Alien Bill of Rights, 173
Aliens, 10, 194, 247n3; in Canada, 210; citizenship and, 175; education and, 175–76; exclusion of, 173, 175, 210; hiring, 172–73, 175; protection for, 55–56, 171–76; as suspect class, 174–75, 176
Ambach v. Norwick (1979), 175
Amelioration. *See* Remediation
American Anti-Slavery Association, 143

American Dilemma, An (Myrdal), 218
American Equal Rights Association, 143
American Woman Suffrage Association, 144
Andrews v. Law Society of British Columbia (1989), 210, 211
Anthony, Susan B., 38, 143
Anti-miscegenation laws, 53–54, 182
"Anti-Okie" law, 188, 247n8
Apartheid, 21, 98, 212, 213
Apsit et al. v. Manitoba Human Rights Commission (1985), 208, 249n8
Arizona Governing Committee v. Norris (1983), votes on, 168
Atchison, Topeka & Santa Fe Railway Co. v. Vosburg (1915), 68–69
Attendance zones, 98, 100, 103, 105, 106; racially neutral, 96; remediation by, 104, 110
Attorney General of New York v. Soto-Lopez (1986), 181
Austin Independent School District v. United States (1976), 111

Backward classes, promotion of, 198–201
Backward Classes Committee (India), 199
Baer, Judith, 174; on *Califano*, 154; on Fourteenth Amendment, 35, 41, 42; on *Kahn*, 150; on *Rostker*, 160; on *Schlesinger*, 152; on sex discrimination, 150, 153
Baker v. Carr (1962), 176, 178, 179, 247n5
Bakke, Alan, 116; suit by, 118. *See also* *Regents of the University of California v. Bakke*
Bakke, DeFunis and Minority Admissions (Sindler), 116
Balaji v. State of Mysore (1963), 199, 200, 208
Barbier v. Connally (1884), 54, 64
Bayefsky, A. F., 206–7, 208
Beale, Howard K., 61, 62
Beard, Charles A.: on Fourteenth Amendment, 62–63
Beitz, Charles, x

County (1981), 158–59, 165, 209; votes on, 167
Military, women and, 159–60. *See also* Veterans' preferences
Miller, Justice: on *Bradwell*, 142; on equal protection, 47, 48; on Equal Protection Clause, 46; on *Slaughter-House Cases*, 62
Milliken v. Bradley (1974), 9, 107–15, 140
Mills v. Habluetzel (1982), 185
Minnesota Rate Case (1889), 66
Minor, Virginia, 143
Minors. *See* Children
Minor v. Happersett (1875), 56, 144
Miscegenation, 41, 44; laws against, 53–54, 182
Mississippi University for Women v. Hogan (1982), 160–61; votes on, 167
Missouri ex rel Gaines v. Canada (1938), 76, 77, 79
Model of Social Justice, 140, 234
Monroe v. Board of Commissioners of the City of Jackson, Tennessee (1968), 101
Moore v. City of East Cleveland (1977), 186
Morales, Roberto, 181
Morality, 226; concerns for, 192
Morgan v. Virginia (1946), 77, 240n6
Moynihan Report, 204
Muckrakers, 64
Muller v. Oregon (1909), 144
Munn v. Illinois (1877), 52
Munro, R. F., 40–41
Murry, Lula Mae, 186. *See also U.S.D.A. v. Murry* (1973)
Myrdal, Gunnar, 3; on racism, 218

NAACP, 74, 81, 82; busing and, 113; *Corrigan* and, 240n1; *Guinn* and, 75; *Murray* and, 240n4; segregation and, 89; straightforward equality and, 27; *Sweatt* and, 80
Narrow domain, 28, 31, 35, 39, 56, 59, 84, 85, 239n12. *See also* Broad domain
Nashville Gas v. Satty (1977), votes on, 167
National American Woman Suffrage Association, 144
National Woman's party, 146, 245n4
National Woman Suffrage Association, 143, 144
Natural rights, 16, 35, 41–44
Natural selection, 222–24
Neal v. Delaware (1881), 50–51
Negroes: fear of, 60; legal status of, 30–31
New Jersey Welfare Rights Organization v. Cahill (1973), 183
Newport News Shipbuilding & Dry Dock Co. v. EEOC (1983), votes on, 168
Nicomachean Ethics (Aristotle), 16
Nineteenth Amendment, 144

Nixon, L. A., 75
Nixon, Richard: busing and, 102; China visit of, 5–6
Nixon v. Condon (1932), 75–76
Nixon v. Herndon (1927), 74, 75, 82–83
Nyquist v. Mauclet (1977), 174–75

O'Brien v. Skinner (1974), 177
Occupational Safety and Health Administration (OSHA), 164
O'Connor, Sandra Day: on affirmative action, 135; on burden of proof, 132; on *Mississippi University for Women*, 160–61; on *Paradise*, 131; on preferential protection, 129; on *Price Waterhouse*, 163, 164; on racial preference cases, 136–38, 140; on sex discrimination cases, 166–70; on Title VII, 130; on *Watson*, 131–32, 163; on *Wimberly*, 161
"On and Off the Bus in Charlotte" (Gaillard), 102
O'Neill, T. J., 122; on group-regarding equality, 121
O'Neill, Tip, 1
Opportunity. *See* Equality of opportunity
Orient Insurance Co. v. Daggs (1899), 65
"Original Understanding of 'Equal Protection of the Laws' " (Frank and Munro), 40–41
Orr v. Orr (1979), 155; votes on, 167
Ortwein v. Schwaab (1973), 188; due process and, 189
Orwell, George: on equality, 13
OSHA. *See* Occupational Safety and Health Administration

Pace v. Alabama (1883), 53, 56, 59
Parham v. Hughes (1979), 155–56; votes on, 167
Parker, John J.: on *Briggs*, 89–90, 92, 95, 97
Parks, Rosa, 78–79
Pasadena City Board of Education v. Spangler (1976), 110–11
Passion for Equality, The (Cauthen), x
Past discrimination, 135; effects of, 139, 140; women and, 155. *See also* Discrimination
Paternalism, 149, 190–91
Paternity, establishing, 185. *See also* Fathers
Patsone v. Pennsylvania (1914), 172, 173
Pecking orders, examination of, 2, 6–7, 14, 217
Perlman, Philip, 79
Personnel Administrator of Massachusetts v. Feeney (1979), 157, 163; votes on, 167
Pickett v. Brown (1983), 185
Planned Parenthood of Central Missouri v. Danforth (1976), 191